LATINA LEGACIES

VIEWPOINTS ON AMERICAN CULTURE

Viewpoints on American Culture offers timely reflections for twenty-first century readers. A sensible guide to knowledge in a scholarly field, something one can pick up—literally and figuratively—seems to be facing extinction. Volumes in our series will provide intellectual relief and practical solution.

The series targets topics where debates have flourished and brings together the voices of established and emerging writers to share their own points of view in compact and compelling format. Our books offer sophisticated, yet accessible, introductions into an array of issues under our broad and expanding banner.

Sifters: Native American Women's Lives
Edited by Theda Perdue

Long Time Gone: Sixties America Then and Now
Edited by Alexander Bloom

Votes for Women: The Struggle for Suffrage Revisited
Edited by Jean H. Baker

Race on Trial: Law and Justice in American History
Edited by Annette Gordon-Reed

Latina Legacies: Identity, Biography, and Community
Edited by Vicki L. Ruiz and Virginia Sánchez Korrol

LATINA LEGACIES

Identity, Biography, and Community

**Edited by Vicki L. Ruiz and
Virginia Sánchez Korrol**

OXFORD
UNIVERSITY PRESS

2005

OXFORD

UNIVERSITY PRESS

Oxford University Press, Inc., publishes works that further
Oxford University's objective of excellence
in research, scholarship, and education.

Oxford New York
Auckland Cape Town Dar es Salaam Hong Kong Karachi
Kuala Lumpur Madrid Melbourne Mexico City Nairobi
New Delhi Shanghai Taipei Toronto

With offices in
Argentina Austria Brazil Chile Czech Republic France Greece
Guatemala Hungary Italy Japan Poland Portugal Singapore
South Korea Switzerland Thailand Turkey Ukraine Vietnam

Published by Oxford University Press, Inc.
198 Madison Avenue, New York, New York 10016

www.oup.com

Oxford is a registered trademark of Oxford University Press

Library of Congress Cataloging-in-Publication Data
Latina legacies: identity, biography, and community / edited by Vicki L. Ruiz and Virginia
Sánchez Korrol.
p. cm.—(Viewpoints on American culture)
Includes bibliographical references and index.
ISBN-13 978-0-19-515398-9; 978-0-19-515399-6 (pbk.)
ISBN 0-19-515398-7; 0-19-515399-5 (pbk.)
1. Hispanic American women—Biography. I. Ruiz, Vicki. II. Sánchez Korrol,
Virginia. III. Series.
E184.S75L36245 2005
920.72'089'68—dc22   2004050131 (Rev.)
[B]

[Cover photographs: From left to right: Lola Rodríguez de Tió, courtesy of Proyecto de
Digitalización de la Coleccion de Fotos del Periódico *El Mundo*, Universidad de Puerto Rico,
Recinto de Río Piedras; Nina Otero-Warren, courtesy of Museum of New Mexico, negative
number 89756; Loreta Janeta Velázquez, call number E605.V43 1876 (Wilson Annex),
courtesy of University of North Carolina at Chapel Hill; Pura Belpré, The Pura Belpré
Papers, courtesy of Centro de Estudios Puertorriquenos, Hunter College, CUNY; Dolores
Huerta, courtesy of Walter P. Reuther Library, Wayne State University; Ana Mendieta, The
Estate of Ana Mendieta Collection, courtesy of Galerie Lelong, New York; Jovita González
Mireles, E.E. Mireles and Jovita González Mireles Papers, Special Collection and Archives,
courtesy of Texas A&M University-Corpus Christi Library; Luisa Moreno, courtesy of
Dr. Vicki L. Ruiz; and Antonia Pantoja, The Antonia Pantoja Papers, courtesy of Centro de
Estudios Puertorriquenos, Hunter College, CUNY.]

1 3 5 7 9 8 6 4 2

Printed in the United States of America
on acid-free paper

ACKNOWLEDGMENTS

We would like to recognize all of the contributors for their intellectual insights, hard work, and encouragement for this project. Thank you for sharing your passionate commitment to Latina history. Perhaps it makes sense that, given our own bicoastal perspectives, the overarching framework for *Latina Legacies* would come from a brilliant historian rooted in the Midwest—María Montoya of the University of Michigan. Indeed, Montoya read successive drafts of the introduction, pressing us to see the forest for the trees, and this volume's intellectual edge and conceptual reach owe much to her critical prodding. Series editor Catherine Clinton provided unflagging enthusiasm and a deft editorial pen. Her queries and those of Oxford senior editor Susan Ferber strengthened both the substance and style of the text that follows.

We are most grateful to Susan Ferber for all of the time and attention she placed in this endeavor over the past three years. She is a superb editor in every respect. More than an acquiring editor, she is an inquiring one. Ferber really digs into the text, at times making comments line by line. Our own prose and that of our contributors certainly benefited from her astute intellect. We also thank her for her patience, encouragement, and pragmatic counsel.

We appreciate the comments of the anonymous reviewers for their generous support and sharp questions and to Jay Kleinberg at Brunel University for her prescient remarks on the Moreno, Pantoja, and Mendieta essays. Carlos Cruz, managing editor of *Latinas in the United States: An Historical Encyclopedia*, deserves special mention. With boundless enthusiasm, he lent his artistic talents to the design of the cover. From our casual conversations at a café in Florence, he created a spectacular image for the book.

We also acknowledge the production staff at Oxford and our terrific copyeditor, Bethany Johnson Dylewski.

All of the essays are original, unpublished work with the exception of three chapters: one is a direct reprint, and two are adaptations from previous work. We thank Rose Robinson and Marge Dean at the University of California Press and Nick Kanellos of Arte Público Press for granting us permission to include these pieces in the collection.

Finally, we acknowledge our families—our partners and children. Victor Becerra and Chuck Korrol provided encouragement, patience, laughter, and love (and remember we took you to Italy for a women's history conference).

CONTENTS

CONTRIBUTORS

EDNA ACOSTA-BELÉN is Distinguished Service Professor of Latin American and Caribbean Studies, and Women's Studies, at the University at Albany (SUNY), where she directs the Center for Latino, Latin American, and Caribbean Studies. She is co-founder and editor of the *Latino(a) Research Review*. The author or editor of eight books, she has recently published *"Adiós Borinquen Querida": The Puerto Rican Diaspora, Its History, and Contributions* (with Margarita Benítez et al., 2000).

MARÍA RAQUEL CASAS is an Associate Professor of History at the University of Nevada, Las Vegas, where she teaches undergraduate and graduate courses on American history, specializing in Chicano/a history, gender, and the Spanish borderlands. She is the author of *"Married to a Daughter of the Land": Interethnic Marriages in California, 1820–1880* (2005).

ALICIA CHÁVEZ is a doctoral candidate in American history at Stanford University. She is completing her dissertation, "Laboring in Los Angeles: Mexican Americans, Unionization, and Working-Class Identity, 1973–1988."

MARÍA EUGENIA COTERA is an Assistant Professor in the Program in American Culture/Latino Studies and the Women's Studies Program at the University of Michigan. She authored "Refiguring the Historical Representations of the Texas Mexican Border" in *Western American Literature* (Spring 2000). She holds a Ph.D. in Modern Thought and Literature from Stanford University.

CARLOS A. CRUZ is managing editor of *Latinas in the United States: An Historical Encyclopedia*. His areas of specialization are computer graphic arts, social anthropology, and art history. He was an art critic for *El Diario-La Prensa* in New York City. He holds an MFA from Brooklyn College.

AMY DOCKSER MARCUS is a journalist for *The Wall Street Journal* and the author of *The View from Nebo: How Archaeology Is Rewriting the Bible and Reshaping the Middle East* (2000). She has written extensively about women soldiers during the Civil War and is preparing a book on the subject.

DEENA J. GONZÁLEZ is Professor and Chair of the Department of Chicana/o Studies at Loyola Marymount University in Los Angeles. She has published extensively on nineteenth-century New Mexico and has authored *Refusing the Favor: The Spanish-Mexican Women of Santa Fe, 1820–1880* (1999). She and Suzanne Oboler are coediting *The Encyclopedia of Latinos and Latinas in the United States*, in preparation for Oxford University Press.

NANCY A. HEWITT is a Professor of History and Women's and Gender Studies at Rutgers University, New Brunswick. Her scholarship focuses on women's community-based activism in the nineteenth and twentieth centuries. She is the award-winning author of *Women's Activism and Social Change in Rochester, New York, 1822–1872* (1984) and *Southern Discomfort: Women's Activism in Tampa, Florida, 1880s–1920s* (2002).

BRIAN O'NEIL is an Assistant Professor of History and the Director of the International Studies Program at the University of Southern Mississippi. He is completing a book manuscript, *Pan-American Visions: Hollywood's Good Neighbor Policy and U.S.–Latin American Relations, 1938–1946*. He received his Ph.D. in history from the University of California, Los Angeles.

MARIAN PERALES is a doctoral candidate in American history at the Claremont Graduate University. She is completing a dissertation on the life and times of Teresa Urrea.

BEATRICE PITA teaches in the Spanish section of the Department of Literature at the University of California, San Diego. She has edited and written the introduction to María Amparo Ruiz de Burton's two novels, *The Squatter and the Don* (1992) and *Who Would Have Thought It?* (1995), with Rosaura Sánchez. She and Rosaura Sánchez also coedited *Conflicts of Interest: The Letters of María Amparo Ruiz de Burton* (2001).

VICKI L. RUIZ is a Professor of History and Chicano/Latino Studies at the University of California, Irvine. The author or editor of ten books, she has written *From Out of the Shadows: Mexican Women in Twentieth-Century America* (1998) and *Cannery Women, Cannery Lives: Mexican Women, Unionization, and the California Food Processing Industry, 1930–1950* (1987). She has coedited three editions of *Unequal Sisters: A Multicultural Reader in U.S. Women's History* (with Ellen DuBois). She and Virginia Sánchez Korrol are the coeditors of *Latinas in the United States: An Historical Encyclopedia* (2005).

ELIZABETH SALAS is an Associate Professor of American Ethnic Studies at the University of Washington. She authored *Soldaderas in the Mexican Military: Myth and History* (1990; Spanish edition, 1995). She is completing a manuscript on Mexican Federal soldiers in American internment camps from 1913 to 1915, in addition to her current research on Chicanas in Washington State and British Columbia.

ROSAURA SÁNCHEZ is a Professor of Latin American and Chicano Literature in the Department of Literature at the University of California, San Diego. The author of *Telling Identities: The Californio Testimonios* (1995), she has edited and written the introduction to María Amparo Ruiz de Burton's two novels, *The Squatter and the Don* (1992) and *Who Would Have Thought It?* (1995), with Beatrice Pita. She and Beatrice Pita also coedited *Conflicts of Interest: The Letters of María Amparo Ruiz de Burton,* (2001).

LISA SÁNCHEZ GONZÁLEZ is an Assistant Professor of English at the University of Connecticut, Storrs. She is the author of *Boricua Literature: A Literary History of the Puerto Rican Diaspora* (2001). She is preparing a book on the life and work of Pura Belpré. She received her Ph.D. in English from the University of California, Los Angeles.

VIRGINIA SÁNCHEZ KORROL is Professor and Chair of the Department of Puerto Rican and Latino Studies at Brooklyn College, City University of New York (CUNY). Her publications include *From Colonia to Community: The History of Puerto Ricans in New York City* (1994); *Women in Latin America and the Caribbean* (with Marysa Navarro, 1999); and *Teaching U.S. Puerto Rican History* (1999). She and Vicki L. Ruiz are the coeditors of *Latinas in the United States: An Historical Encyclopedia* (2005).

LATINA LEGACIES

INTRODUCTION

Vicki L. Ruiz and Virginia Sánchez Korrol

In 1800, seven-year-old Apolinaria Lorenzana and her mother stepped off the ship *Concepción* onto the docks at Monterey, California, as members of a manifest of orphans and potential wives sent by the Spanish colonial government in Mexico to the remote province of Alta California. As an elderly woman, Lorenzana remembered, "Upon our arrival in Monterey, the governor distributed some of the children like puppies. . . . I remained with my mother and various other women. . . . Those that were already women, Francisca and Pascuala, were married very soon. . . . My mother also married an artilleryman."[1] Civil authorities and mission priests had high expectations for these potential brides. They would bear Catholic citizens of New Spain and contribute their physical labor for the welfare of their kin and their settlements.

But these passengers were not the first Hispanic women to arrive on North American shores. Since the founding of St. Augustine in 1565, Spanish-speaking women had made homes for themselves and their families in the farthest reaches of Spain's North American empire. In such far-flung destinations as St. Augustine, Santa Fe, San Antonio, and Los Angeles, Latinas created homes and created communities. How did they change as the country around them changed? How did they make meaning in their own lives? How did they make history?

This collection features fifteen fascinating individuals whose lives offer insight into the legacies left by women of Latin American birth or heritage to the economic, intellectual, and cultural development of what is today the United States. Through narrative biographies, *Latina Legacies* provides a glimpse into diverse histories predicated on race, region, gender, culture, and social location and on a past of multiple conquests and migrations. More than a sampling of notable women, the volume places their lives in the context of their historical moments. Readers, for example, explore the conquest of the Mexican North by the United States though the entrepreneurship of Gertrudis Barceló and the writings of novelist María Amparo Ruiz de Burton. They experience a sense of homeland and heritage as expressed through the fervor of Lola Rodríguez de Tió and Teresa Urrea. They also negotiate the mean streets of New York City during the 1930s and 1940s alongside newcomers Pura Belpré, Luisa Moreno, and Antonia Pantoja.

These women represent a re-envisioning of Latina history, one that takes into account gendered genealogies of power as mapped through grassroots activism, literature, education, and entrepreneurship. Much of the current scholarship revolves around women as trade union and community heroines; and while acknowledging this important historical tradition, *Latina Legacies* complicates the notion of labor to include women who work for themselves and those who create literature and art. The entrepreneur and the writer stand shoulder to shoulder with the rabble-rousing reformer to render a fuller recounting of Latina history. Indeed, the production and dissemination of knowledge by Latinas reveal much about their own worldviews and historical agency.[2]

Historical agency involves not only individual decision making, but also "the creative orchestration of cultural elements."[3] Emphasizing transnationalism, identity formation, and on occasion, feminist consciousness, these fifteen biographical profiles explore how women made meaning in their own lives and in the lives of others. They underscore both structural and cultural *fronteras* or borders, ranging from the impact of colonialism in Puerto Rico to segregation in the Southwest to traditional gendered expectations that cut across region and class. Women's motivations should not be judged on a continuum with resistance on one end and accommodation on the other, but instead "should be placed within the centrifuge of negotiation, subversion, and consciousness."[4]

The concept of voice also calls for critical reexamination. Perhaps voice has become a fashion victim spoiled by overexposure. It is not a matter of "giving voice," but rather of situating the spaces in the text whereby narrators and historical subjects reveal themselves in their own words. Furthermore, inflections of memory (despite its many frailties) may be central to crafting more satisfying constructs of agency and voice. Memories crystallized in literature and visual art speak eloquently to historical experience. In her writing, Jovita González Mireles recreated the past of her South Texas ancestors, while Ana Mendieta through performance art and photography sought a visceral, physical connection with Cuba, the land she left as a child. Both women imparted a strong sense of homeland and historical memory.

In addressing agency and voice, *Latina Legacies* emphasizes the fluidity of identities. To varying degrees, each biographer focuses on the politics and poetics of identity formation, locating the body, in the words of anthropologist Rebecca J. Lester, "as *both* a locus of experience *and* an object of analysis."[5] These fifteen public women, as writers, educators, entertainers, entrepreneurs, labor organizers, community activists, mystics, and artists, traversed and transgressed the cultural conventions and social boundaries of their time. Visible and vocal, they represent a panoply of Latina experiences.

Nomenclature for Latinas in and of itself reveals much about the diversity of Spanish-speaking peoples in the United States, past and present. There has never existed a single signifier of self-identification from Tejanos and Californios of the nineteenth century to Latinos and Hispanics today. In this volume, Latina is an umbrella term referring to all women of Latin American birth or heritage, including women from North, Central, and South America and the Spanish-speaking Caribbean. Mexicana and Mexicano refer to those born in Mexico, with Mexican American indicating birth in the United States. Chicana and Chicano reflect a political consciousness that emerged out of the Chicano student movement, often a generational marker for those who came of age during the 1960s and 1970s. Nuyorican refers to Puerto Ricans born on the mainland, not just in New York, while Puertorriqueña and Puertorriqueño include islanders and Nuyoricans alike. Boricua signifies endearment, empowerment, and unity for all Puerto Ricans. For some, regional identification becomes synonymous with nationality—Tejanos in Texas and Hispanos in New Mexico and Colorado. Others situate themselves in terms of racial location, preferring perhaps an Iberian connection (Hispanic) or emphasizing indigenous (mestizo/a) or African (Afro-Latino/a) roots. Cultural/national identification remains strong—Salvadorans, Dominicans, Brazilians, and Cubans (to name just a few). With the Latino population, reaching 37.4 million in 2002, these Americans will be referred to by many names, with Latino and Hispanic as the most ubiquitous.[6] Keeping in mind this mosaic of identities, it is important to place the fifteen biographies that follow within a brief chronology of Latina history, beginning with the settlement of St. Augustine.

Since the earliest periods of Hispanic life in the Americas, the presence of women has been essential. Established before the colonization of what would become the southwestern United States, the settlement of St. Augustine, Florida, serves as a fair example of life in the colonial periphery of the viceroyalty of New Spain and offers interesting glimpses into women's roles. Founded in 1565 during the golden age of Spanish exploration and conquest, and ceded to England in 1763, St. Augustine was one of three military units in the primary line of defense established by the Spanish Crown throughout the Caribbean and the Gulf of Mexico to protect the treasure ships that plied the seas. Fraught with constant danger of foreign invasion, colonists in this frequently neglected frontier settlement faced enormous obstacles merely to survive. St. Augustine settlers were subject to British attacks, like the unsuccessful one staged in 1702 by James Moore of Carolina and the even stronger assault in 1740 led by James Oglethorpe of Georgia. In addition to foreign interlopers, the colonists, who included people of Spanish, Indian, and African heritage, suffered the instability of financial support from the Crown and the injustices of life within a rigid class, color, and labor system that privileged Spaniards. Yet the inability to implement royal policy from so great a distance already marked colonists with a degree of self-sufficiency and determination endemic to colonial development.

Women were critical to forging livable settlements out of such inhospitable sites. St. Augustine women participated in every aspect of colonial life, but their accumulation of land and wealth were particularly important. They married young, usually to much older husbands, and widows frequently remarried. As widows, women not only inherited land and other forms of wealth, but also became potential donors for financing convents or chapels. Although women's economic positions were firmly based on familial or marital connections, their lives were also conditioned by race, class, and marital status. Indian and black women, often enslaved or indentured laborers in the house and the fields, were concentrated at the bottom rungs of the social scale. However, evidence indicates that free blacks, recent immigrants, and non-elites could also own property. By 1763, St. Augustine included some Catalan immigrants, Christianized Indians, and free blacks, who added to an already diverse and shifting demographic profile of the colony. Juana Ana María Paniagua, for example, was a *mujer mercenaria* (prostitute) who owned slaves and property. Although most women were not, in fact, landowners, over a quarter of all landowners in the colony were single women, probably widows. When St. Augustine came under British rule in 1763, many citizens migrated to the Spanish colonies of Cuba, Puerto Rico, Santo Domingo, and other parts of the Hispanic Caribbean.[7]

Women also journeyed to northern New Spain, an area that would become better known as the Spanish borderlands, the Mexican North, and later, the southwestern United States. Women participated in the founding of Santa Fe in 1610, San Antonio in 1718, and Los Angeles in 1781. The colonists themselves were typically mestizos (Spanish/Indian) or mulattos (Spanish/African). For those settlers who garnered economic and social power, they and their children would often position themselves as "Spanish," putting into practice the truism "money buys color," common throughout colonial Latin America.

In the early years, the concern was less on status than on survival, as settlements, especially in Texas, New Mexico, and Arizona, teetered on the brink of extinction through starvation or combative relationships with native peoples. As the missions, pueblos (towns), and presidios (forts) took hold over the course of three centuries, however, Spanish/Mexican women raised families on the frontier and worked alongside their fathers and husbands herding cattle and tending crops.

Women also participated in the day-to-day operation of area missions. Whether heralded as centers of godliness and civilization or condemned as concentration camps, the missions, particularly in California, played instrumental roles in the economic development of an area and in the acculturation and decimation of indigenous peoples. In an environment of social indoctrination, acculturation, and servitude, missions relied on Indian labor to feed the growing colony and produce essential goods for trade. To support their endeavors, mission friars recruited women into service as housekeepers, midwives, cooks, healers, teachers, seamstresses, and business managers. The experience of Apolinaria Lorenzana, who became the housekeeper at the San Diego mission after her arrival in California, was typical of the period. Lorenzana cared for the church sacristy and priestly vestments, supervised the work of Indian seamstresses, shopped for supplies, healed the sick, and operated an informal school for the daughters of settlers. Her own education demonstrates the resourcefulness that characterized Spanish-speaking women on the borderlands. "When I was a young woman in California, I learned alone to write, using for this the books I saw, imitating the letters on whatever white paper I found discarded. Thus I succeed in learning enough to be make myself understood in writing."[8]

The close proximity of Indian and Spanish/Mexican women engendered little pretense of a shared sisterhood. Indentured servitude was prevalent on the colonial frontier and persisted well into the nineteenth century, with Indians and, to a lesser extent, people of African heritage pressed into bondage. For instance, in 1735, Antonía Lusgardia Ernandes, a mulatta, sued her former master for custody of their son. Admitting paternity, the man claimed that his former servant had relinquished the child to his wife since his wife had christened the child. The court, however, granted Ernandes custody. In other cases, this pattern continued with tragic results. As noted by historian Miroslava Chávez-García, the murder of the Indian servant known only as Ysabel at the hands of her mistress, Guadalupe Trujillo, in 1843 offers but one example of the violence inflicted by one group of women on another. While "captives" could become "cousins," to quote distinguished scholar James F. Brooks, race and class hierarchies significantly shaped the daily lives of indigenous actors on the Spanish/Mexican borderlands.[9]

The story in this volume of the accomplished Hispanicized Indian, Victoria Reid, provides a fascinating view of the shifting definitions of race, privilege, and social position. Born in a *ranchería* near the San Gabriel mission and schooled in a convent, Reid crossed class and color lines more than once within her lifetime. Her identity as an Indian woman altered to Spanish/Mexican when she married Hugo Reid, a Scotsman, in 1836. During her marriage, she proved an astute businesswoman, ably managing the family ranchos. But once widowed, she again became an Indian woman. Set against a code of conduct that frowned on intermarriage, her world offered limited opportunities, even for a woman with her entrepreneurial abilities.

Spanish/Mexican women (and Indians, like Victoria Reid, who "passed") were not cloistered señoritas uninterested in matters of property or business. Married women on the Spanish borderlands had certain legal advantages not afforded their Euro-American peers. Under English common law, women, when they married, became *femme covert* (or invisible in the eyes of the legal system), and they could not own property separate from their husbands'. In contrast, Spanish/Mexican women retained control of their land after marriage and held one-half interest in the community property they shared with their spouses. In archives throughout the Southwest, property records reveal that Spanish/Mexican women took active roles in managing both larger ranches and small family farms.

In a thriving commercial center like Santa Fe, crossroads for Mexican and U.S. trade, women also found opportunities as entrepreneurs. María Gertrudis Barceló, known as La Tules, owned a saloon and gambling hall frequented by Euro-Americans and Mexicans alike. A shrewd negotiator of the shifting cultural terrains of Santa Fe, she provided an exotic respite for settlers and soldiers and exposed newcomers "to Spanish-Mexican

music, habits, and humor" as they "unloaded their money at the table."
La Tules was a very wealthy woman by all accounts on the eve of the
United States's war with Mexico; her story offers a unique opportunity to
compare life before and after the American occupation.[10]

A number of military confrontations took place during the nineteenth
century that completed the demise of Spanish control of the Americas.
The wars of Latin American independence spanning the period from 1810
to 1824 left Spain with control of only two former colonies, Cuba and
Puerto Rico. Colonialism intensified in these provinces, resulting in a
century of increased slavery, landless peasantry, a landed elite, and political oppression that drove countless Cuban and Puerto Rican reformers
and insurgents into exile, where they sought a new future and formed
new communities in the eastern and southern United States.

Life on the Spanish borderlands changed dramatically in 1848 with the
conclusion of the U.S.–Mexican War, the discovery of gold in California,
and the signing of the Treaty of Guadalupe Hidalgo. This treaty ceded almost one-half of Mexico's territory to the United States, with California,
Arizona, and New Mexico joining Texas under the American flag. The treaty
also assured Mexican residents that after one year, they would become full
U.S. citizens, secure in their property and privileges, but in practice these
provisions were frequently ignored. Mexicans on the U.S. side of the border,
even those who had wealth and identified as "Spanish," became second-
class citizens, divested of their property, political power, and cultural en-
titlements. Segregated from the Euro-American population, Mexican
Americans in the barrios of the Southwest sustained their identities and
cherished their traditions. With little opportunity for advancement, they
were concentrated in the lower echelon of industrial, service, and agricultural jobs. This period of conquest and marginalization, both physical and
ideological, intensified stereotypes that affected rich and poor alike.

Some historians have asserted that elite families believed they had a
greater chance of retaining land if they acquired a Euro-American son-in-
law. Intermarriage, however, was no insurance policy. In 1849, María
Amparo Ruiz married Lieutenant Colonel Henry S. Burton, and five years
later the couple purchased Rancho Jamul, a sprawling property of over
500,000 acres. When Burton died in 1869, the ownership of Rancho Jamul
came into question. After seven years of litigation, the court awarded his
widow only 8,926 acres. Chronicling her experiences, Ruiz de Burton, who
is considered the first Mexican American novelist, penned *The Squatter
and the Don* (1885), a fictionalized account of the decline of the Californio
ranching class. Her writings convey a sense of loss and displacement but

with a steely defiance and attitude. The lives of Victoria Reid, Gertrudis Barceló, and María Amparo Ruiz de Burton reveal how individuals interpreted and travailed in a new political, economic, and social order.

On a community level after 1848, Spanish-language newspapers in the Southwest could be read as bastions of cultural resistance to pervasive U.S. influence. Courageous editors reported stories of violence and gross injustice elided by the English-language press, such as the lynching of Mexican men accused of crimes by Euro-American vigilantes. Regarding women, the same editors upheld a double standard by often reinforcing traditional norms where women were expected to abide without question the wishes of fathers, husbands, and brothers. Indeed, in the name of protecting the purity of young girls, some residents of New Mexico, including several priests, protested the establishment of coeducational public schools.

Nonetheless, few women stretched the bonds of convention more than Loreta Janeta Velázquez, a Cuban American woman who, disguised as a Confederate officer, fought for the South in the Civil War. Her adventures seem even more remarkable as she chronicled them in a memoir entitled *The Woman in Battle*. Although some scholars claim that Velázquez was a fictional character, growing evidence suggests otherwise. Indeed, historians who study the lives of nineteenth-century Latinos have generally overlooked women's literacy. Profiles of such figures as María Amparo Ruiz de Burton, Loreta Janeta Velázquez, Lola Rodríguez de Tió, and Luisa Capetillo assume telling importance in recovering women's motivations and aspirations, their worldviews as heterogeneous as the women themselves—from Velázquez's pro-Confederate memoir to Capetillo's socialist-feminist manifesto. Furthermore, many women, far less publicly, expressed their innermost thoughts in prose and poetry, and some shared their writings in a myriad of Spanish-language newspapers that connected Latino communities in the United States with each other and with their countries of origin.

Latino presses and cultural institutions mirrored the communities they served. Often rebuking the United States for its failure to live up to the accords of the Treaty of Guadalupe Hidalgo or to the guarantees set forth under the U.S. Constitution, Spanish-language newspapers reinforced Latino heritage, contested discrimination, and organized communities for political action. In the cigar factories of Ybor City and West Tampa, for instance, Cuban workers eagerly read *Herencia*, their local paper. By the 1890s, Spanish-language presses such as *Patria* and *Porvenir*, in New York, Tampa–Ybor City, Key West, and other regions of the eastern seaboard, strongly promoted the struggle for Cuban and Puerto Rican independence. They also rallied these nascent communities around trade unions, working-class culture, and integrative concepts of *latinismo.*

The most prominent woman of nineteenth-century Puerto Rico, Lola Rodríguez de Tió, was among the staunchest supporters for the island's independence, steadfast in her belief that the people of Puerto Rico could govern themselves free of Spanish rule. After the Spanish-Cuban-American War of 1898, she was disappointed that although the U.S. government granted Cuba its independence in 1902, it made Puerto Rico a nonincorporated American territory. While her story conveys the hardships faced by political exiles, it also underscores the depth of her devotion to homeland and independence.

Another extraordinary exile, Teresa Urrea, created, claimed, and blended public and spiritual spaces. A gifted *curandera* (folk healer), Urrea, the daughter of an Indian servant and the local *patron*, ministered to poor mestizos and indigenous peoples in her home state of Sonora, Mexico. When the Mexican government seized the lands of local natives and villagers, many fought back, some carrying Urrea's image over their hearts as they went into battle. Steeped in indigenous traditions, she was deemed a saint by her followers and a heretic by the Catholic Church; and after the ill-fated rebellion (one that foreshadowed the Mexican Revolution of 1910), she fled to Arizona in 1892. Years later she attracted considerable publicity as the first woman in the United States to hold public, religious revival–style, faith healings during a national theatrical tour.

A contemporary of Urrea though worlds away, Luisa Capetillo emerged at the turn of the twentieth century as a fiery labor organizer who mobilized Latino workers against their exploitation by tyrannical landowners and manufacturers both in Puerto Rico and in the continental United States. Like Emma Goldman, one of the most famous radicals of her day, Capetillo refused to separate women's rights from workers' rights. Like Goldman, she lived life on her own terms, flouting traditional gendered conventions. Capetillo's feminist writings emphasized women's education, suffrage, and, in keeping with many anarchists' ideals, free love.

A suffragist with more mainstream views, Adelina Otero Warren was both a rural New Mexico aristocrat and modern feminist. A Progressive-era reformer who worked in a settlement house in New York City, she helped secure her home state's ratification of the Nineteenth Amendment, which granted women the right to vote. Two years later, in 1922, she became the first Latina to run for the U.S. Congress, but her campaign was rocked by scandal. A force to be reckoned with in New Mexico public education, she wrote *Old Spain and Our Southwest* as an effort to preserve Hispano cultural traditions and folkways for later generations.

In the cities on the eastern seaboard during the 1920s and 1930s, Latinas, the majority of whom were Puerto Rican, created organizations that were dedicated to fostering community ties and maintaining cultural roots. The first Latina librarian in the New York City library system, Pura Belpré, offers a good example of these civic-minded women. Concerned that the children of this growing migrant community were losing their Puerto Rican culture and their Spanish language, Belpré initiated a series of bilingual library programs that focused on island culture and folklore. As a mulatta, Belpré was certainly cognizant of her gendered racial location in the continental United States, a location marked as much by phenotype as by class and culture. In her library work and in the children's books she authored, her dedication to cultural conservation is striking during an era when Americanization policies in U.S. schools typically denigrated ethnic backgrounds and languages.

A sense of homeland also resonated in the writings of folklorist Jovita González Mireles. A native Tejana, she was very well educated, earning a master's degree from the University of Texas. She channeled her passion for recording the legends and stories of Tejanos on the border into numerous articles and two novels. Her coauthored *Caballero* affords a fascinating fictional glimpse into daily life for a Tejano ranching family after the U.S.–Mexican War. Her works provide important countermemory to the typical tales of Euro-American cowboys and heroic pioneers that filled popular Texas history books. On parallel paths, Adelina Otero Warren, Pura Belpré, and Jovita González Mireles created classroom curricula and shaped educational policy. All three authors wrote during a time of U.S. prosperity followed by global depression and marked in the Southwest by large-scale immigration from Mexico and on the East Coast by a growing stream of migrants from Puerto Rico.

In 1900, more than 100,000 Mexicans lived in the Southwest; by 1930 this figure would increase tenfold as more than 1 million Mexicanos, pushed out by a devastating revolution at home and lured in by the promise of jobs, came to the United States. Settling into existing barrios and forging new communities in the Southwest and Midwest, Mexican immigrants sought wage employment in railroads, steel mills, restaurants, hotels, canneries, and commercial laundries or in the agricultural fields as migrant workers. Like their Puerto Rican and Cuban counterparts, Mexicanas also earned money within the home, taking in boarders and laundry, doing piecework, and babysitting neighborhood children whose mothers worked outside the home. Across the United States, Latinas labored in factories, particularly in the garment industry, where poor conditions and low wages set the stage for union organization.

The onset of the Great Depression shook immigrant hopes to the core, due to the deepening financial crisis and widespread deportations and repatriations to Mexico. From 1931 to 1934, an estimated one-third of the 1.5 million Mexicans in the United States were either deported (summarily taken off the streets and transported across the border) or repatriated (leaving on their own, frequently under the threat of deportation), even though most were native U.S. citizens. Mexicans, notably in the West, were either deported by immigration agents or persuaded to depart voluntarily by duplicitous social workers who exaggerated the opportunities available south of the border. In the East, the Depression prompted many Puerto Ricans to return to the island, where conditions were also poor, but where family connections could provide food and shelter. Discrimination and segregation in housing, employment, schools, and public recreation also served as bitter reminders of Latino second-class citizenship. Color counted—Mexican Americans with indigenous features in California and their Afro-Latino Caribbean counterparts in Florida were both subjected to the daily humiliations of segregation, from "White Trade Only" signs in shop windows to separate, woefully inadequate schools. To address the needs of Latino communities, a number of mutual aid, civil rights, and trade union organizations emerged during this period. Women and men made common cause in such diverse groups as the middle-class League of United Latin American Citizens (LULAC) in the Southwest to the more worker-oriented, New York–based *La Liga Puertorriqueña y Hispana* (Puerto Rican and Hispanic League).

A dynamic immigrant from Guatemala, Luisa Moreno was the first and only transcontinental Latina labor organizer. Her work carried her from the sweatshops of New York's Spanish Harlem to cigar plants in Florida to fruit and vegetable canneries in California. The first Latina officer of a major union, she cultivated local leadership among workers, especially women. Moreno also served as the driving force behind *El Congreso de Pueblos de Hablan Española* (the Spanish-speaking Peoples' Congress), the first national Latino civil rights assembly, held in 1939. While her activism came at great personal cost to her family life, she is remembered for her unwavering commitment to worker and immigrant rights.

During World War II, the Brazilian entertainer Carmen Miranda emerged as a U.S. box office sensation. Her films exemplified Hollywood's role in promoting President Franklin Delano Roosevelt's Good Neighbor policy with Latin America. As a celebrity goodwill ambassador, Miranda revealed strength of character that went beyond the graceful ability to sing and dance while wearing an elaborate headdress filled with fruit. The inspiration for the advertising icon Chiquita Banana, Carmen Miranda was an actor with a superb sense of comedic timing and a popular diplomat of great skill.

After World War II, Puertorriqueños migrated from the island in significant numbers, with more than 40,000 arriving per year from 1946 to 1956. Arriving in New York City from Puerto Rico in 1944, Antonia Pantoja, a young schoolteacher, devoted over four decades to improving the material conditions, political standing, and educational opportunities for Latinos, especially in New York City. In developing grassroots leaders, Pantoja focused not on labor unions but on neighborhood organizations and educational programs for youth. By the 1960s, more than 1 million Boricuas lived in the continental United States, the majority of them in New York. Bridging the postwar generation, the student activists of the 1960s, and contemporary Latino public policy networks, Pantoja helped prepare successive cadres of college-educated individuals to tackle the problems facing Latino communities.

Since 1960, these communities have experienced significant demographic change. Fleeing revolutions and civil wars, significant numbers of Cubans and Central Americans have made the United States their home. From the nineteenth century onward, Cubans had settled in the United States, but their numbers were small. Since 1959, however, well over 500,000 Cubans have come to the United States. Although initially an exile community, two to three generations of Cuban Americans over the last forty years have changed the demographic and political landscape of South Florida, with Miami as the heart of Cuban American life. Historian María Cristina García has emphasized the diversity of Cuban experiences with her question: "What does it mean to be a black, Chinese, or Jewish Cuban?"[11]

Changes in immigration laws that favored family reunification further opened the borders to Latin American immigrants, especially Mexicanos. Grinding poverty, limited job opportunities, and grossly uneven economic development continue to push people north (*al otro lado*). Some of these new immigrants hail from indigenous communities in Mexico and Guatemala and identify themselves as Mixtecs, Zapotecs, or Mayans (to name a few).[12] According to recent census figures, Latinos represent almost 50 percent of the foreign-born population in the United States (15 million out of 31 million total). In 2002, the Latino population could be categorized as follows: 67 percent Mexican; 14 percent Central and South American; 8 percent Puerto Rican; 4 percent Cuban; and 6 percent other groups (for example, Dominicans). Moreover, 40 percent of all U.S. Latinos are foreign-born.[13] This layering of generations and of diverse cultural groups, ranging from Hispanos in New Mexico whose roots extend back four centuries to recently arrived Salvadoran immigrants in Washington, D.C., speak to an array of Latino identities. Latinos include foreign nationals and U.S. citizens; gay and straight; Spanish and non-Spanish speakers; Catholics, Protestants, Jews, and Mormons, as well as practitioners of *Santería* and Native American beliefs. Latinos embody all colors—white, black, and varying shades of brown. Not surprisingly, political beliefs run the spectrum from conservative to liberal. The Republican Party in the last few years has made inroads into the general Latino electorate, which, with the exception of Cuban Americans, has been considered solidly Democratic.

The civil rights movement of the 1960s and 1970s galvanized Latinos into a political force. As part of the global student movements, Mexican and Puerto Rican youth created a myriad of organizations to address continuing problems of discrimination, particularly in education and political representation. Embracing the mantle of cultural nationalism, Mexican Americans transformed a pejorative barrio term "Chicano" into a symbol of pride. Chicano/a implies a commitment to social justice and to social change. From Los Angeles to Chicago to New York, Latino youth desired greater access to higher education, a revamped curriculum to reflect their experiences (Chicano/Latino Studies), expanded public services for their communities, and perhaps most of all, meaningful political representation. They also protested the Vietnam War, the forced sterilization of poor women, U.S. policy in Central America, and the exploitation of immigrants. Moreover, they proved to be tireless volunteers for the United Farm Workers, staffing boycott campaigns and organizing in the fields. Bursting with cultural pride, some students dreamed of revolution, others of social reform.

Participating in all facets of the movement, Latina feminists have made their voices heard through political action, community organizations, academic scholarship, and creative expression. Latina feminist motifs so eloquently expressed in literature by writers, like the influential Dominican intellectual Camila Henríquez Ureña, are accentuated in the works of contemporary artists. The Cuban American performance artist Ana Mendieta combined drama, experimentation, earthworks, and photography in exploring themes like women's relationship to the body, nature, and heritage. Integrating sexual and cultural identities in her work, Mendieta displayed a clear political consciousness that incorporated pre-Hispanic civilizations and fertility icons with Afro-Cuban beliefs. Mendieta's avant-garde work continues to receive acclaim long after her death.

The only living woman profiled in this collection is arguably the most prominent U.S. Latina in the twentieth century—Dolores Huerta. Cofounder of the United Farm Workers with César Chávez, Huerta served as the union's vice president, chief contract negotiator, lobbyist, and strategist. In addition to agitating for improved wages, she has tackled issues of migrant health, housing, and education and has been at the forefront of the campaign to end pesticide poisoning in California fields. Huerta, the mother of eleven children, exemplifies the intertwining of community, family, and self in the pursuit of social justice.

Latina Legacies traces individual lives through the pen, the purse, and the picket sign. Yet such categories are not mutually exclusive. Indeed, reclaiming the intellectual lives of Latinas is as vital a historical project as acknowledging their trade union and political activism. Given the situated nature of racial location, these fifteen narratives reveal how class and culture meet at the level of the individual and of the community.

"Stories are the spirit threads passed on from generation to generation."[14] Latina history has often been a private one, narratives told at the kitchen table. We hope this collection inspires a new generation of historical research, including recording family memoirs and writing scholarly monographs. Many histories remain to be discovered and interpreted, especially of women with Central American, South American, and Caribbean roots. The preponderance of Mexican and Puerto Rican biographies in *Latina Legacies* reflects the current state of the field. As coeditors, we emphasize interdisciplinarity in research and theoretical approaches, recruiting authors from literary criticism, visual art, journalism, and cultural studies. Only nine of the sixteen contributors are historians. As biographers, we share a passionate commitment to conveying women's lives, aspirations, and decisions within their historical moments, interrogating "the process by which the past becomes memory and then memory becomes history."[15] Focusing on identity, biography, and community, this collection privileges the public presence and concrete contributions of U.S. Latinas across time, region, and cultural group. Simply stated, they made history.

NOTES

1. Doña Apolinaria Lorenzana, "Memories of Doña Apolinaria Lorenzana" (1878), San Diego Historical Society Research Archives, San Diego, California. Lorenzana went on to note that when her stepfather was later transferred back to Mexico, her mother accompanied him, but she did not. "He took my mother with him. Thus I remained separated from my mother and I did not see her again. She died almost upon her arrival at San Blas, perhaps from the grief of having left me."

2. Although we define it differently, we are grateful to Florencia Mallon, the renowned historian of Latin America, for bringing the term "genealogies of power" to our attention.

3. Rebecca J. Lester, *Jesus in Our Wombs: Embodying Modernity in a Mexican Convent* (Berkeley and Los Angeles: University of California Press, forthcoming), 329.

4. Vicki L. Ruiz, *From Out of the Shadows: Mexican Women in Twentieth-Century America* (New York: Oxford University Press, 1998), 145.

5. Lester, *Jesus in Our Wombs*, 31.

6. U.S. Bureau of the Census, *The Hispanic Population in the United States: March 2002* (Washington, D.C.: Government Printing Office, 2003), 1. For more information on nomenclature, see Suzanne Oboler, *Ethnic Labels, Latino Lives: Identity and Politics of (Re)presentation in the United States* (Minneapolis: University of Minnesota Press, 1995); and Clara E. Rodríguez, *Changing Race: Latinos, the Census, and the History of Ethnicity in the United States* (New York: New York University Press, 2000).

7. Susan Pickman and Dorca R. Gilmore, "St. Augustine Settlement," in *Latinas in the United States: An Historical Encyclopedia*, ed. Vicki L. Ruiz and Virginia Sánchez Korrol (Bloomington: Indiana University Press, forthcoming).

8. "Memories of Doña Apolinaria Lorenzana."

9. Miroslava Chávez-García, "Guadalupe Trujillo: Race, Culture, and Justice in Mexican Los Angeles," in *The Human Tradition in California*, ed. Clark Davis and David Igler (Wilmington, Del.: Scholarly Resources, 2002), 31–46; James F. Brooks, *Captives and Cousins: Slavery, Kinship, and Community in the Southwest Borderlands* (Chapel Hill: University of North Carolina Press, 2002).

10. Deena J. González, "La Tules of Image and Reality: Euro-American Attitudes and Legend Formation on a Spanish-Mexican Frontier," in *Building with Our Hands: New Directions in Chicana Scholarship*, ed. Adela de la Torre and Beatríz Pesquera (Berkeley and Los Angeles: University of California Press, 1993), 75–90 (quotations on p. 83).

11. María Cristina García, "Adapting to Exile: Cuban Women in the United States, 1959–1973," *Latino Studies Journal* 2 (May 1991): 32. Cuban Americans can be found across the United States, with significant numbers in New York, New Jersey, Illinois, and California.

12. For more information on recent indigenous immigrants, see Devra Weber, "Historical Perspectives on Mexican Transnationalism," *Social Justice* 26 (Fall 1999): 39–58; and Michael Kearney, "Transnational Oaxacan Indigenous Identity: The Case of Mixtecs and Zapotecs," *Identities* 7 (June 2000): 173–95.

13. Social Science Data Analysis Network, "Nativity and Citizenship, 1990–2000," available online at http://www.censusscope.org/us/chart_nativity.html (accessed June 20, 2004); U.S. Bureau of the Census, *Hispanic Population in the United States*, 1, 3.

14. Chicana visual artist Irma Lerma Barbosa quoted in María Ochoa, *Creative Collectives: Chicana Painters Working in Community* (Albuquerque: University of New Mexico Press, 2003), 68.

15. Vicki L. Ruiz and Ellen Carol DuBois, eds., *Unequal Sisters: A Multi-cultural Reader in U.S. Women's History* (3d ed.; New York: Routledge, 2000), xv.

1

VICTORIA REID AND THE POLITICS OF IDENTITY

María Raquel Casas

Madame looks like a rose from Castile.

Hugo Reid

Sometime in September 1836, the widow Victoria Bartolomea married Hugo Reid at the San Gabriel mission, located near the small town of Los Angeles, California.[1] After the ceremony, the couple attended to their landholdings, became part of the small San Gabriel community, and raised Victoria's four children from her previous marriage. Socially and culturally, little distinguished this couple from their neighbors, except for race. Victoria Bartolomea, a Comicrabit Indian, was born near the San Gabriel mission and raised as a neophyte under the authority of the Catholic fathers.[2] Hugo Reid was born in Scotland, lived in Mexico for several years, and then migrated to California. Intermarriage in the Spanish colonies was fairly commonplace between Spanish-Mexicans and Indians, resulting in a caste society defined primarily by race. Although it was initially a triracial society that included people of Spanish, Indian, and African descent, colonial New Spain, and specifically the territory that would become Mexico, had by the mid-1700s become a mestizo (person of mixed race) society, where the mixture between Spanish and Indian predominated. Though the Spanish, and to a lesser extent the French, freely intermarried in their colonial settlements, within the British and American traditions of colonization, few Euro-American or British men intermarried with full-blooded Indian women.[3] This reason alone makes Victoria

Bartolomea Reid rather unique within California history, but her story, which has often been ignored or silenced by various historical and literary accounts, reveals several intriguing aspects not only of this particular woman's life, but also of Californio society in the mid-nineteenth century.

Using intermarriage as a historical lens illuminates the ways in which various peoples came in contact and negotiated social and cultural space through the institution of marriage. The theme of intermarriage in the Spanish borderlands has received a tremendous amount of historical attention, yet intermarriages did not take place at consistent rates, and their meaning shifted depending on time and place. For example, in New Mexico, marriage between Spanish-Mexican settlers and Indians was common in the first one hundred years of settlement but declined thereafter.[4] In California, however, intermarriages with Indians were rare, even during the initial wave of settlement, and the number declined still further in the nineteenth century.[5] Why, then, did Victoria Bartolomea and Hugo Reid intermarry? What advantages did this union afford to these two people? Most important, how did it change Victoria's life and personal identity, and why? Victoria Bartolomea Reid provides an exceptional example of how race, gender, and marriage functioned and shifted in the Spanish borderlands and within American society as well.

From the American perspective, intermarriage between Indians and Euro-Americans was discouraged, excused, and preferably ignored because it affronted conventional ideas that sexual mixing between the races was unnatural and should be neither sanctioned nor valued. Due to these socioracial attitudes, invading Americans after the Mexican-American War commented on the Reids' marriage and wondered why a "white" man would marry an "Indian squaw." To Euro-Americans, Victoria, as an Indian woman, had a specific and inimitable racial identity. In their eyes, Indians and Mexicans were for the large part seen and defined as racially inferior to "white" people. Victoria's association with Hugo Reid thus disturbed Euro-Americans, whose references to this marriage frequently expressed their racial anxiety about miscegenation. What these Americans failed to recognize, however, was that in nineteenth-century Spanish-Mexican California, racial identification was flexible; how individuals negotiated and maneuvered their social status and privileges depended on their local conditions and social opportunities. While race certainly distinguished this couple, an analysis of how race and marriage were intertwined and functioned within the Reids' transforming communities deepens our understanding of how gender and racial identities were constructed and imbued with meaning along the California frontier.

Such an examination of Victoria's negotiation of her own marriage and the Spanish race system not only reveals some of Victoria's personal agency and why she was an extremely desirable mate for Hugo, but it also opens other windows into the sociocultural lives of women in early nineteenth-century California. In terms of frontier societies, comparisons are too often solely made with Euro-Americans and specific indigenous, non-Euro-American populations. By placing Victoria in a Spanish-Mexican colonial context, we can more closely examine how women were valued and how racial ideas functioned in this community. Through Victoria, we can see how certain women were important colonizers, and how subjugated individuals understood and took advantage of colonial contradictions. Very few indigenous people were given the opportunity to cross over, or to "pass," into the elite echelon of society, but Victoria did cross over. For these reasons, her silenced personal history deserves to be told.

Moreover, these interethnic unions have too often been studied from a male perspective; the impulses, desires, and decisions made by the women have rarely been taken into account. Although interethnic marriages were exceptional in many ways, they still reflected the larger collective values and social processes of Californio society.[6] Furthermore, in order to grasp the significance of marital relationships in California during the 1820s and 1830s, it is first necessary to understand the central and continuous role that marriage played, in both Spain and its colonies, in the expansion of the Spanish empire.

Throughout the frontier regions of the Spanish empire, the shortage of Spanish women temporarily elevated and accentuated female status. Spanish women were already accorded certain legal privileges denied to other European women, the most important being a married woman's right to own, inherit, and convey property. As property holders, Spanish women could engage in contractual obligations and address the court of law for redress. These legal privileges were instigated and perpetuated in Spain during a seven-hundred-year period, from 711 to 1492, when the Moors invaded from Africa and controlled the Iberian Peninsula. During this period, known as the *Reconquesta*, the Spanish engaged in and perfected the art of frontier warfare and settlement. Recognizing that winning battles did not necessarily dissuade or dislodge the Moors from their control over conquered territories, battle had to be followed by successful town settlements by Christian citizens. The establishment of these towns and cities demanded the recruitment of women in order to establish a thriving Christian population along the war zone. To this end, Spanish Christian women were granted *fueros* (special legal privileges) that largely protected and granted them property rights in these frontier cities. Over seven hundred years, Spanish society became accustomed to these legal privileges that distinguished Spanish women from their European sisters. In order to recruit women to the new settlements, marriage as an institution was further modified to accommodate frontier conditions through a series of social legislation and regulations that kept expanding women's fueros. It was this marriage ideology that was also transplanted to New World; these rights would eventually be granted to all women who entered the Spanish marriage system, regardless of race.[7]

By 1769, when California was first founded, the Spanish marriage system was especially suited to frontier conditions, as it had slowly been evolving for almost 1,500 years to accommodate expansionist settlement. Because California was Spain's last major colonizing effort along the northern frontier in the eighteenth century, the knowledge that colonial Spanish officials had gained of conquest and of colonizing successes and failures in the previous two centuries informed the colony. When Spanish officials finally decided to maintain a permanent colonizing presence along its empire's northernmost border to discourage Russian encroachment, women and families were key to these colonizing schemes after the initial military conquest. Authorities heavily advocated the recruitment of women as the most effective means of accomplishing the goals of colonization. Continuous efforts targeted women but bore poor results. Small numbers of women volunteered to follow the soldiers and Catholic fathers northward. Juan de Bautista de Anza's 1775–76 expedition exemplified the difficulties of female recruitment. Drawing colonizers primarily from the Nueva Vizcaya province, and particularly from the region now called Sinaloa, Mexico, the Crown offered a variety of incentives to the male settlers, including grants of animal stock when they settled in the new territory, the reimbursement of transportation costs, a promised two years' pay, and five years' rations. To encourage women to move and to properly equip them for their journey and eventual settlement, they were "outfitted with two skirts, one underskirt, three blouses, three white cotton petticoats, two pairs of shoes, linen material for two jackets, two pairs of Brussels stockings, two pairs of hose, two *rebozos* (shawls), a hat, and six yards of ribbon."[8] Even with these incentives, only thirty-four women, including twenty-nine wives, accompanied their soldier-husbands north with de Anza, indicating the harsh economic and physical conditions these colonists knew they would encounter if they chose to resettle.

Officials, concerned with the potentially destabilizing effects of long-term, long-distance separation, encouraged Spanish couples to reunite as quickly as possible, preferring that wives join their husbands in the colonies. The presence of single males on the frontier, especially due to their likely participation in illicit sexual relations, also troubled the authorities of the Catholic Church and Spanish state, who therefore sought to provide stable conjugal relationships. Officials would support and reinforce the stability and growth of families, just as families would support and obey the church and state. Successful marriages were thus a crucial building block in the process of successful long-term colonization. These policies also guaranteed that Spanish-Mexican women were active and privileged conquerors in this region. In British-American colonies, settler women were seen merely as helpmates to their men. In Spanish-Mexican society, women were an important component of conquest.[9]

Because race and social status were so vitally important to the Spanish-Mexican population, individuals constantly strived to advance to more elevated caste classifications or to be called *Don* or *Doña,* depending on their gender, forcing those around them to acknowledge their personal and social status. Given the shifting definitions of racial and economic privilege, individuals could sometimes easily "pass" into another social and racial category, and at other times they could not. As Ann Twinam writes, some Spanish colonists "achieved an alternative public status, not because of what they really were but because they 'were treated as if they were'—and here one could append a number of desired variables: 'white,' 'legitimate,' 'honorable,' 'Don,' 'Doña.' Such ability to pass made it possible for some individuals to achieve racial, natal, and many other kinds of status in the public sphere that differed from their reality."[10] If these were the socioracial rules, marriage was just another tool that men and women used in their personal and public battles to achieve greater social standing and status, as interpreted by their local peers. Along frontier settings, once this cultural schema was in place and everyone understood the avenues of advancement, everyone, including Indians, tried to "pass" as non-Indians when permitted. Nevertheless, there were a great number of variables throughout the Spanish borderlands that allowed or disallowed Indians to take advantage of the Spanish-Mexican caste system.

In the case of California, the level of sexual violence inflicted on native women by soldiers alarmed church officials, who vociferously reported and condemned such acts of sexual violence, including numerous raids upon Indian villages, to the Crown. Not only did soldiers rape and abduct these women, they often murdered the Indian men who attempted to protect them. As early as 1771, church officials recognized that these acts of sexual and physical violence hindered their

Christianization/Hispanicization efforts. They demanded a better class and more disciplined type of soldier, as well as the recruitment of marriageable females. They chastised military authorities for the lax punishment of guilty soldiers and petitioned the Crown to encourage marriage between solders and neophytes—baptized Indians who were in the process of becoming fully Christian—in order to curb the soldiers' brutal sexual appetites. Officials anticipated that these sanctioned permanent unions would help build a trusting and enduring bond between the native communities and the Spanish intruders. To encourage these marriages, ecclesiastical authorities proposed economic incentives, including retirement from the army, a grant of land near the woman's mission, a seaman's salary for two years, and rations for five years. Unfortunately for the Spanish officials, these economic incentives were insufficient to persuade many Spanish-Mexican men to marry neophytes, the most available single women.[11]

By 1790, Californian settlements were slowly and steadily growing, particularly the mission settlements, which became the most important economic institutions in the region before 1820. One of the largest and most productive missions was the San Gabriel mission, which was built in close proximity to the Comicrabit people's traditional lands, where Victoria Bartolomea was born in a village between 1808 and 1810. The proximity of the village assured that the Comicrabit people were incorporated into the daily religious rituals and agricultural cycles of the mission. Victoria, along with other girls of her generation, underwent the full cycle of Hispanicization and the prescribed indoctrination for female children. Victoria was allowed to live with her parents until the age of six or seven, and then she was removed to the *monjeria* (nunnery) of the mission. Within the mission walls she was schooled in the principles of Christianity, was taught to read and write, and was instructed in fundamental household skills in the manner of the Spanish. Although she would have learned to cook, sew, do laundry, garden, and maintain her personal hygiene in her traditional culture, the mission system was an active attempt at erasing native traditions and acculturating children toward Spanish, Christian culture.[12] While at the mission, Victoria received special attention from Eulalia Pérez, the mission's *llavera* (key keeper), who chose her to be an assistant.

When the girls reached puberty, the mission fathers encouraged marriage. They pressured Victoria to accept the neophyte Pablo María, whose family belonged to the neighboring Ytucubit village and who, like Victoria, had undergone forced acculturation. Throughout the mission system, the Catholic fathers discouraged neophytes from marrying outside their affiliated missions in order to retain their valuable labor. This was the opposite of the traditions of the San Gabriel Indians. Prior to the Spanish-Mexican invasion, they practiced exogamy: marriage within their communities was interpreted as incest. Their marriage did not remove Victoria or Pablo from service to the mission, and Victoria continued as one of Eulalia Pérez's assistants. In 1822, when Victoria was approximately fifteen years old, she gave birth to her first child, Felipe. Three more children, José Dolores, María Ygnacia, and Carlitos, would follow. The couple's services and their accommodation to the mission system were clearly valued by the mission fathers, who rewarded them with two plots of land, known as *parajes*, sometime during the early 1830s. Theoretically, when missions were established among Indian peoples, it was understood that the Indians did not lose right to their land. Missions were only holding and safeguarding the land for the people until the conversion process was completed, and then the land would revert back to the people. Unfortunately, it was the mission fathers who decided when an individual had become completely Christianized/ Hispanicized. Victoria and Pablo had accomplished a tremendous feat, as relatively few neophytes were ever granted land rights.

As the husband and head of the household, Pablo María was granted the land, but when he died around 1836, all the property was now in Victoria's hands. If Victoria was forced into accepting her first marriage partner, widowhood gave her full control over choosing her next mate. As a landholding, Christian, and Hispanicized person, Victoria's potential choices for a new husband now expanded beyond the neophyte population. Land ownership was crucial to Victoria's new social status and personal ethnic identity. This shift in social and ethnic identity was further accentuated by Victoria's selection of Hugo Reid as her second husband.

Born in Essex, Milchin, Renfrew County, Scotland, in 1810, Hugo Reid first came to Mexico in the mid-1820s. He and business partner William Keith established a trading house in Hermosillo, Sonora. Seemingly on a whim, Hugo traveled to California in the summer of 1832 and became acquainted with the foreign traders residing in the Los Angeles area. Speculating that greater profit might be found in California, Reid and Keith, along with California trader Jacob P. Leese (who had emigrated from Denmark), established a small store selling sundry goods in the Los Angeles plaza in 1834. Within the year, however, Reid left California after being accused of abetting a short-lived Sonoran emigrant uprising, the *Apalátegui* revolt, and because he could no longer tolerate Leese's quarrelsome nature. During his initial stay in Los Angeles, Hugo Reid must have met Victoria Bartolomea. They clearly had formed some connection during his time in Los Angeles because news of Victoria's widowhood quickly brought Reid back to California. As early as 1835, Hugo made known to other foreign traders his desire to own land; whatever other considerations influenced Reid's decision to marry, he had struck on the most convenient method of gaining land. Indeed, a foreigner was not allowed to own land unless he was Catholic, a Mexican citizen, and married to a Mexican woman.[13] Victoria's land turned Reid into a ranchero. Soon after their marriage in September 1836, Reid purchased more land near the Mission San Gabriel and built a house for his new family, and from there he managed his properties.

Genuine affection existed between Victoria and Hugo, as evidenced by Hugo's adoption and protection of all four of Victoria's children. After 1836, the children were always referred to as Reid's. Had Pablo María survived, Victoria and her children would only have been referred to by their first name, followed by the signifier, *indio*, but by having a European surname, Victoria and her children were exempted from having to refer to themselves as indios.[14] By giving them his European surname, Reid allowed Victoria and her children to more fully integrate into the elite Californio class. As a father, Hugo accepted his responsibilities and was protective of his new charges. For example, in 1843, Abel Stearns, the most influential and important merchant in Los Angeles, employed the Reids' son José Dolores to work in Stearns's Los Angeles warehouse. But when one of Stearns's employees "made use of an oath stamping his foot at him [José Dolores] saying moreover he was shaming [*sic*] illness," Hugo quickly removed José Dolores from the disagreeable situation. In an otherwise cordial correspondence, this was the only letter in which Reid ever reproached his esteemed friend.[15] Marriage to a European male furthered the socioracial distance of Victoria's family from their Indian ethnicity, strengthening the social ties within the Californio society for all the Reids.

For Hugo Reid, the adoption of Victoria's children had another social benefit: as a parent, Reid could utilize the Catholic *compadrazgo* (god-parenting) system. Primarily a symbolic religious relationship, the compadrazgo system was also a means of enlarging fictive kin through relationships of reciprocity. Through compadrazgo, Reid strengthened his friendship and business relationship with Abel Stearns. Hoping to purchase the Rancho Alamitos but lacking the necessary funds, Reid approached Stearns to join him in this land venture. Anxious to "accelerate our compadrasgo [*sic*]," Hugo sent along four loaves of bread made by

Victoria, not because Stearns needed food, "but merely to put you in mind of what bread we will eat on our own ranch of the Alamitos."[16]

Reid's correspondence reveals Victoria's personal contributions to maintaining and overseeing the two ranchos, Rancho Santa Anita and Huerta de Cuati. Constant bouts of stomach pains often debilitated Hugo, leaving Victoria in charge. Though bedridden, Reid informed Stearns that the wheat harvest was going well under Victoria's supervision. Victoria estimated that it would take all of the following week to complete since "it is hard because in some places they absolutely have to pick it by hand and I have told them not to waste any. Nevertheless there are more ways than one to kill a dog according to the proverb of those gentiles called English."[17] Furthermore, while Reid ran Rancho Santa Anita, Huerta de Cuati was under Victoria's care. By 1844, Huerta de Cuati was growing 20,500 grapevines, with room to expand to 40,000 vines. Along with the vines, the Reids cultivated a variegated orchard of 430 trees, including 21 fig trees, 7 plum, 25 pear, 5 apple, 32 orange, 40 pomegranate, 2 honey mesquite, 240 peach, 8 blood orange, 3 walnut, 7 olive, and 40 lemon. In another letter to Stearns, Hugo wrote, "Please let Jim [Reid's *mayordomo*] have the *cuneta* [barrel] filled with Brandy—it perteneces [*sic*: pertains] to my wife's line of business—You and I will settle in the afternoon its price as it is a cash account."[18] The brandy, also known as *aguardiente* throughout Latin America, was a locally distilled spirit that was often used as a form of exchange. Given the lack of monetary currency in California, aguardiente provided a staple commodity that facilitated economic exchanges. In one letter she wrote to Abel Stearns, Victoria clearly indicated her authority in making day-to-day decisions concerning the business of the rancho:

> My dear Sir, Having received your message through Don Mariano Roldan, requesting my sending the rest of the *aguardiente* and *panocha* [cakes of brown sugar], which I had taken a few days ago from your home. Of the said *panocha* it seems to me that it has been paid for; and of the *aguardiente* it is true that I said I would sell it for you but as I found myself unable to pay the servants: I took the said *aguardiente*, however if you are in such need of it; please send word with the driver; I will myself will go to the city and give over the *aguardiente*.[19]

In all likelihood, the brandy was used as payment for Indian labor at both Huerta de Cuati and Rancho Santa Anita.

Like other rancheros, Victoria and Hugo Reid used alcohol as both a means of payment and a means of maintaining dependent relations with Indian labor. In another letter to Abel Stearns, Hugo itemized the account of a runaway Indian laborer named Alejo, who "had not presented himself before me because he knows very well that he owes me more than two dollars, if he is at the ranch and denies the account, I shall be obliged to send for him."[20] In the two months he worked for the Reids, Alejo purchased rum from the Reids five separate times, twice "for the medical attendants of his wife."[21] Producing and controlling the rancho's aguardiente, paying and commanding Indian servants, and being the wife of a European offered Victoria identification with the ranchero elite. This identification was further solidified by her social acceptance by her Californio neighbors.

Because Indian servants and workers surrounded her, speculation over Victoria's racial identity and the unavoidable social dilemmas and racial contradictions she encountered daily must be considered. Her marriage to a white man deepened the patina of Victoria's Hispanicization, but neither she nor her children completely erased or negated their racial categorization. Victoria's "Indianness" caused people to remark on the uniqueness of this union. Recent California histories often make references to this interethnic marriage but only name Hugo and usually refer to Victoria as his Indian wife. Hugo, rather than Victoria, has thus remained the most important historical actor in this interesting union.

These histories draw their depictions from nineteenth-century accounts and absorb the biases of the earlier accounts. For example, in his personal memoir recounting his sixty years in California, William Heath Davis described his 1844 visit to the Reids. Before he recountes his visit, he noted that the Californios "seldom intermarried with the Indians; but they mixed with them to a certain extent; and in visiting the Missions, one would sometime see fine looking children belonging to the Indian women, the offspring of their associations with California men."[22] Having enjoyed the Reids' hospitality, he remarked that he was "surprised and delighted with the excellence and neatness of the housekeeping of the Indian wife, which could not have been excelled. The beds which were furnished us to sleep in where exquisitely neat, with coverlet of satin, the sheets and pillow cases trimmed with lace and highly ornamented."[23] Davis recognized and called attention to Victoria's wifely talents, but he clearly viewed Victoria as an exception to Indian habits of cleanliness and domesticity; indeed, throughout his memoir he constantly expressed his low opinion of Indians.

The most intimate and personal account of Victoria and her racial dichotomy comes not from Hugo's correspondence but from Laura Evertson King, a young white neighbor. Intending to defend Hugo from an unfavorable characterization in the Thompson and West publication *History of Los Angeles County*, in an 1898 article King criticizes the implication that Reid was eccentric, as well as the book's assertion that he was not an expert on the life and customs of the San Gabriel Indians. In an attempt to be appointed as an Indian agent in the San Gabriel Valley, King contended, Hugo wrote a series of essays that proved his expertise in Indian matters. "If my memory does not play me false," King wrote, "he was not eccentric, unless his marriage with an Indian woman could have been considered an eccentricity. He might have 'gone farther and fared worse,' as she was a noble woman in many respects, but being an Indian, her noblest characteristics were left to be discovered by those who loved her and who knew her best."[24] Defending Hugo Reid may have been the prime motivation for the article; however, King's description of Victoria clearly indicates Victoria's strong self-assurance and her contributions to advancing the family's fortunes. King wrote that Victoria clearly believed that only through her had Hugo "acquired his wealth, and through her he was enabled to write his essays on the life and customs of the Indians of San Gabriel Valley."[25]

Unlike William Heath Davis, King described a simpler, more intimate household. When King visited the Reids, Victoria was often seated on the ground, directing an Indian servant in the making of tortillas. While the meal was simple, Victoria was "dressed in a costly gown of black satin, with an embroidered shawl of crepe around her shapely shoulders, daintily taking the broiled beef in her fingers, she would give me a lesson in Indian etiquette. Not all the dainty dishes of a king's banquet could equal the unforgotten flavor of that simple supper."[26] Beyond demonstrating the tremendous affection and regard King held for Victoria, King also contextualized Victoria's shifting identity in the transforming California society. Everyone used the honorific title of Doña Victoria, King noted; within Spanish-Mexican social constructions, Victoria had risen into the highest ranks of society. As Antonia Castañeda has written, Euro-Americans held a dichotomous view of Spanish-Mexican women, whom they defined as being either "Spanish," and thus seen as racially pure, socially elite, virtuous, and highly moral, or "Mexican," and thus seen as racially mixed, lower class, morally lax, and of easy virtue.[27] By calling Victoria a Doña, Californios, and by extension Euro-Americans, were classifying her as Spanish. But Victoria's obvious "Indianness" continued to make Euro-Americans uneasy. No costly gown could completely cover up Victoria's ethnicity. As long as Hugo Reid's social position remained intact, Victoria occupied a social space that subsumed her ethnic identity. Whereas Victoria's land and economic contributions bolstered Hugo Reid's social status in the Mexican period, in the American period, Victoria's social status solidly rested on Hugo's protection and legitimacy. As long as Hugo maintained his wealth, Euro-Americans could accept an eccentric Scotsman married to an "Indian wife." Euro-Americans, like William Heath Davis, continuously interpreted the refined and poised Victoria as exceptional, but it is important to note that this definition did not fully protect Victoria in American society.

How Euro-Americans expressed their racial anxiety over Victoria's daughter, María Ygnacia, took a curious bend. While both Davis and King referred to Victoria as being merely an "Indian wife," Davis radically rewrote and transformed Ygnacia Reid's ethnic identity. Describing her as "a beautiful girl of about eighteen, born some years before their marriage, of another English father," Davis remarked that Ygnacia "was English in feature, with blue eyes and auburn hair, very luxuriant." No mention was made of Ygnacia's brothers and their coloring, even though Carlitos was still living with Hugo and Victoria at the time of Davis's visit in 1844. For Davis and his contemporaries, accepting Ygnacia in social interactions exposed deep psychological delusions and racial rationalizations. Similarly, various accounts by U.S. soldiers stationed in southern California during the U.S.–Mexican War mentioned the loveliness of the Bandini sisters and a certain "half-English, half-Indian" young woman whose companionship was as greatly appreciated as her Californio friends. Unable to consider a "full-blooded" Indian female beautiful, the only possible alternative was a blue-eyed Indian female. In order to socially interact with Ygnacia and Victoria Reid, Euro-Americans needed to create psychological and social distance with "common" Indians for their own peace of mind. They could and did make some exceptions in the case of Victoria and María Ygnacia, but their social and racial attitudes against Indians persisted.

In terms of marital strategies, Victoria's choice of Hugo benefited and protected her children. Upon her mother's marriage, Ygnacia escaped the mission cycle that removed children from their homes. The Reids' friendship and associations with the Californio elite, especially the Bandini family, advanced the women's cultural capital as defined by the local society. Ygnacia became a frequent visitor to the Bandini home and often accompanied the youngest Bandini sister, Arcadia, to local social events.

Californio acceptance of the Reid children was most evident when Felipe Reid married María de la Resurección Ontiveros on August 18, 1843. Throughout the Spanish borderlands, few Spanish-Mexican women married Indians, and the women who did generally belonged to the lower working class. The Ontiveros were a middling landholding family who settled in the Los Angeles region in the first wave of Spanish colonization.[28] María de la Resurección was the only female in her family to intermarry with an Indian, though by 1843 Felipe was not, strictly speaking, an Indian. Rather he was Hispanicized, Spanish-speaking young man, with Indian heritage, who had received some formal education. Felipe looked and comported himself more in the manner of the Californio elite than an Indian. How acceptable Felipe would have been to the Ontiveros if his father, Pablo María, were still alive is a matter of speculation, but clearly Victoria's children moved up vertically within the community's social ranks rather than decline into the ranks of dispossessed neophytes, at least prior to the influx of Euro-American immigrants.

Regrettably, the Reids' matrimonial happiness closely followed the ups and downs of Hugo's business interests. In 1841, Hugo purchased and refitted the cargo ship *Esmeralda* for the China trade. Writing to Abel Stearns, Hugo's affection toward Victoria was readily apparent, as he lovingly wrote, "Madame looks like a rose from Castile and is at this moment sitting in front of me and saying with her eyes: Give him my regards."[29] In Hugo's mind, Victoria was clearly a Californiana, not an Indian woman. The ship set sail in early October for the Sandwich Islands, and not only did the venture prove unsuccessful, but on redocking in San Pedro, Hugo was accused of smuggling. To settle the smuggling charges and dispose of the cargo at a loss, Hugo Reid was forced to sell either the Rancho Santa Anita or Huerta de Cuati; he chose the former. This downturn in business instigated a growing estrangement in the Reids' marriage.

After the *Esmeralda* fiasco, Hugo's attention turned to the development of their lands; however, his election as *juez de paz* (justice of the peace) for the pueblo of San Gabriel kept him away from his properties and family. Forced to handle civil disputes as well as attend to the secularization of the San Gabriel mission, Hugo hired his friend Jim McKinley as *major-domo* (overseer) to run the rancho in his absence. Many Californio landowners hired overseers due to their multiple landholdings. But given Victoria's experience at overseeing the rancho's laborers, Hugo's actions indicated that he no longer trusted Victoria as a business partner. Had Victoria been preoccupied with bearing and taking care of young children, hiring an overseer would have made sense; but Victoria and Hugo never had children together, and thus Victoria was able to expend a great deal of time on the maintenance of their diminishing landholdings. As juez and a friend of the governor, Pio Pico, Hugo was advantageously positioned to purchase the former lands of the San Gabriel mission when the governor put them up for sale. After Hugo purchased a tract of land on June 8, 1846, his economic hopes were temporarily bolstered, but like many of the rancheros, he overextended himself financially.

When the California gold rush erupted, Hugo rushed into the mines, further weakening his already compromised health. Like so many other miners, he failed to strike gold and instead drew on his previous merchant skills to open a store, in partnership with Jim McKinley, to sell goods to the miners. Victoria was left behind and in charge of the lands. The store initially provided some profits, but McKinley's lack of business acumen and Hugo's election as a representative to the California Congressional Convention in 1850 ended the enterprise. Directing his attention to governmental affairs brought both economic and marital setbacks. Forced to sell land in order to pay outstanding debts, by 1850 the Reids' landholdings totaled a mere 188 acres. In May 1851, an anxious Victoria wrote to Stearns: "We have not heard from him, and we are very much surprised that he had not written a single letter since he left."[30] A strong possibility exists that Hugo had temporarily abandoned his family. Ironically, it was during this possible estrangement from his wife—his purported informant—that Hugo wrote his collection of essays, *The Indians of Los Angeles County*.

Originally published in 1852 as letters to the *Los Angeles Star* newspaper in twenty-four weekly installments, this collection of essays described the history, habits, beliefs, and language of the California Indians prior to European contact. According to Robert F. Heizer, Benjamin Davis Wilson's "temporary appointment as Indian Agent for the southern district of California" prompted Hugo to claim himself an "authority on the subject" of California Indians in order to gain the next appointment as permanent Indian agent.[31] The Reids' diminishing fortunes made the position quite attractive, and his marriage to Victoria legitimized Reid's claim as an authority. Wilson wrote in 1852 that beyond Reid's twenty years of residence and his scholarly accomplishment was the fact that his "opportunities of knowing the Indians perhaps exceeded those of any in the State."[32] Wilson obviously believed that being married to Victoria gave Reid a unique entrée into the cultural world of the Indians—a view, if Laura King's personal account is correct, that Victoria also shared.

After the Mexican-American War, American businessmen came to dominate the Californian economy. Common sense would suggest that

Euro-American men who were bilingual and were incorporated into California society had greater advantages and chances of succeeding in the new economic and social environment; however, Hugo's experience belies this assumption. His economic opportunities were dwindling by the early 1850s, and neither his personal nor business associations were proving economically beneficial, which increased Hugo's dissatisfaction with marriage. By 1851, Hugo made his dissatisfaction quite evident in his letter to the newly engaged Emilio Onofrio. As he wrote to the younger man:

> Well friend, being the bachelor which you are now, very casually you could enter into one of those hotels and make yourself a beef *taco* without anyone knowing of it—but once married (if you ever come to getting roped into it) you'll see the difference—Even if you want to you won't be able to because even if it's only ten o'clock in the morning, in wanting to step out into the street the wife will greet you with Emilio, soul of mine, don't go, the table is already set. Whether you want to or not, at that moment you'll take off your hat for two reasons, one for that soft voice, and the other because your conscience condemns you. I say this is how it'll be because never will you suppose that one day you'll have taken a heretic as a consort.[33]

Was Hugo speaking from experience? If so, Victoria had transformed from being "a rose from Castile," with European gentility and beauty, into a nagging heretic, within the span of their ten-year marriage. Not only was Hugo feeling the constraints of marriage, but he also suffered the socioracial constraints of being married to an Indian woman as defined by the Euro-Americans. In an undated note entitled "Anecdote of a Lawyer," Hugo copied the following:

> In a justice of the Peace Court on one occasion two lawyers were engaged on one side, one of them had recently been married to an Indian girl, the other had an American wife. The opposite side was defended by a young lawyer who was not married but lived with one Indian girl. The client of the first had been proven by his own lawyer to have been going to *the* Ranchería to sleep!— The American wife's lawyer *feeling* his superiority over all others, to the total disregard of the *feelings* of others—Made the following remark—Any man who would cohabit with an Indian places himself on the level of the brutes![34]

Why was this note kept? Did Hugo need a reminder of how the expanding number of newly arrived Euro-Americans viewed the men who cohabited with "Indian" women? Did Reid identify with the lawyers or with someone else in the anecdote? Before the Mexican-American War, Californios accommodated the union of a white man and a neophyte woman, but in the solidifying world of Euro-American dominance and hegemony, as the note indicated, interracial or interethnic alliances were unacceptable. With only Spanish-Mexican neighbors, Victoria had conducted herself honorably and had reaped the privileges of elite social status. With new Euro-American neighbors, and after Hugo Reid died in 1852, the social forces that had supported her marital union were swept aside. In Euro-American California, race became the defining social category, and Victoria once again became a mere Indian, like the tens of thousands of other Indians who were being pressed to the lowest rung of the Californian economic and social ladder.

As the ranks of the Californios were overrun by the Euro-American masses and social interaction declined, the concessions previously granted to Victoria evaporated. After Hugo's death, Victoria was assigned a conservator, Benjamin Davis Wilson, to oversee her personal well-being and property. He proved a deceitful guardian. In 1854, Wilson produced a deed to the Huerta de Cuati, claiming to have paid $8,000 to Victoria, who signed the deed with a cross.[35] Why would the literate Victoria sign with a cross rather than with her name? Most likely the document was fraudulent, and Wilson took advantage of Victoria's vulnerability. In 1855 a court appointed Agustin Olvera as Victoria's administrator "because the court considered her incompetent to arrange her own property."[36] This final act signaled the complete erasure of the social and personal advancements Victoria had worked so hard to achieve.

According to Laura Evertson King, Victoria made a point shortly before her death of seeking King out for one last visit. The Doña who once wore black satin and expensive lace shawls was now robed in common cotton cloth, wrapped in a quilt, and attended by a single Indian servant.[37] On December 23, 1868, Victoria, the former Señora and Doña, died like so many other California Native Americans—ignored, destitute, and erased from the historical record by the notion that she was a mere Indian squaw. Ironically, while most Americans have paid little attention to her death or to her unique life experiences, Victoria's shadow continues to haunt California lore through one of the greatest California novels of all time, *Ramona*.

In the 1880s, two Americans, Hubert Howe Bancroft and Helen Hunt Jackson, busily researched and wrote seminal works that left indelible images of early nineteenth-century California on the American imagination.[38] The motivation and intent of both writers differed greatly, but the outcomes and impact of their writings—Bancroft in his seven volumes of Californian history and Jackson in her 1884 novel *Ramona*—effectively encased Californios before the Mexican-American War as tragic, romantic figures living a pastoral lifestyle in a halcyon age. Unlike Bancroft, who interviewed and collected vital historical narratives from aging Californios, Jackson was not interested in writing an accurate history. Instead, she intended to write the *Uncle Tom's Cabin* of the Californian Mission Indians, a novel that would set "forth some Indian experiences in a way to move people's hearts."[39] And she succeeded, to a certain extent; however, rather than moving the hearts of easterners to champion the Californian Mission Indians, *Ramona* sparked interest in Californio society.

The key to *Ramona*'s popularity was "not that it translate[d] fact into fiction, but that it translate[d] fact into romantic myth."[40] A retelling of William Shakespeare's *Othello*, the novel centers on two star-crossed lovers, the beautiful Ramona Gonzaga and the full-blooded Mission Indian Allesandro. Orphaned, Ramona is reared by the wealthy "Spanish" Doña Moreno, who never tells the young girl the circumstances of her birth—that her father was a wealthy Scottish merchant, Angus McPhail, who married an Indian woman whom he later disparaged. Although Jackson never names Victoria and refers to her as merely an Indian squaw, Victoria's shadow was made forever part of California's history.

Jackson knew enough of Victoria's marriage to Hugo Reid to use it as a motif within her novel, but she failed to understand Victoria's importance. Jackson's treatment of Victoria reminds us that not all Indian women, just as not all Spanish-Mexican women, can easily be classified and contained within the romantic and tragic images Americans tried to impose on them throughout the nineteenth century. How women negotiated their local cultural and social privileges are an important part of how Spanish borderlands history must be written. Race, class, social status, and marriage were constantly fluid and dependent on the specific configurations of greater social and historical forces. Through cultural and historical studies of specific life stories of women in the Spanish borderlands, a new and stronger light is helping to remove them from the shadows of American society and history.

NOTES

1. The exact date of their marriage has been lost, but Hugo Reid's correspondence clearly indicates that he and Victoria were married as early as

1836. Although literate, Victoria left only a handful of letters. Nineteenth-century Californianas left few written materials that would help contextualize and reveal what life was like for women of this time and place. Because Victoria never directly wrote about herself, this essay carefully reconstructs her life from contemporary accounts and mainly from Hugo Reid's personal and business letters, which reveal more about Hugo than Victoria.

2. Throughout the colonial Spanish borderlands, the Catholic Church commanded its missionaries to *reducir* (Latin for "to lead back") the Indians to Christianity. Unable to coerce the Indians into accepting Christianity, the church fathers systematically incorporated the Indians into mission life by forcing them to live in pueblos near missions, to wear clothes, to speak Spanish, and to learn reason in order to accept the true faith. Until the Indians accepted conversion, they were considered neophytes and apprenticed to the mission. Traditionally, apprenticeship should only have lasted ten years, after which the fathers would reward the new Christians with plots of land. As the missions became the most economically prosperous institutions in California, however, the church fathers were reluctant to give up such valuable landholdings, and therefore they arbitrarily dictated when the period of servitude would end. Thus, many neophytes served the mission far longer than ten years.

3. Gary B. Nash, "The Hidden History of Mestizo America," in *Sex, Love, Race: Crossing Boundaries in North American History*, ed. Martha Hodes (New York: New York University Press, 1999), 10–32.

4. See Ramón Gutiérrez, *When Jesus Came, the Corn Mothers Went Away: Marriage, Sexuality, and Power in New Mexico, 1500–1846* (Stanford, Calif.: Stanford University Press, 1991), 103–4, 285–92; and James F. Brooks, *Captives and Cousins: Slavery, Kinship, and Community in the Southwest Borderlands* (Chapel Hill: University of North Carolina Press, 2002), 196.

5. Antonia I. Castañeda, "Presidarias y Pobladores: Spanish-Mexican Women in Frontier Monterey, Alta California, 1770–1821" (Ph.D. diss., Stanford University, 1990), 250–62.

6. The term "Californio" became a popular form of self-identification by the Spanish-Mexican settlers in the 1830s. Californio was largely a political term, used mainly by second- and third-generation children born in California, who resented the lack of attention and funding that Mexico paid to their territory.

7. Heath Dillard, *Daughters of the Reconquesta: Women in Castilian Town Society, 1100–1300* (Cambridge, U.K.: Cambridge University Press, 1984), 2–9, 213–20.

8. Virginia M. Bouvier, *Women and the Conquest of California, 1542–1840: Codes of Silence* (Tucson: University of Arizona, 2001), 60.

9. Castañeda, "Presidarias y Pobladores," 114–73.

10. Ann Twinam, *Private Lives, Public Secrets: Gender, Honor, Sexuality, and Illegitimacy in Colonial Spanish America* (Stanford, Calif.: Stanford University Press, 1999), 29.

11. Castañeda, "Presidarias y Pobladores," 248–52; Douglas Monroy, *Thrown among Strangers: The Making of Mexican Culture in Frontier California* (Berkeley: University of California Press, 1990), 109.

12. Monroy, *Thrown among Strangers*, 59–62.

13. David J. Weber, *The Mexican Frontier,1821–1846: The American Southwest under Mexico* (Albuquerque: University of New Mexico Press, 1982), 158–64; Monroy, *Thrown among Strangers*, 157–61.

14. Marie E. Northrop, *Spanish-Mexican Families of Early California: 1769–1850* (2 vols.) (Burbank, California: Southern California Genealogical Society, 1987).

15. Perfecto Hugo Reid to Abel Stearns, July 21, 1838, SG Box 52, Manuscript Collections, Huntington Library; San Marino, California (hereinafter cited as MCHL).

16. Perfecto Hugo Reid to Abel Stearns, March 24, 1843, San Gabriel, SG Box 52, MCHL.

17. Perfecto Hugo Reid to Abel Stearns, June 29, 1841, San Gabriel, SG Box 52, MCHL.

18. Perfecto Hugo Reid to Abel Stearns, August 25, 1839, SG Box 52, MCHL.

19. Victoria Bartolomea Comicrabit Reid to Abel Stearns, July 16, 1842, San Gabriel, SG Box 51, MCHL.

20. Perfecto Hugo Reid to Abel Stearns, July 17, 1843, Rancho Uva Espina, SG Box 52, MCHL.

21. Ibid.

22. William Heath Davis, *Seventy-Five Years in California, 1831–1906* (San Francisco: John Howell, 1929), 109.

23. Ibid.

24. Laura Evertson King, "Hugo Reid and His Indian Wife," in *Historical Society of Southern California and Pioneer Register* (Los Angeles, 1898), 111.

25. Ibid.

26. Ibid., 112.

27. See Antonia I. Castañeda, "The Political Economy of Nineteenth-Century Stereotypes of Californianas," in *Between Borders: Essays on Mexicana/ Chicana History*, ed. Adelaida R. Del Castillo (Encino, Calif.: Floricanto Press, 1990), 213–38; and David J. Langum, "Californio Women and the Image of Virtue," *Southern California Quarterly* 59 (Fall 1977): 245–50.

28. Virginia L. Carpenter, *The Ranchos of Don Pacífico Ontiveros* (Santa Ana, Calif.: First Pioneer Press, 1982).

29. Perfecto Hugo Reid to Abel Stearns, June 15, 1841, San Gabriel, SG Box 52, MCHL.

30. Victoria Bartolomea Comicrabit Reid to Abel Stearns, May 30, 1849, SG Box 51, MCHL.

31. B. D. Wilson, *Los Angeles Star*, July 18, 1868, as quoted in Robert F. Heizer, ed., *The Indians of California: Hugo Reid's Letters of 1852* (Los Angeles: Southwest Museum, 1968), 1.

32. Ibid.

33. "Letter to Emilio Onofrio, no date, 1851," Hugo Reid Collection, Seaver Research Center, Museum of Natural History, Los Angeles, Calif.

34. "Anecdote of a Lawyer, undated," Hugo Reid Collection; emphasis in original.

35. Reid; Maria Victoria Bartolomea (Comicrabit) Reid to Benjamin Davis Wilson, deed to Rancho Huerta de Cuati, February 1854, WN 1528, MCHL.

36. U.S. Courts. District Court, California. Proceedings of Land California Land Cases, Southern District Case 171 (Rancho Huerta de Cuati or Quati), Maria Victoria Bartolomea (Comicrabit) Reid, claimant, 1852–1857, FAC 70 (455). MCHL. See also King, "Hugo Reid and His Indian Wife," 113.

37. King, "Hugo Reid and His Indian Wife," 113.

38. For Helen Hunt Jackson's travels and investigations in California, see Valerie Sherer Mathes, *The Indian Reform Letters of Helen Hunt Jackson, 1879–1885* (Norman: University of Oklahoma Press, 1998).

39. Ibid., 298.

40. Kevin Starr, *Inventing the Dream: California through the Progressive Era* (New York: Oxford University Press, 1985), 60–61.

2

GERTRUDIS BARCELÓ

La Tules of Image and Reality

Deena J. González

In the summer of 1846, Doña Gertrudis Barceló stood at an important crossroad. Exempted from the hardships and tribulations endured by the women around her, Barceló had profited enormously from the "gringo" merchants and itinerant retailers who had arrived in Santa Fé after the conquest. The town's leading businesswoman, owner of a gambling house and saloon, and its most unusual character, Barceló exemplified an ingenious turnaround in the way she and others in her community began resolving the problem of the Euro-American, now lodged more firmly than ever in their midst. Barceló also epitomized the growing dilemma of dealing with newcomers whose culture and orientation differed from hers.

Since 1821, people like Barceló had seen traders enter their town and change it. But local shopkeepers and vendors had done more than observe the developing marketplace. They had forged ahead, establishing a partnership with the adventurers who brought manufactured items and textiles to Santa Fé while exporting the products of Nuevo México, including gold, silver, and equally valuable goods, such as Navajo blankets and handwoven rugs.[1]

Barceló's life and activities were indisputably anchored in a community shaped by a changing economy, as well as by other political, social, and cultural demands. Orthodox interpretations of her life have overlooked the primacy of the surrounding turmoil. Moreover, by 1846, she would become the female object of the easiest, most exaggerated misunderstandings bred by such complicated frontier situations. The exaggerations have been examined from several perspectives, but standard works have failed to assess the role that sex and gender played in discussions of Barceló's business and personality.[2] The outcome has been the creation of a legend around her, one directly shaped by the disruptions experienced by her generation and focused on her business and her sex.

Gertrudis Barceló was said to have controlled men and to have dabbled in local politics, but these insinuations do not form the core of her legend. Rather, reporters of her time, professional historians today, and novelists have debated her morals, arguing about her influence over political leaders and speculating about whether she was operating a brothel. These concerns are consistently revealed in early accounts of Barceló by writers and soldiers recalling their experiences in the "hinterlands" of northern Mexico. The negative images and anti-Mexican stereotypes in these works not only stigmatized Barceló but also helped legitimize the Euro-Americans' conquest of the region. Absorbed and reiterated by succeeding generations of professional historians and novelists, the legend of Barceló has obscured the complex reality of cultural accommodation and ongoing resistance.

Moreover, the legend evolving around Barceló affected the lives of other Spanish-Mexican women. Her supposed moral laxity and outrageous dress were generalized to include all the women of Santa Fé. Susan Shelby Magoffin, the first Euro-American woman to travel down the Santa Fé Trail, observed in 1846 that "These were dressed in the Mexican style; large sleeves, short waists, ruffled skirts, and no bustles—which latter looks exceedingly odd in this day of grass skirts and pillows. All danced and smoked cigarittos, from the old woman with false hair and teeth [Doña Tula], to the little child."[3]

This was not the first account of La Tules, as Barceló was affectionately called (in reference either to her slimness or to her plumpness, because *tules* means "reed")[4] Josiah Gregg, a trader during the 1830s, said that La Tules was a woman of "loose habits," who "roamed" in Taos before she came to Santa Fé.[5] In his widely read *Commerce of the Prairies*, Gregg linked local customs—smoking, gambling, and dancing—to social and moral disintegration. La Tules embodied, for him and others, the extent of Spanish-Mexican decadence.

La Tules's dilemmas predated 1846 and, at a social and economic level, portended a community's difficulties, which were not long in developing. Governing officers in Chihuahua had already sent word of a crackdown on illegal trafficking.[6] Bishop Zubiría in Durango issued a pastoral limiting church holidays and celebrations, in an effort to economize on expenses but also on priests' time. This pastoral gave added emphasis to the regulations descending on New Mexicans, who now became aware that the Catholic Church, too, was reconsidering its obligations. In this period, Barceló and other Spanish-Mexicans experienced the tightening grip of the Mexican state, which was bent on rooting out uncontrolled trading; but they gained a reprieve accidentally. As orders arrived from the church concerning the condition of Christians on the northern frontier, the United States chose to invade, hurling General Stephen Kearny and his troops toward the capital city.[7]

Barceló's activities and business acumen demonstrated, despite these pressures, the *vecinos'* (residents') proven resilience and the town's characteristic adaptability. But in the 1840s Barceló also became the object of intense Euro-American scrutiny and harsh ridicule. She was an expert dealer at monte, a card game named after the *monte* (mountain) of cards that accumulated with each hand. She drew hundreds of dollars out of merchants and soldiers alike; it was the former who embellished her name and reputation, imbuing her facetiously with characteristics of superiority and eccentricity.

Josiah Gregg, the trader, first brought Barceló notoriety because his book described her as a loose woman. But Gregg also argued that money from gambling eventually helped elevate her moral character.[8] A Protestant, and a doctor in failing health, Gregg respected only her gift—the one he understood best—for making money. During her lifetime, she became extraordinarily wealthy, and for that reason as well, Gregg and others would simultaneously admire and disdain her.

In the face of such contradictory attitudes toward her, Barceló ventured down a trail of her own choosing. Not quite as rebellious as Juana Lopes, who had defied husband and judge alike, she nevertheless achieved personal autonomy. Several times, she appeared before magistrates to pay fines, testifying once against an indicted judge who had pocketed her money. She even involved her family in her pursuits, and they were fined along with her.[9] As early as 1825, she was at the mining camp outside of Santa Fé, Real del Oro, doing a brisk business at monte.[10] By the 1830s, the card dealer was back in town, enticing Euro-Americans to gamble under terms she prescribed. At her saloon, she served the men alcohol as she dealt rounds of cards. Controlling consumption as well as the games, Barceló accommodated the newcomers, but on her own terms. "Shrewd," Susan Shelby Magoffin, wife of the trader Samuel Magoffin, called Barceló in 1846.[11]

Barceló had proven her shrewdness long before that. Since the 1820s, Barceló had engaged in an extremely profitable enterprise. Gambling, dubbed by observers the national pastime, was ubiquitous, and by the mid-1830s nearly every traveler and merchant felt compelled to describe Barceló's contributions to the game.[12] Matt Field, an actor and journalist from Missouri, depicted Barceló's saloon as a place where her "calm seriousness was alone discernible, and the cards fell from her fingers as steadily as though she were handling only a knitting needle. . . . Again and again the long fingers of Señora Toulous swept off the pile of gold, and again were they replaced by the unsteady fingers of her opponent."[13] By any account, Euro-Americans could understand what drove Barceló. Because they recognized in her their own hungry search for profit, they embellished their stories and, just as frequently, maligned her.

When Barceló died in 1852, she was worth over ten thousand dollars, a sum twice as high as most wealthy Spanish-Mexican men possessed and larger than the average worth of Euro-Americans in Santa Fé.[14] Her properties were extensive: she owned the saloon, a long building with large rooms, and she had an even larger home not far from the plaza. She made enough money to give generously to the church and to her relatives, supporting families and adopting children.[15] Military officers claimed that she entertained lavishly and frequently.[16]

Dinners, dances, gambling, and assistance to the poverty-stricken elevated Barceló to a special place in New Mexican society, where she remained throughout her life. The community respected her since it tolerated atypical behavior in others and rarely seemed preoccupied with what Barceló represented. Even her scornful critics were struck by how well received and openly admired the woman with the "red hair and heavy jewelry" was among Santa Fe's "best society."[17]

What was it about Nuevo México in the two decades before the war that allowed a woman like Barceló to step outside the accepted boundaries of normal or typical female behavior, make a huge sum of money, undergo excessive scrutiny, primarily by newcomers to Santa Fé, and yet be eulogized by her own people? Some answers lie within her Spanish-Mexican community, which, although beset by persisting problems, had flexibility and an inclination toward change. Others lie in the general position and treatment of women in that society.

Court records and other documents reveal that Santa Fé's women were expected to defer to men but did not, that they were bound by a code of honor and respectability but often manipulated it to their advantage, and that they were restrained by fathers and brothers from venturing too far out of family and household but frequently disobeyed them. One professional historian has argued that social codes in colonial New Mexican society, with their twin emphasis on honor and virtue, were primarily metaphors for expressing hierarchical relationships but also served to resolve conflict as much as to restrict women.[18] Women's behavior and the espoused social ideals of restraint, respectability, and deference were at cross-purposes, especially in a community that was supremely concerned about the appearance of honor if not its reality. Separate requirements based on gender—or what the society would label appropriate masculine and feminine virtues—occupied an equally important place in these social codes and also concerned power and the resolution of conflict.

Barceló's gambling and drinking violated the rigid codes that organized appropriate female behavior, but such behavior was not the key to her distinctiveness. Rather, her success as a businesswoman and gambler gave her a unique independence ordinarily denied women. Thus, the most hostile comments about her frequently came from Spanish-Mexican women. In particular, complaints filed against Barceló reveal the extent of other women's animosity, not men's, and were usually thinly disguised as aspersions on her honor. In 1835, Ana María Rendón remonstrated that Barceló and Lucius Thruston, a migrant from Kentucky, were cohabiting.[19] In fact, Barceló's husband lived in the same house, indicating that Thruston was probably a boarder. Honor lay in the proof, and Barceló achieved both by defending herself and her husband as well. Another time, Barceló complained about a slanderous comment made by Josefa Tenório and was also exonerated.[20] Spanish-Mexicans of Santa Fé remained a litigious people, and they waged battles on many fronts. The *alcalde* court (local court) prevailed as the best place to seek resolution. However, Catholic Spanish-Mexican *vecinos* were generally a forgiving people, especially where slander and gossip were involved. Barceló forgave Ana María Rendón's complaint when Rendón retracted it, and the records are filled with similar recantations in other cases.[21]

At issue, then, were not Barceló's violations of gender and social codes—she had in part moved beyond that—but the others' violations of her good name and reputation. On one level, their hostility and outright distrust of Barceló were vendettas directed against a neighbor on the road to wealth and prestige. On another, women upheld the gender code (albeit with some trepidation) because, in complaining about Barceló, they defended themselves and their society. Even when she was fined for gambling, the amounts were so minuscule that they neither halted Barceló's gambling nor conveyed a forceful message about modifying social behavior.[22]

Barceló, a married woman, would not have been able to step outside the boundaries of her society, nor would Manuela Baca or Juana Lopes in the previous decade, if there were no disjunction between the idealized married life and the conditions that stood in the way of its realization—conditions such as taking in boarders or having children out of wedlock. Rallitas Washington, Barceló's grandniece born out of wedlock, as well as hundreds of other women whose mothers were unmarried, formed a decidedly heterodox, yet devoutly Catholic, community.[23] In relationships as in personal behavior, these women's lack of conformity did not shake the conscience of a community as much as needle it.

Beyond cultural mores and behavioral codes, though, what might go unrecognized is that women of the Far West who defied the rules might have been viewed from the outset as marginal. When not ignored completely, women who have existed outside the boundaries of a society of community—or who have been ostracized for various reasons—have frequently been termed outlaws and burdened with characteristics obscuring their social or economic conditions. That may have been standard procedure for marginal women everywhere.[24]

But marginality signifies not only the transgression of social boundaries but also the aftermath of such transgression; it represents the fate of people who press against those boundaries and afterward must live on the edges of society. Barceló cleverly crossed social and sexual barriers to gamble, make money, buy property, and influence politicians, but she avoided marginality. She did not regard herself as a marginal woman, nor was she necessarily marginalized, except by Euro-Americans. She was unusual and she was mocked for it, but not by her own people. In fact, her life and legend are interesting precisely because, in the eyes of observers, she came to represent the worst in Spanish-Mexican culture while, as a Spanish-Mexican, she mastered the strategies and methods of the Americanizers; she achieved what they had professed in speeches and reports originally to want for all New Mexicans.[25]

Barceló's life and her legend contradict orthodox notions of marginality in a situation of conquest. In their writings, conquerors maligned and ostracized her. The opinions they expressed and the images they drew of her sealed her legend in the popular imagination because their works were distributed throughout the United States. Translated into several languages, Gregg's *Commerce of the Prairies* was reprinted three times between 1844, when it first appeared, and 1857. Thousands of readers learned through him of the "certain female of very loose habits, known as La Tules."[26] What Gregg and the others could not communicate to their audience was that La Tules was adaptable, and that, before their eyes, she had begun disproving their notion that Spanish-Mexicans were "lazy and indolent."[27] She contradicted James Josiah Webb's contention that all Spanish-Mexicans did was "literally dance from the cradle to the grave."[28] Barceló's busy saloon hosted nightly fandangos, or dances, and their organizer easily became the target of Webb's manipulation of stereotype. Dancing, drinking, and gambling—the order was often changed according to how much the writer wanted to emphasize licentious behavior—gave these Protestant travelers pause, and they quickly made use of the observations to fictionalize Barceló's, and all women's, lives.

But the tales about La Tules are important in another respect. Fictitious representations marginalized Barceló because they shrouded her life in mystery and called forth several stereotypes about Mexicans. Yet Barceló was hardly the excessive woman the travelers depicted. Instead, she became pivotal in the achievement of their conquest. Worth thousands of dollars, supportive of the army, and friendly to accommodating politicians, Barceló was in the right place to win over Spanish-Mexicans for the intruders. Using business and political skills, she made the saloon the hub of the town's social and economic life, and at the hall she kept abreast of the latest political developments. Politicians and military officers alike went there seeking her opinion or involved her in their discussions about trade or the army.[29] As adviser and confidante, she took on a role few other women could have filled. If she existed on the fringes of a society, it was because she chose to place herself there—a woman with enormous foresight who pushed against her own community's barriers and risked being labeled by the travelers a madam or a whore.

Such caricatures denied her contributions to the economy and the society. Had she not been a gambler, a keeper of a saloon, or a woman, she might have been praised for her industry and resourcefulness, traits that antebellum Euro-Americans valued in their own people.[30] But from the point of view of the writers, the admirable qualities of a woman who lived by gambling and who was her own proprietor would have been lost on Protestant, middle-class readers. Furthermore, they could hardly imagine, let alone tolerate, the diversity Santa Fé exhibited. It became easier to reaffirm their guiding values and walk a literary tightrope by making La Tules a symbol of Spanish-Mexican degeneracy or an outcast altogether. Barceló had exceeded their wildest expectations, and in their eyes she was an outlaw.

Yet the aspersions heaped on Barceló were not designed solely to obscure her personality and life or to make her activities legendary. They created an image that fit the Euro-Americans' preconceptions about Spanish-Mexicans. Thus described to the readers, the image of Barceló in travel documents merely confirmed older, pernicious stereotypes. Many recalled the *leyenda negra* (black legend) of the sixteenth century, when Spaniards were objectified as a fanatical, brutal people.[31] Historians and others have traced another critical stage in the development of anti-Mexican fervor to the antebellum period, when expansionist dreams and sentiments of such politicians as Senator Thomas Hart Benton gave rise to a continued confusion about Spanish-Mexican culture.[32] Not only travelers from the United States but also residents in general harbored deep prejudices toward Spanish-Mexicans.[33] The travelers of the nineteenth century thus represented broader racial attitudes and demonstrated the ethnocentrism of a population back home.

Racial slurs and derogatory comments about Mexicans appeared regularly in the *Congressional Record*, in newspapers, and, not coincidentally, in travel accounts.[34] Speeches and statements consistently equated brown skin with promiscuity, immorality, and decay. Albert Pike, who arrived in New Mexico from New England in 1831, called the area around Santa Fé "bleak, black, and barren";[35] New Mexicans, he said, were "peculiarly blessed with ugliness."[36] The chronicler of a military expedition to New Mexico in the 1840s, Frank Edwards, said that all Mexicans were "debased in all moral sense"[37] and amounted to little more than "swarthy thieves and liars."[38] The same judgments were made later, long after the war had ended, and reflect the persistence of the same thinking. The historian Francis Parkman argued that people in the West could be "separated into three divisions, arranged in order of their merits: white men, Indians, and Mexicans; to the latter of whom the honorable title of 'whites' is by no means conceded."[39] In the same period, William H. Emory of the boundary commission declared that the "darker colored" races were inevitably "inferior and syphilitic."[40]

These select references—and there are hundreds of other comments like them—depict a set of racist attitudes and ethnocentric beliefs from the Jacksonian period that carried into Santa Fé. Travelers thus mirrored the intrinsic values of a nation encroaching on Mexican territory and were fueled by the heightened fervor over destiny and superiority.

Scholars have assessed the genre of travel guides and recollections as contributions to literature and have debated its special characteristics of construction, organization, and distortion.[41] But the books had something besides literary appeal; they sold rapidly in a country hungry for information about the West. Many planned visits and escapes to the healthier climates of the Southwest, while others intended to live in warmer areas and to find markets for their goods: such motives had inspired Gregg to leave Missouri for Santa Fe. Although he and his fellow adventurers were genuinely curious about Mexicans and about what the West had to offer, one important consequence of their visits, vacations, and reports, at least for Barceló, was that the migrants also brought capital to Santa Fé.[42] The accounts cannot, therefore, be considered only as travel literature; they do not, as some have argued, simply unveil anti-Mexican, anti-Catholic sentiment.[43] Rather, they describe—from the outside in, from the perspective of the colonizer—the systematic movement of an ethnocentric people to Santa Fé and reveal the interest in the promise of continued prosperity in the Southwest.

Travel writers of the nineteenth century, however, were also conscious of the desires and proclivities of their readers. Hence, these writers described the unsavory material culture (Matt Field gazed upon the adobe buildings and labeled Santa Fé's houses a testament to "the power of mud")[44] and the miserable conditions because they thought the objectionable portraits would suit their audience. Assessed today, the writers and their reflections continue to convey the overwhelmingly persistent attitudes, values, and ideas of a conquering group interpreting others. Except for a government official, Brantz Mayer, whose book indicted United States travelers by citing their prejudices against Mexicans, these writers mainly exhibited condescension and an implied, if not outspoken, sense of superiotity.[45]

This uniformity in outlook is not the only characteristic binding these works and suggesting their significance in conquest. Many of the writers patterned their books after previously published accounts, such as Zebulon Pike's narrative of his reconnaissance trips in the early nineteenth century.[46] Imitating his organization and style, such writers as Gregg exaggerated La Tules's appearance, blamed her for the ruin of many "wayward youth," and imitated previous travelogues in other ways to portray and dismiss the wretched condition of the Spanish-Mexicans. Barceló's smoking and gambling were but two of the most widely reported vices. George Brewerton, writing for *Harper's Magazine* in the 1850s, continued the tradition. To the growing list of those at fault, he added the duplicitous New Mexican priests, for stifling individuality and stunting well-being:

> Here were the men, women, and children—the strong man, the
> mother, and the lisping child—all engaged in the most debasing
> of vices, gambling, the entire devotion to which is the besetting

sin of the whole Mexican people. . . . What better could you have expected from an ignorant, priest-ridden peasantry, when those whom they are taught to reverence and respect, and who should have been their prompters to better things, not only allow, but openly practice this and all other iniquities?[47]

The popularity of gambling and drinking among all people prompted Brewerton and his predecessors to decry the pervasive debauchery—which, it seemed, only they, as Euro-Americans, could relieve. They failed to understand that Spanish-Mexicans loved celebration and socializing. The church organized parties, pageants, and social affairs on varied occasions; yet even officially sanctioned church holidays or the days when patron saints were honored did not escape Euro-American comments.[48] Brewerton found "rude engravings" of saints everywhere, among rich and poor, which he said would be "decked out by the females of the family with all sorts of tawdry ornaments.[49] He wondered about people who would use a doll to represent the Virgin Mary. Brewerton failed, in his rigid anti-Catholic viewpoint, to understand the beauty and intricacy of the *bultos* and *retablos* (icons and altarpieces). Catholicism, in Brewerton's opinion, did nothing but give Spanish-Mexicans occasion to revel in superstition, or to drink and dance. A community's way of celebrating—even the pious processions when the Virgin and the saints were paraded through town for all to worship in the annual outpouring of public devotion—was lost on Protestants: "During this whole time the city exhibited a scene of universal carousing and revelry. All classes abandoned themselves to the most reckless dissipation and profligacy. . . . I never saw a people so infatuated with the passion for gaming."[50] Whether commemorating saints or gathering for entertainment and diversion, Spanish-Mexicans appeared lascivious.

To the Protestant mind, nothing short of the complete elimination of gambling would lift New Mexicans out of their servility and make them worthy of United States citizenship. The Jacksonian Americans wanted to replace gambling with industry and enterprise. To them, gambling stemmed from a fundamental lack of faith in the individual, and it was risky besides. Travelers called monte a game of chance; they said that it required no particular skills and brought undeserved wealth.[51] By that logic, La Tules, a dealer par excellence, was not an entrepreneur; her wealth was undeserved because it sprang from "unbridled passions."[52] Her gravest sin against Protestant ethics became not the unskilled nature of her trade or her undeserved success but her lack of restraint: her wealth was uncontrolled. Yet initial misgivings about Barceló and the games passed after many entertaining evenings at the gambling house. Once soldiers and others began going there, they lingered, and returned often.[53] Deep-seated anti-Mexican feelings and moralistic judgments gave way to the profits that awaited them if they won at monte, or the pleasures to be savored each evening in Santa Fé even if they lost.

At the numerous tables that lined Barceló's establishment, men who could not speak Spanish and people who did not understand English learned a new language. Card games required the deciphering of gestures and facial expressions but did not depend on any verbal communication. Soldiers and travelers new to Santa Fé understood easily enough what was important at the gaming table. Over cards, the men and women exchanged gold or currency in a ritual that emblazoned their meetings with new intentions. Drinking, cursing, and smoking, the soldiers and others unloaded their money at the table; if Barceló profited, they lost. But the game was such a diversion for the lonely soldiers that they hardly seemed to mind. The stakes grew larger at every turn, and many dropped away from the table to stand at the bar. Barceló's saloon took care of those who did not gamble as well as those who lost. Sometimes a group of musicians arrived and began playing. Sometimes women—who, if not gambling, had been observing the scene—cleared a space in the long room, and dancing began.[54]

Barceló did more than accommodate men by inviting them to gamble. She furthered their adjustment to Santa Fé by bringing them into a setting that required their presence and money. At the saloon, the men were introduced to Spanish-Mexican music, habits, and humor. They could judge the locals firsthand and could observe a community's values and habits through this single activity. After they had a few drinks, their initial fears and prejudices gradually yielded to the relaxed, sociable atmosphere of the gambling hall.

In the spring of 1847, Lieutenant Alexander Dyer first visited the saloon. By June, his journal listed attendance at no fewer than forty fandangos and described numerous visits to La Tules's saloon. Frequently, cryptic citations indicated his rush to abandon the journal for the card games: "at the Me. House tonight" meant a visit to the monte house, and it appeared dozens of times in any given month.[55] Dyer's "Mexican War Journal" leaves the distinct impression that a soldier's life, for those of his stripe, involved a constant round of entertainment; visits and parties at Barceló's hall were part of an officer's busy social life.

Thus, rhetoric about gambling or cavorting lessened with time. If visitors did not entirely accept the sociable atmosphere, they were sufficiently lonely for Euro-American women and companionship to go to Barceló's saloon and attend other events to which they were invited. When Kearny and his officers went to Mass on their first Sunday in town, they endeared themselves to Spanish-Mexicans.[56] Some soldiers at the fort, like Dyer, had little choice but to adapt, because they were assigned to Santa Fé for two years. Other newcomers, however, were shocked into submission.

Finding much to upset them, visitors were nevertheless impressed by the scenic grandeur of Santa Fé and the environs. James Ohio Pattie remained as awed by Taos Mountain, stretching fifteen thousand feet high, as he was intrigued by the native life below it. He puzzled over differences: "I had expected to find no difference between these people and our own, but their language. I was never so mistaken. The men and women were not clothed in our fashion."[57]

Nine days later, Pattie reached Santa Fé, and this time his tone grew prosaic:

> The town contains between four and five thousand inhabitants.
> It is situated on a large plain. A handsome stream runs through it,
> adding life and beauty to a scene striking and agreeable from the
> union of amenity and cultivation around, with the distant view
> of snow clad mountains. It is pleasant to walk on the flat roofs of
> the houses in the evening, and look on the town and plain
> spread below.[58]

In a few weeks, Pattie had reached Chihuahua City, traveling the considerable distance in a short time. He described it as the "largest and handsomest town I had ever seen."[59] The trek across treacherous deserts, the long unbroken plain, and probably the fact that Spanish-Mexicans were much friendlier to him than Indians (whom he feared and loathed) changed Pattie's original reservations.

But travel records contain an underlying difficulty: they tend to freeze their author's thoughts in time and do not reveal the extent of the adaptations or changes a writer might have experienced. Many travelers evidently did not find anything to admire or enjoy in Santa Fé, but some did. Although locked into a particular time and a special setting, the men, after consistent reflection and observation, relaxed their worst fears. Pattie's descriptions might not have been atypical in that regard.

Court cases offer other impressions of how sojourning Euro-Americans changed their organizing concepts and values. The evidence is especially suggestive for those who began making a transition to becoming settlers. In the 1820s, Julian Green was fined for gambling at monte; on the same day, the judge assessed a fine against Barceló.[60] In 1850, the census lists Green, with a woman named María, in a household containing six children; all have Spanish first names.[61] Another *vecino*, Marcelo Pacheco, sued William Messervy for slander in the 1840s, calling the merchant "a trespasser who thinks he owns everything."[62] He won his case, and Messervy had to pay a fine. Perhaps Green and Messervy were perplexed about Santa Fe's ways, as many migrants had been, but because they paid their fines and stayed in Santa Fé, they changed.

Investigations in these records delineate the onset of the newcomers' accommodation. Barceló was not the only one practicing accommodation; it worked in two directions. Whether obeying the community's laws or breaking them, new men were adjusting to life away from home. Santa Fé modified the settling Euro-Americans, at times even the sojourning ones, and Barceló had begun to socialize them in the traditions of an older settlement. The people of the Dancing Ground continued their practice of accepting newcomers, particularly those who seemed able to tolerate, if not embrace, the community's religious and secular values.

At the same time, the conquering soldiers were armed, as the merchants Gregg and Webb were, with purpose and commitment. Military men brought plans and realized them: a fort above the town was begun the day after Kearny marched into Santa Fé. Soldiers built a two-story-high flagstaff, and the imposing structure on the plaza attracted visitors from the Dancing Ground who came supposedly to admire it, but probably also were there to assess the military's strength.[63] What better symbol than a new garrison and an obtrusive monument rising high for all the people to notice? Soldiers hailed these crowning achievements as signs of blessings from God to a nation destined to control the hemisphere, but locals were not so pleased.

A new wave of resistance derailed Barcdó's efforts to help resettle Euro-Americans in Santa Fé. Nevertheless, even after her death in 1852, Barceló's legend continued to indicate that her role extended beyond the immediate helping hand she had lent Euro-Americans. No documents written by her, except a will, have survived to tell whether she even recognized her accomplishment or if she read much into the assistance she had given the American cause. Her wealth would suggest that she might have harbored an understanding of her influential status in the process of colonization. One fact remains, whether she realized it or not: beginning with her, the accommodation of Euro-Americans proceeded on several levels. Barcdó had inaugurated the first, at the gambling hall, and she set the stage as well for the second, when women began marrying the newcomers.

But as one retraces the original surrounding tensions—deriving from the steady and continuing presence of traders, merchants, and soldiers— and juxtaposes them against Barceló's achievement as an architect of a plan that reconciled the Euro-American to Santa Fé, the realities of displacement and encroachment must not be forgotten. Lieutenant Dyer reported problems as he observed them, and he commented a year after his arrival in Santa Fe: "Still it began to be apparent that the people generally were dissatisfied with the change."[64] In January 1847, resisters in Taos caught and scalped Governor Charles Bent, leaving him to die.[65] In the spring, a lieutenant who had been pursuing horse thieves was murdered, and forty-three Spanish-Mexicans were brought to Santa Fé to stand trial for the crime.[66] In October of the same year, some months after several revolts had been suppressed and their instigators hanged, Dyer reported "a large meeting of citizens at the Palace," where speakers expressed "disaffection at the course of the commissioned officers."[67]

Local dissatisfaction and political troubles had not subsided, in spite of Barceló's work. In the late 1840s, Navajos and Apaches stepped up their raids, and reports filtered in of surrounding mayhem.[68] The garrisoned soldiers grew impatient and acted rashly, and Dyer reported that "a Mexican was unfortunately shot last night by the sentinel at my store house. Tonight we have a rumor that the Mexicans are to rise and attack us."[69] The government in Santa Fé was being forced again to come to terms with each new case of racial and cultural conflict, because it was still charged with trying murders and treason, and it had now become the seat for initiating solutions. Problems no longer brewed outside; they had been brought home by accommodated Euro-Americans.

But Barceló should not be blamed here, as she has been by some, for so many problems. She symbolized the transformations plaguing her people. She symbolized as well how an older community had handled the arrival of men from a new, young nation still seeking to tap markets and find a route to the Pacific. Moreover, she exemplified contact and conflict between independent female Catholics and westering male Protestants. The political and social constraints within which she existed had not disappeared as a community contemplated what to do with the strangers among them.

The people of Santa Fé did not kill any newcomers as residents of Taos had. Surrounding the Dancing Ground, stories and legends of other people resisting Americanization were about to begin, and these no longer empha-sized accommodation. Barceló was unusual in that way as well. She was of a particular time and a special place. The famed resister to American en-croachment, Padre Antonio José Martínez of Taos, opposed (in his separat-ist plans and principles) all that Barceló had exemplified. A legend developed around him that stands in interesting contrast to La Tules's.[70]

Yet in New Mexico and throughout the West, resistance was giving way to Euro-American encroachment. Richard Henry Dana, traveling in Cali-fornia during the 1830s, mourned the seemingly wasted opportunity pre-sented by land still in the possession of Spanish-Mexicans: "In the hands of an enterprising people, what a country this might be!"[71] His fellow sojourners to New Mexico concurred. What Dana and the other Euro-Americans failed to see was that the land and its communities were al-ready in the hands of such enterprising persons as Barceló. But rather than acknowledge the truth, they disparaged her; as conquerors their minds could not comprehend her intellect, enterprise, and success. Barceló, they believed, had erred. Yet in giving herself to the conquest, but not the conquerors, she survived and succeeded. She drew betting clients to her saloon; they played but lost; she gambled and won. In the end, the sa-loon that attracted conquerors released men who had been conquered.

NOTES

1. Josiah Gregg, *The Commerce of the Prairies,* ed. Max Moorhead (Norman: University of Oklahoma Press, 1964), 105–6 (originally published 1844).

2. Fray Angélico Chavez, "Doña Tules: Her Fame and Her Funeral," *El Palacio* 62 (August 1950): 227–34; Janet Lecompte, "The Independent Women of Hispanic New Mexico, 1821–1846," *Western Historical Quarterly* 22 (January 1981): 25–26.

3. Stella Drumm, ed., *The Diary of Susan Shelby Magoffin, 1846–1847: Down the Santa Fe Trail and into Mexico* (Lincoln: University of Nebraska Press, 1982), 145.

4. Tules was the diminutive for Gertrudis. See Marc Simmons, *The Little Lion of the Southwest: A Life of Manuel Antonio Cháves* (Chicago: University of Chicago Press, 1983), 55.

5. Gregg, *Commerce of the Prairies,* 168.

6. Howard R. Lamar, *Far Southwest* (New York: Norton, 1970), 55.

7. On the church, see "Zubiría Pastoral," 1840, Archives of the Arch-diocese of Santa Fe, Coronado Collection, University of New Mexico,

microfilm, LDD, no. 2; and "Bishop Zubiría's Visitation," 1845, Archives of the Archdiocese of Santa Fe, box 4, book 89.

8. Gregg, *Commerce of the Prairies,* 168–69.

9. See Trinidad Barceló, June 9, 1825, Probate Court Journals, Mexican Archives of New Mexico, New Mexico State Records Center, microfilm, roll 26, frame 187.

10. Janet Lecompte, "La Tules and the Americans," *Arizona and the West* (Autumn 1978): 220.

11. Drumm, *Diary of Susan Shelby Magoffin,* 120.

12. For Gregg's comments, see *Commerce of the Prairies,* 168–69; for other comments, see William Clark Kennedy, *Persimmon Hill: A Narrative of St. Louis and the Far West* (Norman: University of Oklahoma Press, 1948), 191; and John E. Sunder, ed, *Matt Field on the Santa Fé Trail* (Norman: University of Oklahoma Press, 1960), 206.

13. Sunder, *Matt Field,* 209.

14. Angelina F. Veyna, "Z & Zs My last wish that . . .": A look at colonial Nuevo Mexicanas through their testaments," in *Building with Our Hands: New Directions in Chicana Studies,* eds. Adela de la Torre and Beatriz Pesquera (Berkeley: University of California Press, 1993): 91–108. For comparison, see table 6.2 in the essay by Angelina Veyna in this volume.

15. Will of Gertrudis Barceló, Santa Fe County Records, Wills and Testaments, 1848–1856, book A-1, 154.

16. John Galvin, ed., *Western America in 1846–1847: The Original Travel Diary of Lieutenant J. W. Abert, Who Mapped New Mexico for the United States Army* (San Francisco: J. Howell, 1966), 75; see Abert's report in *Senate Executive Document* no. 23, 29th Cong., 1st sess.

17. Gregg, *Commerce of the Prairies,* 168–69.

18. Ramón Arturo Gutiérrez, in a paper presented at the annual meeting of the Western Historical Association, Salt Lake City, October 12, 1984.

19. See Lecompte, "La Tules," 222; and the source, Complaint of Ana María Rendón to the alcalde, Probate Court Journals, 1835, roll 20.

20. Complaint of Ana María Rendón.

21. Lecompte, "La Tules," p. 222; for recantations, see Complaint against José Tenório, January 15, 1828, and November 14, 1829, Probate Court Journals, roll 8, frame 310; Petition of Juan Francisco Gonzales, Probate Court Journals, 1829, roll 10, frame 177.

22. Gertrudis Barceló, June 9, 1825, Probate Court Journals, roll 26, frame 186.

23. On the issues of illegitimacy and legitimacy, see Ramón Arturo Gutiérrez, "Marriage, Sex, and the Family: Social Change in Colonial New Mexico, 1690–1846," Ph.D. diss., University of Wisconsin–Madison, 1980.

For examples of the church's stance on legitimacy and baptism, see Books of Baptisms, 1826–1841, Archives of the Archdiocese of Santa Fe, New Mexico State Records Center, microfilm.

24. On the Far West, see George M. Blackburn and Sherman L. Richards, "The Prostitutes and Gamblers of Virginia City, Nevada: 1870," *Pacific Historical Review* 48 (May 1979): 239–58; and Lawrence B. de Graaf, "Race, Sea and Region: Black Women in the American West, 1850–1920," *Pacific Historical Review* 49 (May 1980): 285–313. For earlier periods and for women of two different worlds, see Adelaida del Castillo, "Malintzin Tenépal: A Preliminary Look into a New Perspective," in *Essays on La Mujer*, ed. Rosaura Sánchez and Rosa Martínez Crux (Los Angeles: Chicano Studies Research Center, University of California, 1977), 124–49; and Marina Warner, *Joan of Arc: The Image of Female Heroism* (New York: Knopf, 1981).

25. For speeches, see Kearny's in Ralph Emerson Twichell, *The Story of the Conquest of Santa Fe: New Mexico and the Building of Old Fort Marcy*, A.D. *1846* (Santa Fe: Historical Society of New Mexico, 1923), 30; for another, see *Santa Fe Republican*, January 22, 1848; and for an earlier version of the same ideas but espoused in the United States, see *Richmond Esquire*, May 11, 1847. For a report and discussion on the benefits a railroad would bring, see the *Western Journal*, vol. 1, 260; and the *Richmond Daily Union*, May 13, 1847.

26. Gregg, *Commerce of the Prairies*, 168.

27. Waddy Thompson, *Recollections of Mexico* (New York: Wiley and Putnam, 1846), 23.

28. James Josiah Webb, "Memoirs, 1844–1889," Museum of New Mexico, History Library, Santa Fe, manuscript, 46; James Ohio Partie, *The Personal Narrative of James O. Pattie, of Kentucky* (Ann Arbor: University of Michigan Press, 1960), 120 (originally published 1831).

29. Simmons, *Little Lion*, 55; for the officers at the game of monte, see Walter Briggs, "The Lady They Called Tules," *New Mexico Magazine* 39 (1971): 9–16.

30. For an overview, see Edward Pessen, *Jacksonian America: Society, Personality and Politics* (Homewood., Ill.: Row, Peterson, 1969). For criticism of the attendant values, see Herman Melville, *The Confidence-Man: His Masquerade* (New York: New American Library, 1964; originally published 1857); for an interpretation of the novel, see Roy Harvey Pearce, "Melville's Indian Hater: A Note on the Meaning of 'The Confidence-Man,'" *Publications of the Modern Language Association* 67 (1952): 942–48.

31. The legend's origins have been traced to several sources, among them Bartolomé de las Casas, *In Defense of the Indians*, trans. Stafford Poole (De Kalb: Northern Illinois University Press, 1974). For other arguments

about the origins, see Stanley T. Williams, *The Spanish Background of American Literature* (New York: Shoe String Press, 1968), 1:3; and Philip Wayne Powell, *Tree of Hate: Propaganda and Prejudices Affecting United States Social Relations with the Hispanic World* (New York: Basic Books, 1971).

32. Thomas Hart Benton, Speech on the Oregon Question, May 28, 1846, Senate Document, *Congressional Globe*, 29th Cong., 1st sess., 915, 917.

33. For earlier statements, see Joel Roberts Poinsett, *Notes on Mexico Made in the Autumn of 1822* (New York: Praeger, 1969), 40, 120–22 (originally published 1824); for a detailed survey of attitudes toward Mexicans, see Philip Anthony Hernández, "The Other Americans: The American Image of Mexico and Mexicans, 1550–1850," Ph.D. diss., University of California, Berkeley, 1974.

34. Dr. Adolphus Wislizenus, "Memoir of a Tour to Northern Mexico," *Senate Miscellaneous Document,* 30th Cong., 1st sess., 2–3. For an example of an anti-Mexican travel account in Texas, see Mary Austin Holley, *Observations, Historical, Geographical, and Descriptive* (Austin: University of Texas Press, 1935), 128 (originally published 1833); in California, see Alfred Robinson, *Life in California* (New York: Da Capo, 1969), 73 (originally published 1846).

35. Albert Pike, *Prose Sketches and Poems, Written in the Western Country with Additional Stories,* ed. David Weber (Albuquerque: University of New Mexico Press, 1967), 7.

36. Ibid., 275. For a Euro-American woman's reactions during visits to Santa Fe, see Jane Austin, Letter to her "Dear Brother," October 23, 1846, Museum of New Mexico, History Library, Santa Fe, box 4, 1.

37. Frank S. Edwards, *A Campaign in New Mexico with Colonel Doniphan* (Philadelphia: Carey and Hart, 1847), 132.

38. Ibid., 50.

39. Francis Parkman, *The California and Oregon Trail: Being Sketches of Prairie and Rocky Mountain Life* . . . (New York: Putnam, 1849), 360.

40. W. H. Emory, "Notes of a Military Reconnaissance from Fort Leavenworth, in Missouri, to San Diego, in California . . . Made in 1846–7, with the Advanced Guard of the Army of the West," *House Executive Document* no. 41, 30th Cong., 1st sess., 110.

41. Mabel Major, Rebecca Smith, and T. M. Pearce, *Southwest Heritage: A Literary History with Bibliography* (Albuquerque: University of New Mexico Press, 1938). For deciphering distortion, see Robert A. LeVine and Donald Campbell, *Ethnocentrism: Theories of Conflict, Ethnic Attitudes, and Group Behavior* (New York: Wiley, 1972).

42. Richard Onofre Ulibarri, "American Interest in the Spanish-Mexican Southwest, 1803–1848," Ph.D. diss., University of Utah, 1963, 80.

43. Ray Allen Billington, *The Protestant Crusade, 1800–1860: A Study of the Origins of American Nativism* (1938; rpt. Gloucester, Mass.: Peter Smith, 1963), 75, 223–30. For a comment by Webb, see Ralph Bieber, ed., *Adventures in the Santa Fe Trade; 1844–1847, by James Josiah Webb* (Glendale, Calif.: Arthur H. Clark, 1931), 102.

44. Sunder, *Matt Field*, 194.

45. Brantz Mayer, *Mexico, as It Was and as It Is* (Philadelphia: G. B. Zieber, 1847); for an example of an observer who vacillated in his opinions about Mexicans, see Abiel Abbot Livermore, *The War with Mexico Revised* (Boston: American Peace Society, 1850).

46. Susan Reyner Kenneson, "Through the Looking-Glass: A History of Anglo-American Attitudes toward the Spanish-Americans and Indians of New Mexico," Ph.D. diss. Yale University, 1978, 130.

47. George Brewerton, "Incidents of Travel in New Mexico," *Harper's Magazine* 47 (April 1854): 589.

48. Gregg, *Commerce of the Prairies*, 173, 179–80.

49. Brewerton, "Incidents," 578.

50. Thomas James, *Three Years among the Indians and Mexicans* (Philadelphia: Lippincott 1952), 88–89 (originally published 1916).

51. Gregg, *Commerce of the Prairies*, 167–68.

52. Brewerton, "Incidents," 588.

53. Alexander B. Dyer, "Mexican War Journal, 1846–1848," Museum of New Mexico, History Library, manuscript, 80–81, 84, 118–19.

54. "Gen. Kearny and the Army of the West: Extracts from the Journal of Lieut. Emory," *Niles National Register* 71 (November 7, 1846): 158.

55. Dyer, "Mexican War Journal," 96.

56. Drumm, *Diary of Susan Shelby Magoffin*, 138; for an example of the continuing partnership between the church and the military, see the inauguration of Governor David Merriwether in Gunther Barth, *Instant Cities: Urbanization and the Rise of San Francisco and Denver* (New York: Oxford University Press, 1975). 70.

57. Pattie, *Narritive*, 41.

58. Ibid., 44.

59. Ibid., 110.

60. Testimony of Julian Green, June 9, 1825, Probate Court journals, roll 20, frame 188.

61. United States Bureau of the Census, Seventh Census of Population, for Santa Fe, 1850 (microfilm, New Mexico State Records Center).

62. Complaint of Marcelo Pacheco, April 11, 1846, Probate Court Journals, roll 32, frame 185. See also the Euro-Americans fined for "making fandangos without licenses," Jury Book, 1848–1856, Probate Court journal, Santa Fe County Records, 137–40.

63. James Madison Cutts, *The Conquest of California and New Mexico by the Forces of the United States in the Years 1846–1847* (Philadelphia: Carey and Hart, 1847), 84.

64. Alexander Dyer to Robert Johnston. February 14, 1847, Museum of New Mexico, History Library, box 4, 2.

65. Lamar, *Far Southwest,* 68.

66. Dyer to Johnston, February 14, 1847, 2–3.

67. Dyer, "Mexican War Journal," 97.

68. Ibid., 62 on Navajo and Apache raids, see David J. Weber, *The Mexican Frontier, 1821–1816: The American Southwest under Mexico* (Albuquerque: University of New Mexico Press, 1982), 92–93.

69. Dyer, "Mexican War Journal," 82.

70. On Martínez's activities, see Lamar, *Far Southwest,* 72; on the legend, see E. K. Francis, "Padre Martínez: A New Mexico Myth," *New Mexico Historical Review* 31 (October 1956): 265–89; for a short biography, see Pedro Sánchez, "Memorias sobre la vida del presbitero don Antonio José Martínez," in *Northern Mexico on the Eve of the United States Invasion,* ed. David Weber (New York: Arno Press, 1976); in the same collection, see "Historia consisa del cura de Taos Antonio José Martínez" (originally published in El *Historiador,* May 4, 1861).

71. Richard Henry Dana, *Two Years before the Mast* (New York: New American Library, 1864), 136 (originally published 1840).

3

THE ADVENTURES OF
LORETA JANETA VELÁZQUEZ

Civil War Spy and Storyteller

Amy Dockser Marcus*

This gave me a real pang. . . . But there was no help for it.

Loreta Janeta Velázquez, on cutting her hair

Loreta Janeta Velázquez served as a soldier, spy, and secret agent during the American Civil War, but even after she was criticized for her behavior, jailed, and called a charlatan, the only regret that she ever expressed was about having to cut her long hair. "This gave me a real pang," she wrote in her 1876 memoir documenting her many adventures, "but there was no help for it."[1] Velázquez wanted to leave her hometown of New Orleans and go out into the world, and the only way she could do it was dressed as a man.

The sixth and last child of a Spanish *hacendado* (landowner), Loreta Janeta Velázquez was born in Havana, Cuba, on June 26, 1842. Her father, whom she described in her memoir as a well-to-do, devout Catholic, was a native of Cartagena, Spain. An educated, learned man, he had been appointed to an official position in the Spanish colony of Cuba two years before Velázquez's birth. Her English-speaking mother was an American of French descent, the daughter of a prominent merchant family. Raised in a Spanish cultural ambience where Don Velázquez exercised

* With Virginia Sánchez Korrol.

59

paternalistic authority over his wife and children, Loreta Janeta was none-theless fluent in both Spanish and English. Her father never spoke the English language without an accent, in spite of his wife's efforts to teach him.

The family relocated to San Luis Potosí in central Mexico in 1844, when Don Velázquez inherited vast landed estates. Unfortunately, the family's fortunes were cut short with the outbreak of the war between Mexico and the United States (1846–48). The Velázquez family supported Mexico in the conflict, and their estates were devastated by the United States at the end of the war, a misfortune that embittered Don Velázquez against Americans for the remainder of his life. An impressionable child and her father's favorite, Loreta Janeta perhaps remembered these events in her later decision to side with the Confederacy against the United States. Growing up as the privileged child of wealthy landowners on yet another inherited estate in Cuba, Loreta Janeta Velázquez was conditioned to so-cial and political beliefs comparable to those of the American South. Plan-tation life in nineteenth-century Cuba rested on the power, position, and luxury that came from productive agricultural properties worked by en-slaved labor. A rigid class and race system was the defining factor in Cuban society. These influential experiences, along with an impetuous and romantic nature, motivated Velázquez to commit her life to the Confed-erate cause.

We do not know for sure how many women donned male clothing and went off to fight in the Civil War, although some estimates run as high as four hundred or more.[2] Few ended up writing their stories for poster-ity. Velázquez's book is one of only two memoirs that we have about women soldiers in the Civil War and the only one written by a Latina. The other book, written by a Union soldier and spy named Sarah Emma Edmonds, was a national bestseller when it first appeared in 1864.[3] Velázquez's reception was far different. Ten years after the end of the Civil War, the public seemed uninterested in hearing the perspective of a Con-federate woman—a Latina, no less.

Written in a style akin to popular Spanish and English language nov-els of the day, Velázquez's provocative and engaging memoir, which sen-sationalized her liaisons and flirtations with both men and women and her daring exploits as a spy, tested her readers' credulity. Jubal A. Early, a former Confederate general, accused Velázquez of inventing her tale and deemed it an "affront to the honor of Southern men and women."[4] Velázquez never became an accepted popular figure as Edmonds did, in her own time or in ours. While Edmonds was careful to say that she went to war because she wanted to help others, Velázquez openly admitted that she became a soldier mainly to further her own adventurous interests. An intelligent, bilingual, bicultural woman who was educated in the United States, as was customary among elite Cuban families in the nineteenth century, Velázquez sought excitement, and the pay she could receive as a soldier was much higher than what one could make working in a factory or as a domestic servant. Edmonds donated the profits from her book to help soldiers who had been wounded in the war. But Velázquez's memoir was written a decade after the war, in a different political and social climate, for the immediate purpose of earning money for herself and her small child. After the war, Edmonds slipped quietly back into the traditional role expected of women at that time, marrying and raising a family. Velázquez, who married four times, cared for her son on her own and continued to travel and to promote reactionary Confederate rhetoric long after the war was over. Indeed, committed to the southern secessionist cause and marketing her Spanish language skills, she even served as the interpreter for an ill-fated colonizing expedition to Venezuela by a group of filibustering ex-Confederates. The last time Velázquez was heard from was in a letter she sent while working as a newspaper correspondent in Brazil. After that, she disappeared from the historical record.

While Edmonds's story can be viewed as that of a woman who pushed the boundaries of her time, in many ways Velázquez's story is about a woman who trod right over them. Nonetheless, Velázquez's book offers a vivid Latina legacy. Hundreds of Latinos and Latinas who resided in the southern states or who were drawn to the conflict from Caribbean countries because of common commercial and ideological interests died in the American Civil War. Their role in the conflict is virtually expunged from the historical record.[5]

Much of what we know about Velázquez's story comes from her book, *The Woman in Battle: A Narrative of the Exploits, Adventures, and Travels of Madame Loreta Janeta Velázquez, Otherwise Known as Lieutenant Harry T. Buford, Confederate States Army*. In over six hundred pages and fifty-two chapters, Velázquez chronicled her many adventures. Her book was written in the sensational tone familiar to pulp fiction readers of the day. Relating to her Spanish roots more than to her American heritage, Velázquez claimed that she was descended from Don Diego Velázquez, conquistador and first governor of Cuba, and the prominent Spanish painter Don Diego Rodriguez Velázquez. It is probable that these familial connections existed, as it was not unusual for members of honored Spanish families to serve the Crown in the Latin American and Caribbean colonies over several generations. However, Velázquez also admitted in her memoir to an "impulsive and imaginative disposition" and that she was often prone to romanticize even the smallest episodes of her life. "I could not even write a social letter to my father to inform him of the state of my health, or my educational progress, without putting in it some romantic project which I had on hand. This propensity of mine evidently annoyed him greatly, for he frequently reprimanded me with much severity."[6]

Like other Latinas of her station in the United States during this time, claiming a "Spanish" identity was an important class and racial marker. Throughout the narrative, Velázquez frequently identified herself as a "Spanish" woman. Following Hispanic cultural norms, she kept the Velázquez family name, rather than assuming the surnames of any of her husbands. On at least one occasion, she described herself as a "Cuban and true Southern sympathizer," seemingly emphasizing a proud colonial heritage and traditional elite concepts of class and race. Indeed, Cuba and the American South were linked by common political concerns over slavery, imperialism, and commercial interactions based on the exchange of food and clothing for cotton. By the time of the Civil War, Havana had become a center for Confederate trade and transportation disrupting the Union blockade. During the period of Reconstruction, when Velázquez was writing her memoir, Cuba launched its own aborted attempts to break the Spanish colonial yoke. Following the island's Ten Years' War, from 1868 to 1878, Cuban patriots in exile found safe havens in New Orleans and other southern cities.[7]

Velázquez's earliest encounters with American culture took place when she was sent to New Orleans to live with her mother's sister and to complete her education. It was not unusual for Cuban families to send their sons and daughters abroad for education. Sons in particular studied in Spain or in France, like Velázquez's brother Josea. Daughters were often sent to Catholic girls' schools in the United States to learn English and the domestic arts.

While she was living in New Orleans, Velázquez's family had arranged for her to marry a young Spaniard, named "Raphael R." in her memoir. Velázquez might not have questioned her arranged betrothal had not her American friends at school found the idea so peculiar. "I had been educated under very old-fashioned ideas with regard to the duties which children owe to their parents," Velázquez noted in her memoir, "for, among my father's country people, children, even when they have arrived at years of discretion, are supposed to be under the authority of their fa-

ther and mother, and marriages for love, having their origin in a spontaneous affection of young people for each other, are very rare. It is the
custom in Spain."[8] As a means of escape, she decided to elope with the
boyfriend of her best friend, an American army officer whom she identified only as William in the memoir. According to Velázquez, by the time
William joined the Confederate army and set off for the front in June 1861,
she had given birth to three children, all of whom had died. Only nineteen years old, Velázquez embarked on what would be the first of many
transformations.

On the evening before William departed, Velázquez suggested to her
husband that she disguise herself as a man and accompany him into battle.
When he withheld permission, Velázquez decided to go ahead anyway.
She was not alone in seeking a military adventure. Both Union and Confederate women tried to sign up for battle. Army recruitment physical
exams were superficial at best, rarely going beyond a demonstration that
the recruit could shoot a gun. There was also a widespread assumption
that anyone wearing pants must be a man. Many women thus passed
themselves off as pre-adolescent boys eager to join the soldiers' ranks.

Velázquez, however, chose a different path to military service. She did
not attempt to join an already existing unit. Instead, as she reported, she
went back to New Orleans, enlisted a friend's help in cutting her hair, and
bought a uniform and false mustache. Then, she set out to recruit soldiers
to join a battalion, ultimately convincing 246 men to enlist. She paid for
their equipment out of her own pocket—certainly a sign that she was a
woman of some economic means. When she presented the men to her
husband at his encampment in Pensacola, Florida, William expressed both
surprise and anger that his wife had ignored his directive that she stay
home. He probably would have sent her back, but soon after her arrival,
William died in an accident. Velázquez decided to leave the Florida camp
and her unit, the "Arkansas Grays," and set off to find a new place for
herself.

In her guise as Lieutenant Harry T. Buford, Velázquez participated in
some of the key battles of the war, including the first battle of Bull Run,
the fall of Fort Donelson, and the battle of Shiloh. At Shiloh, in the wake
of the Confederate defeat, Velázquez was helping to remove dead bodies
from the field, when a burst of shrapnel killed a soldier near her and
wounded her in the arm and shoulder. The surgeon who examined her at
the field hospital realized Velázquez was a female. While some women
soldiers were quickly discovered—one woman recruit had never before
worn pants and tried to put them on over her head—most were detected

when they were hospitalized for illness or battle wounds. The surgeon, however, promised to keep Velázquez's secret. With the very real possibility that she might be jailed for her behavior or be accused of prostitution, Velázquez left the army and headed back to New Orleans. For the time being, she put the uniform of Lieutenant Harry T. Buford away.

It was only a temporary interlude. For the remainder of the war, Velázquez assumed many disguises, including that of an English woman, a white northerner, a French Creole, a Spaniard, an American, a Cuban, and several subsequent incarnations as Buford. She worked as a secret agent and spy, sometimes using a female alias and at other times masquerading as a man. At one point, while disguised as Buford, she was arrested and briefly jailed on suspicion of being a woman. But she always managed to find her way back to the center of the conflict. She took on and cast off new identities on a regular basis, even after the war ended.

Velázquez's devotion to the Confederacy was so genuine that she joined a group of ex-Confederates who journeyed to Venezuela to establish a colony. When it became clear that the organizers of the expedition did not have money or any real plan of how to make the colony work, Velázquez kept moving. She visited Trinidad and St. Thomas, went to Cuba to see family, then returned to New York and traveled across the continent in search of her fortune. In what many contemporaries and some later scholars have interpreted as flights of fancy, she claimed to have mined gold in California (long after the gold rush) and to have lived among the Mormons in Salt Lake City. Her memoir ended in Texas, where she said she planned to settle and to write her book.

The Woman in Battle was challenged almost as soon as it was published. In a May 1878 letter, the former Confederate general Jubal A. Early wrote to Congressman. William Ferguson Slemons, representative from Arkansas, to complain that he had read Velázquez's book and had determined "that the writer of that book . . . had never had the adventures therein narrated." Early questioned whether Velázquez was from the South, or was even Spanish, when he wrote that he had met Velázquez in person and that he believed she was "not of Spanish birth or origin, but is an American and probably from the North." Certainly, this was the highest insult—to be accused of being a northerner by an ex-Confederate general. Early further pointed out that Velázquez never gave the full name of her first husband, who, as an officer in the Confederacy, could have been traced in order to verify the story. He also did not believe for a moment that a woman could raise a battalion of men by herself or pay for it out of her own pocket.

Above all, Early was offended by Velázquez's lifestyle and personality. She was not meek or retiring like a proper woman. Society's conventions clearly meant little to her. Early criticized her for getting married four times and for keeping her maiden name through every marriage. He was furious at her candid descriptions of life in military camp and her depiction of southern soldiers as "drunken, marauding brutes" who sat around the campfire telling dirty jokes and swearing. He was especially incensed by her bragging about her success in drawing the attention of women while dressed in her disguise as Lieutenant Buford. It angered Early that Velázquez claimed that women threw themselves at Buford, that they were so willing to "surrender, without waiting to be asked, all that is dear to women of virtue." He called the book "a libel" against the South and expressed disbelief that forty southern congressmen had come out in support of her story of having served in the Confederate army.

When friends told Velázquez that Early had been publicly attacking her book, she sent him a letter from Brazil, where she was then working as a newspaper correspondent. She pointed out that in the preface to the book, she acknowledged that she had lost her notes and diaries and that, as she was working from memory, some of the events might not be recorded in chronological sequence. Moreover, she had been intentionally vague when using the names of officers and soldiers because she did not want to publicly embarrass them or their families over their wartime behavior. She also tried to appeal to Early's conscience, saying that his attacks would harm book sales, the only source of support for herself and her son. "My health is failing," she wrote to Early, "and my whole soul's direction is the education of him who is to live after I have passed away . . . . [A]ll I ask from you is justice to my child. I live for him and him alone." She ended with an appeal to Early's chivalrous nature, calling him a "gentleman of culture and a patriot."

Early was not quite sure how to respond to Velázquez, and he was not alone in his hesitation. Many newspapers had written glowingly about women soldiers during the war, describing them as heroines. But after the war, the reaction was different. Women who admitted that they had joined the army in search of adventure, rather than to be near a husband or brother or because they were patriots, were lambasted in the press. Those who afterward went back to caring for children, husbands, and homes were more favorably treated when their stories became known.

Early himself had been the commander of two sisters who had disguised themselves as male soldiers and fought for the Confederates. When their true identities were discovered, they were denounced as prostitutes, and Early had them imprisoned. By the time he became embroiled in the debate with Velázquez, Early was no longer a general in an army but a defeated soldier. He had never accepted the South's surrender and spent much of his time after the war writing the history of the conflict and defending both slavery and the South's decision to secede. His feeling of displacement and own loss of power in the postwar society caused him to seek advice on how to proceed against Velázquez. In the end, he sent a copy of a letter setting out his charges against Velázquez to Virginia congressman John R. Tucker and asked whether he should make them public. Apparently, Tucker advised him against it because the response to Velázquez was never sent; all three letters remain in the Tucker family papers.[9]

Velázquez lived at a time when war altered the world in which women lived. With so many men off at war, women found themselves running farms, managing slaves, teaching, and taking nursing jobs—things that had often been off-limits to them before the war. Numerous women recorded in their diaries that they wished that they were men so that they could go off and participate in the great national conflict. Some women even took action and formed home defense brigades. Others joined together to sew uniforms and flags, raised money to buy munitions and support the militia, and became more involved in public political life. Women led bread riots when food shortages became widespread. The war was a catalyst for change in how women wielded power, and Velázquez was not the only one to respond to these new opportunities.[10]

And yet, after the war many women discovered that things had not changed as much as they thought or even hoped. Women still had very limited employment opportunities, and what jobs did exist were poorly paid. Unmarried, working-class women could find work as domestic servants, seamstresses, factory workers, or prostitutes. Women could neither vote nor hold public office, and they had restricted access to higher education. They could not open bank accounts in their own names or even travel without chaperones or male relatives. Seen against this reality, Velázquez's adventures seem all the more extraordinary.

Velázquez was not the only one to find her exploits and reputation challenged after the war. Belle Boyd and Rose Greenhow, both of whom also wrote memoirs about their work as Confederate spies, were accused of gaining their information through sexual favors. At one point, Boyd ended up in a mental asylum. Greenhow drowned toward the end of the war, the gold coins sewn in her dress weighing her down as she tried to make it through the federal blockade of southern ports. Women soldiers were treated particularly harshly in part because they were seen as literally having acted like a man. Jubal Early's criticisms of Velázquez's book ended up informing many of the later histories written about women's roles in the war. Scholars tended to agree that women and men who wrote about their Civil War exploits frequently embellished the truth, mixing historical exaggerations with actual events in recounting their adventures.[11]

The historical records about Loreta Janeta Velázquez are not exactly silent, but it is difficult to trace her life story. Yet unlike many women soldiers during the Civil War who came from poor, agrarian backgrounds and were often illiterate, Velázquez was able to write her own story. In some instances, the families of women who did write diaries burned them because they worried about how their relatives would be viewed by outsiders. After the war, there was a sense among many women that if they spoke about their experiences they would be viewed by their neighbors as having loose morals.

In Velázquez's case, it is almost as if she talked too much. She laid claim to such an extraordinary range of experiences that it is hard to believe that one person could accomplish so much and travel so far in such a short time period, especially in the middle of a war. Jubal Early made several prescient points, and it is true that her book has its share of factual problems. For example, she said she rode on a train line at a time when it did not yet exist. She did not describe a key geographical detail of a battlefield where she said she fought. She gave few identifying details of any of her husbands or her brother, who also served in the army. In other places, however, the information she provided about battles, the weather, and the soldiers with whom she served was accurate. Her descriptions of buildings and places that she visited can be confirmed. Some of her mistakes arise from the fact that she had lost her wartime diary and had to reconstruct many of her adventures from memory. In other cases, she may have wanted to make her tale more sensational in order to sell more books.

The main problem is that Velázquez spent the war essentially in disguise, first as a soldier and then as a spy. She was adept at using different names and telling stories about herself. In her memoir, she reported using the names "Mrs. Williams," "Mrs. Fowler," and "Mrs. Sue Battle" at various times, in addition to her alias as Lieutenant Harry Buford. In searching out references to her in newspaper accounts from the time period, it is difficult to locate the real Velázquez among the various aliases that she used. Her editor and collaborator, C. J. Worthington, a northern naval officer who served the Union during the conflict, is among the few people who provided, in the manuscript's prefatory note, an indication of what she looked like. Eager to validate her credibility, and perhaps in an effort to enhance the sale of the book, he described "Madame Velázquez" as a "typical Southern woman of the war period." "She is rather slender," he continued, "something above medium height, has more than the average of good looks, is quick and energetic in her movements, and is very vivacious in conversation." Worthington further noted that Velázquez was a "shrewd, enterprising and energetic businesswoman" and commented on the wide circle of friends in northern cities, in the South, and the in West who held her in "high esteem" and lauded her talents, social qualities, and "unblemished reputation." He concluded that the memoir was an authentic account of a Confederate heroine.[12]

There are enough historical references to verify that Velázquez most likely did serve as a soldier in disguise using the name Harry Buford. An 1863 record of the Confederate secretary of war, for example, contains a request for an officer's commission from a soldier named H. T. Buford. Velázquez wrote in her book that she had unsuccessfully applied for such a commission. Wartime pay receipts from the U.S. government also indicate that an Alice Williams, an alias Velázquez used, was paid for her work as a spy. A New Orleans newspaper reported that Velázquez did indeed serve as an agent for an emigration company trying to set up a colony in Venezuela.[13]

There were also a number of stories that appeared in a variety of newspapers about a woman dressed as a man and calling herself Lieutenant Buford. Shortly after the outbreak of the war, the *Louisville Daily Journal* reported the arrest of a Mrs. Mary Ann Keith, who had dressed in soldier's clothes and registered at a local hotel as Lieutenant Buford. A few years later, a Lynchburg, Virginia, newspaper recorded the arrest of a woman dressed in Confederate uniform using the name Lieutenant Bensford. As late as 1867, there are references in the newspapers to a woman who served in the Confederate army as Lieutenant Buford or some close spelling of that name. These are all convincing pieces of evidence that Velázquez did in fact do many of the things she claimed.[14]

Velázquez's claims of Spanish identity have also been debated. Jubal Early was one of the first to question this, stating in his letter to Congressman Slemons that after meeting her in person, he did not believe that Velázquez was "a cultivated Spanish lady." Early based his assumptions mainly on the fact that she did not speak English with an accent, assuming that all Latinas, including those educated in the United States (as in Velázquez's case), would have accents. But given her fluency in both languages and her education in New Orleans, it is possible that she did not have one. She certainly claimed Spanish as one of her languages. On her trip to Venezuela, she reported that she was the only one among the Confederates who could speak Spanish. Further, before she dropped out of historical sight, she worked as a newspaper correspondent in South America. Moreover, Spanish legends and stories are woven throughout her memoir. When recounting the many legends that inspired her to disguise herself as a man, she told the story of Catalina de Eraso, the nun-lieutenant who was born in Sebastian, Spain, in 1585 and escaped from her convent to join an expedition to the New World, disguised as a man.

Later, in an emotional part of the book, Velázquez debated whether or not to tell the man who would become her second husband that she had fought by his side in several battles. Captain Thomas DeCaulp had taken command of the army battalion after Velázquez's husband William was killed in an accident. DeCaulp and the widowed Velázquez remained in touch. Their friendship became romantic through letters and a few meetings when DeCaulp was on leave. Eventually, they agreed to marry. DeCaulp had no idea that the soldier called Lieutenant Buford, who had fought beside him, was actually his love interest, Loreta Velázquez. At one point, Velázquez described DeCaulp as pulling out pictures of her from his coat pocket and showing them to his friend Buford. After a battle, DeCaulp became sick and was admitted to a hospital where Velázquez visited him. Velázquez wrote that her unconventional romance with DeCaulp reminded her of an old Spanish *novela* that she had read as a girl in Cuba, about a heroine named Estela who had many adventures disguised as a man until she was reunited with her long-lost lover. Throughout the book, Velázquez drew on Spanish legends when she wanted to make a point or when recounting an incident in her life. She identified with the heroines in these stories, and she imitated the language and style of these romances in the writing of her own book, blurring the borders between the Spanish *novela* and an American adventure tale.

Though a staunch Confederate, for Velázquez, as for so many women of her generation, the military conflict presented an opportunity to take control of her destiny and, just as important, to tell her own story. In that story, it is possible to see the same themes and issues that still concern us today. Prior to the war, Velázquez existed mainly on the margins of Latina history and American society. She was a woman, barred from voting or controlling her own finances. She was an immigrant from Cuba, trying to fit into a new country that tended to look down on newcomers. She lived in the Deep South, outside the Spanish-speaking borderlands of the

Southwest. In her constant traveling, in her willingness to set out for the next new place or territory, and above all, in her ability to continually remake herself, Loreta Velázquez was at her most American.

NOTES

1. Loreta Janeta Velázquez, *The Woman in Battle: A Narrative of the Exploits, Adventures, and Travels of Madame Loreta Janeta Velázquez, Otherwise Known as Lieutenant Harry T. Buford, Confederate States Army* (Richmond: Dustin, Gilman and Co., 1876), reprinted, with an introduction by Jesse Alemán, as *The Woman in Battle: The Civil War Narrative of Loreta Janeta Velázquez, Cuban Woman and Confederate Soldier* (Madison: University of Wisconsin Press, 2003), 63. All subsequent citations refer to the 2003 reprint edition.

2. Historians do not agree on the number of women soldiers who served on both sides of the conflict. Civil War nurse and sanitary-aid activist Mary A. Livermore's estimate of 400 is frequently cited by scholars. Historians DeAnne Blanton and Lauren M. Cook have documented 250 in their book about women soldiers, but they agree that there were many more women who served but either were not detected or for whom documentary records do not exist. See DeAnne Blanton and Lauren M. Cook, *They Fought Like Demons: Women Soldiers in the American Civil War* (New York: Vintage, 2003). Mary Livermore's writings appeared in numerous journals of the time. The citation that seems most likely to include information of women's soldiers of the Civil War is Mary Livermore, *My Story of the War: A Woman's Narrative of Four Years' Personal Experience.* (1887).

3. Sarah Emma Edmonds, *Memoirs of a Soldier, Nurse, and Spy: A Woman's Adventures in the Union Army*, ed. Elizabeth D. Leonard (DeKalb: Northern Illinois University Press, 1999).

4. Velázquez, *Woman in Battle*, ix.

5. Jesse Alemán notes in his introduction to the 2003 edition of Velázquez's memoir that Cubans living in the United States had a "vested interest" in the conflict. Many Cubans had settled in Louisiana and Florida. Alemán cites in particular José Agustín Quintero, a Harvard graduate who served the South as a diplomat and negotiated trade agreements with Latin American countries, Ambrosio José Gonzales, and the Sánchez sisters in Florida, who had occasion to spy on Union troop movements for the Confederate army. Ibid., xxxii–xxxiii.

6. Ibid., 42

7. Alemán links the Confederate cause with the Cuban movement for independence from Spain. Both involved anticolonial or anti-imperialist

struggles. Velázquez vowed in her memoir to fight for Cuban indepen-
dence, yet she was not prepared to promote abolition or a classless society.
These sentiments became more pronounced in Cuba following the Ten
Years' War. See ibid., xxxiii, 502.

8. Ibid., 43.

9. The quotations are from Jubal A. Early to W. F. Slemons, May 22,
1878, and Loreta Velázquez to Jubal A. Early, May 18, 1878, Tucker Family
Papers, Southern Historical Collection, Wilson Library, University of North
Carolina at Chapel Hill.

10. In *They Fought Like Demons*, DeAnne Blanton and Lauren M. Cook
provide an interesting analysis of how newspapers chronicled the story of
women soldiers during the war and the changes in attitudes within society
that took place after the war. Belle Boyd, *Belle Boyd in Camp and Prison*.
(London: Saunders, Otley and Co., 1865); Mrs. Greenshow, *My Imprisonment and the First Year of Abolition Rule at Washing*ton. (London: Richard
Bentley, 1863).

11. Velázquez, *Women in Battle*, 7–13.

12. Jessee Alemán makes the following assertion in the 2003 edition:
On January 5, 1967, the New Orleans *Picayune* reported that 'Mrs. Mary De
Caulp' who had fought in the Civil Was as 'Lieutenant Buford' [sic] joined
the expedition to Venezuela as a Southern Agent. As with other references
to Lieutenant Buford prior to the publication of The Woman in Battle, the
Picayune account does not mention Velázquez's name though some
scholars believe 'Mrs. Mary De Caulp' is Velázquez. See Velázquez, *The
Woman in Battle*, xli. Drew Gilpin Faust describes the way the war changed
many women's lives in *Mothers of Invention: Women of the Slaveholding South
in the American Civil War* (Chapel Hill: University of North Carolina Press,
1996).

13. Many historians who have written about Loreta Velázquez cite the
newspaper articles that mention her name and activities during the war.
See, for example, Elizabeth D. Leonard, *All the Daring of the Soldier: Women
of the Civil War Armies* (New York: W. W. Norton, 1999); and Richard Hall,
Patriots in Disguise: Women Warriors of the Civil War (New York: Marlowe
and Co., 1994).

4

MARÍA AMPARO RUIZ DE BURTON AND THE POWER OF HER PEN

Rosaura Sánchez and Beatrice Pita

And now we have to beg for what we had the right to demand.

María Amparo Ruiz de Burtonp

The relative dearth of information on nineteenth-century Latino/Chicano literary history in the American Southwest has slowly been remedied by the discovery of long-neglected texts such as those written by María Amparo Ruiz de Burton and other nineteenth- and early twentieth-century writers. Ruiz de Burton presents us with an intriguing figure, both historically and literarily—a case of an extraordinarily talented woman with a powerful voice, who addressed crucial issues of ethnicity, power, gender, class, and race in her writing. As an acculturated Californio woman writing for publication in English, Ruiz de Burton participated in a number of contemporary discourses—political, legal, economic, commercial, and literary—all to voice the bitter resentment of nineteenth-century Californios who were faced with despoliation and the onslaught of Anglo-American domination in the aftermath of the annexation of Mexican territory to the United States. Seen in this light, Ruiz de Burton's writings are clearly a precursor to Chicano/a literature, as her novels investigate issues at the core of Chicano/a history and literature: identification, disidentification, dual nationality, citizenship, *latinidad*, and gender constraints. As a woman writer, her work is of special significance, for it brings to the discussion of nineteenth-century texts the perspective of someone who was simultaneously inside and outside of dominant United States culture, and who minced no words in voicing her critique of dominant society.

Born in Loreto, Baja California, on July 3, 1832, María Amparo Ruiz was the granddaughter of José Manuel Ruiz, commander of the Mexican northern frontier in Baja California and later governor of Baja California from 1822 to 1825. Don José Manuel's brother, Captain Francisco María Ruiz, had been the commander of the Presidio at San Diego (1801–13 and 1817–18). María Amparo was related by blood or marriage to several leading Californio families, including the Vallejos, the Guerra y Noriegas, the Carrillos, the Pachecos, the Ortegas, and the Estradas.

As befits her intriguing life story, her immediate family history is shrouded in questions. María del Amparo Ruiz Arango, as her name is given on her marriage certificate, was the daughter of Isabel Ruiz Maitorena and Jesús Maitorena. Her siblings were Manuela and Federico Maitorena. The reason that she chose to use her mother's maiden name, rather than her father's surname, remains uncertain, but certainly the Ruiz name was quite prominent in both Baja and Alta California. It is clear that she grew up as a child of relative privilege in the backwaters of Baja.

María Amparo Ruiz met Captain Henry S. Burton of the United States Army when an expedition of New York Volunteers under his command arrived at La Paz aboard the *Lexington* in July 1847 to take possession of Baja California, just as General Winfield Scott was marching on Mexico City. By the time Burton arrived, La Paz had surrendered, and a number of its citizens had signed articles of capitulation, which allowed them to retain their own officials and laws. A few months after Burton's arrival, and after Mexican resistance on the peninsula had failed, Mexico and the United States signed the Treaty of Guadalupe Hidalgo (1848), which granted Alta California and the rest of the Southwest, but not Baja California, to the invaders. In order to fulfill promises that had been made to residents of Lower California, when the U.S. ships left the area in the fall of 1848, two vessels were reserved for refugee transport. A total of 480 Baja Californians, among them María Amparo Ruiz, then sixteen years old, and her mother Isabel, left for Monterey, in Alta California. Some of the refugees ultimately returned to Baja California, but others remained in the north around the San Francisco area, gaining with the other residents and native Californios full U.S. citizenship when the territory became a state in 1850.

Although raised a Catholic, María Amparo Ruiz married Captain Burton in 1849 in a civil ceremony in Monterey, California, before Samuel Wiley, a Presbyterian minister. The love story of Burton and María Amparo Ruiz, complete with the intervention of a rejected suitor, was a romance that became part of local California lore. It was later recounted by Hubert Howe Bancroft in his *California Pastoral*, by J. Ross Browne in his published letters to his wife, and much later by Winifred Davidson, who wrote several articles for the *San Diego Union* and the *Los Angeles Times* on the Burton-Ruiz love story in the 1930s. Davidson described their love affair in her article "Enemy Lovers" as the union of "natural enemies," given their differences in religion, nationality, and age, during wartime. J. Ross Browne reported that the marriage of the Catholic María Amparo Ruiz to a Protestant caused something of a scandal in Californio society. The Catholic bishop of California himself had to intervene, after the wedding, to grant ecclesiastic legitimacy to the civil ceremony.

Elderly Californios interviewed by Davidson in the early part of the twentieth century still remembered Ruiz de Burton's beauty and aristocratic air, but only a couple spoke of her as a writer. While little is known of her education in La Paz, information provided in letters and book reviews of the period reveals that she was schooled in Spanish and French, and that after arrival in Monterey, she entered a local school to master the English language. Her novels and extensive correspondence in both Spanish and English indicate a strong background in the classics, in English, Spanish, and American literature, in European and American history, and other areas as well.

After their marriage, Captain Burton was assigned first to Monterey, then to San Diego, where he, his wife, and their two children lived for nearly eight years. In 1859, as the conflict escalated between the North and the South, Burton was ordered back east to serve in the Union army. An army engineer by training, Burton saw service in numerous Civil War battles; he was also placed in charge of Fort Monroe in Virginia where Confederate president Jefferson Davis was held after his capture. After Burton's death in 1869 in Rhode Island, his wife was left a thirty-seven-year-old widow with two children. This ten-year period spent on the East Coast as an army officer's wife was a crucial period in Ruiz de Burton's life. Moving in the highest military, political, and social circles, she became an intimate friend of First Lady Mary Todd Lincoln. Ruiz de Burton was thus privy to an insider's view of the scandals, corruption, and inner workings of life in the capital both during and after the Civil War, and she would draw heavily on this experience for her representations and critiques of U.S. society. In addition to describing the plight of prisoners of war during the Civil War, her first novel, *Who Would Have Thought It?* deals pointedly and precisely with the hypocrisy, greed, and moral turpitude among northern abolitionists, clergymen, and politicians.

Her willing acculturation into U.S. society notwithstanding, Ruiz de Burton would always and forever hold on to a Latino cultural specificity and make it a point in her writings to counter the prevailing derogatory portrayals of Mexicans and Latinos. Resentment of the racism directed at Californios-Mexicanos, and their mistreatment and betrayal by both individuals and the state, clearly fueled the critiques in both her novels, *Who Would Have Thought It?* (1872) and *The Squatter and the Don* (1885).[1]

The novel *Who Would Have Thought It?* (published in Philadelphia by J. B. Lippincott) was not Ruiz de Burton's first literary work. While living in San Diego, California, where her husband was stationed in the 1850s, she wrote and produced a five-act comedy based on Cervantes's *Don Quixote,* and several years later, in 1876, she had the play published.[2] *Who Would Have Thought It?*, gives no author on the title-page, but the book is copyrighted under the name Mrs. Henry S. Burton in the Library of Congress. Ruiz de Burton never published her novels under her own name— perhaps as much to conceal her gender as her Latina background—and considering the content of this novel, one can well understand why. The novel is a bitingly satirical narrative, a caustic parody of the United States during the period of the Civil War. It satirizes a prominent scandal of the day, which involved a Presbyterian minister and the wife of one of his friends, and reveals, among a series of insightful critiques, the hypocrisy, pettiness, and racism of a northern abolitionist family and community. Abolitionists in the North are shown to be nativist, xenophobic, and racist. The Mexican perspective, presented through an outsider character, is that of a child, Lola, whose aristocratic Mexican mother—in true romance fashion—has been kidnapped by the Indians. The child is rescued by James Norval, a Yankee geologist who was exploring near the banks of the Gila River, and is brought east to live with his family on the eve of the Civil War. Despite the family's abolitionist rhetoric, Mrs. Norval displays racist and classist prejudices toward (what she considers) the "black" child. Her immediate reaction is to send the child to the kitchen and, later, to sleep with the servants—Irish in this case, who were also considered ethnically and religiously inferior in that New England community. The child's "whitening," as the pigment her mother used to darken her skin and protect her among the Indians wears off (this is, after all, a romance) changes nothing; cultural racism continues to marginalize the child even while Mrs. Norval and the rogue minister Hackwell make plans to benefit from Lola's wealth.

In this text, as later in *The Squatter and the Don,* history and romance are bound up together in the narrative; here, the love story between Lola, the "darkling" from the West, and Norval's son Julian is played out against the backdrop of the Civil War, detailing the moral and political transgressions and corruption of self-righteous easterners. Through this allegory Ruiz de Burton traces the fall of "republican motherhood," that is, the "moral authority" of a Yankee matron; the fall is not so much the fall of the nation, fractured during the Civil War, as the fall of a romantic conception of politics and the unmasking of liberal/democratic ideologies. The geologist Norval has to go into exile to avoid arrest for criticizing the suspension of habeas corpus with the outbreak of the Civil War. Julian, an officer in the Union army, faces dismissal and loss of rank without a court-martial when his father's comments are attributed to him. Julian will be saved, not by constitutional guarantees and protections, but by the intervention of powerful political and financial supporters.

Throughout the novel, Ruiz de Burton counters views that idealized the United States as a just and democratic nation. It is a place, she insists, where dissent is not tolerated, where justice is served only for the economically powerful (like the owners of the telegraph and railroad monopolies), where politicians are ignorant and venal, and where the electoral system is for sale to the highest bidder. Here Ruiz de Burton makes good use of her intimate knowledge of the American political scene—she did, after all, spend many years living on the East Coast and, as a result of her husband's position, had access to high political and military circles in the nation's capital.

Despite the fact that Ruiz de Burton has no basic quarrel with patriarchal values, her representations of women, women's roles, and their capacity for reasoning and agency are particularly noteworthy in *Who Would Have Thought It?* Especially interesting is the novel's intriguing representation of Mrs. Norval, the geologist's wife, whose character gives us a nuanced portrait of feminine psychology and nineteenth-century social norms. In this regard, much remains to be done not only to situate Ruiz de Burton's work within minority literatures in the United States and in relation to women writers like Harriet Beecher Stowe and Lydia Maria Child, but also more generally to examine her novels as a rejoinder to the mainstream Anglo-American literary tradition.

In *The Squatter and the Don,* published by Ruiz de Burton in California thirteen years later, the Alamar family narrative can be seen as a fictional account of the fortunes of many Californio families. It is a composite of many different cases of land loss to squatters and litigation, including that of Ruiz de Burton's friend Mariano Guadalupe Vallejo, whose Soscol rancho is mentioned in the novel, and the author's own legal problems with the

Rancho Jamul in San Diego County. Published after her return with her two children, Nellie and Harry, to San Diego, where she and her husband had earlier purchased the Rancho Jamul, *The Squatter and the Don* was published in San Francisco under the pseudonym "C. Loyal." The "C." stood for *Ciudadano*, or "Citizen," and "Loyal" for *Leal*—that is, *Ciudadano Leal*, a "Loyal Citizen," a common letter-closing practice used in official government correspondence in Mexico during the nineteenth century. The English name, the indeterminacy of the author's gender, and the designation of the author as a "loyal citizen" are even more ironic, considering that the work is severely critical of the political structures of U.S. society. Ruiz de Burton had begun working on this new literary project in 1880, and by 1884 the story had become a full-length narrative. As she indicated in her letters, the novel was as much a commercial venture as a literary and ideological undertaking. She lived on a meager army widow's pension, while engaged in costly litigation to validate her claim to her Rancho Jamul lands, and she was sorely in need of income. Ruiz de Burton knew that whoever controlled reproduction of the novel would benefit from its sale. Given her perilous financial situation (including loans, mortgages, and failed business ventures), which she faced until her death in 1895, it was imperative that she get that control. Her correspondence speaks of the many obstacles she encountered and overcame to get published.

The Squatter and the Don is a historical romance that details the repercussions of the Land Act of 1851, after the U.S. invasion of California, and the rapid rise of the railroad monopoly in the state. The novel is unique in that it is told from the perspective of the conquered Californio population who, despite being promised all the rights of citizenship under the Treaty of Guadalupe Hidalgo of 1848, was by 1870 a subordinated and marginal national minority. The novel's action roughly covers the period of 1872 to 1885 and builds on the tension between the romantic and the historical as it reconstructs conflicts between Californios of Mexican descent and the invading Anglo squatters by focusing on two families: the family of Don Mariano Alamar, owner of a 47,000-acre ranch in the San Diego area, and the family of William Darrell, one of the numerous squatters on the Alamar ranch. Amid the dispossession and disempowerment of the Californios, the youngest daughter of the Don, Mercedes, and the eldest son of the squatter, Clarence, fall in love and encounter the requisite romantic obstacles. While the romantic plot works out happily by the novel's end, the historical issues posed—especially in relation to the disempowerment of the Californios and the rise of corporate monopolies and their power over government policy—are not as easily resolved.

The Squatter and the Don, like all romances, narrates a quest which necessarily involves conflict and resolution, given here as the trials and tribulations standing in the way of the felicitous union of a romantic couple. Because the novel is also marked by its historicity, however, the quest is not merely for the love of a maiden, but also for land and justice. The narrative thus follows two tracks, one historical and one romantic, with the latter serving to frame the reconstruction of a critical period in the history of the Southwest. In this regard, Ruiz de Burton's novel is eclectic, much like other nineteenth-century historical romances. However, with its focus on the demise of a heroic society (the aristocratic/feudal Californios), it differs from other historical romances in that it is not written from the perspective of the conquerors, with the usual portrayal of a "backward" people who are constrained by an outmoded feudal order and unable to cope in the modern postfeudal state. On the contrary, this novel, written from the perspective of the conquered, questions whether the new order did indeed bring progress to the region and, if so, at what cost, in view of the crassness and immorality of much of the invading population (whether squatters or monopolists), its corrupt political leaders and their legislation, and its reprehensible treatment of the conquered. From the invasion of Californio lands, the novel goes on to address other forms of "invasion" that are as much economic and political as geographical. By the novel's end, the victims are seen to be not only the Californios and their immediate antagonists, the squatters, but also the city of San Diego and, in the long run, the entire state population, now subject to the tyranny of the railroad monopoly. The novel concludes by invoking the image of the juggernaut car and stating: "Our representatives in Congress, and in the State Legislature, knowing full well the will of the people, ought to legislate accordingly. If they do not, then we shall—as Channing said—'kiss the foot that tramples us!' and 'in anguish of spirit' must wait and pray for a Redeemer who will emancipate the white slaves of California."[3]

The Squatter and the Don is not, of course, the only novel on nineteenth-century California that deals with the righteous dispossessed or with the voracious monster, the Railroad Trust, as described by Frank Norris seven years later in *The Octopus.* Although Ruiz de Burton's novel does not focus on the dispossession of farmers in the San Joaquin Valley, as Norris's 1901 novel does, *The Squatter and the Don* does provide, years before Norris's publication, a critical portrayal of the railroad monopoly that thwarted the construction of the Texas and Pacific Railroad to San Diego and ends with a mention of the Mussel Slough massacre of 1880, which is the subtext of *The Octopus*. But unlike Norris, who describes "Spanish-Mexicans" as "decayed, picturesque, vicious and romantic," Ruiz de Burton presents by contrast a capable, cultured, even heroic people, who were unjustly deterritorialized, economically strangled, linguistically oppressed, and politically marginalized after 1848. It is precisely to rail against the cultural defamation of Mexicans and Californios—as much perhaps as against the material dispossession—that Ruiz de Burton writes. As Señora Alamar, one of the characters in *The Squatter and the Don*, says, "Let the guilty rejoice and go unpunished, and the innocent suffer ruin and desolation. I slander no one, but shall speak the truth."[4]

But lest one risk reading more into Ruiz de Burton's critiques than is in the text, one must remember, for example, that she attacks corporate monopolies and government collusion, but not the capitalist system per se. Ruiz de Burton rails against corruption and collusion, but her stance is ultimately reformist; she has no problems with capitalism (or patriarchy for that matter) and calls for a "kinder and gentler," more "principled" capitalism. She is nonetheless an astute enough reader of her times to see that the days of nonmonopoly, individual entrepreneur, capitalism will be gone forever, if the "monster" of monopoly is not checked by immediate political action. Consequently, while in *Who Would Have Thought It?* she takes a caustic satiric approach to critique the hypocrisy of U.S. society and the debasement of its government, in *The Squatter and the Don* she exhorts her readers to act while there is still time, to take matters into their own hands, to divest monopoly of its stranglehold on a government ever less "of, by and for the people":

> It seems now that unless *the people of California take the law into their own hands*, and seize the property of those men and confiscate it, to re-imburse the money due *the people*, the arrogant corporation will never pay. They are so accustomed to appropriate to themselves what rightfully belongs to others, and have so long stood before the world in defiant attitude, that they have become utterly insensible to those sentiments of fairness animating law-abiding men of probity and sense of justice.[5]

Although this quotation refers specifically to the power of the railroad monopoly and its stranglehold on California transportation, it also gives voice to Californios' feelings of resentment against the invaders as they faced the loss of their land, social position, and political power in the years following the Treaty of Guadalupe Hidalgo. Ruiz de Burton is not devoid of deeply held class, racial, and patriarchal prejudices; she is, for example, less than generous in her assessment of the Chinese and other "rabble" immigrants, and on occasion she falls back upon stereotypical portrayals of Jews, Indians, blacks, and other groups. And while admittedly deployed strategically to counter anti-Latino cultural biases, Ruiz de Burton argues for an essentialist Latin "difference," believing Latinos to be culturally and morally superior. While both Ruiz de Burton novels thus focus pointedly on matters of race and ethnicity, they go beyond a culturalist perspective as the author widens the scope of her denunciations, by taking to task the ostensible "superiority" of the Anglo, the ignominious state of internal U.S. politics, and the travesties of justice taking place in the halls of Congress, in the prisons and hospitals of the Civil War, in the boardrooms of the railroad monopolies, and in the bedrooms of the wealthy of New York.

The loss of the Southwest and the treatment of its people stand out in Ruiz de Burton's mind and work as a watershed, a forceful caveat for those unwilling or unable to foresee and forestall the onslaught of the juggernaut of U.S. expansionism and the threats posed by monopoly capitalism. The "New World Order," whose political and economic consolidation was witnessed by Ruiz de Burton in the last quarter of the nineteenth century, is the ideology of U.S. expansionism and corporate greed. Ruiz de Burton comes to see the United States as what Cuban writer and patriot José Martí, writing at the same time, termed a "damaged nation," agreeing with him that it is dangerous, in fact hazardous, to one's political and economic health (both within the United States, as well as without) to continue to idealize or admire uncritically the "Colossus of the North."

Interestingly, in both historical romances Ruiz de Burton also carries out an operation in which she figures male agency as handicapped or truncated by the forces of decay and corruption. Thus, the Californio men in *The Squatter and the Don* fall victim to accidents or debilitating illnesses, in addition to suffering land loss and ignominy at the hand of squatters and the government. Likewise, in *Who Would Have Thought It?* the Norval men suffer "compromised male agency," an "emasculation" of sorts, when they are "absented" from the scene as a result of the machinations of scoundrels—male and female—who were in collusion with the government and its policies. In both novels, there is thus a "feminization" of the victims, with gender serving to depict the subordinated status of those "handicapped" by societal constraints. In effect, much like in the nineteenth-century U.S. domestic romance genre, domesticity becomes a space of restricted social agency.

What is also historically important is that in *The Squatter and the Don*—
the first published narrative written in English from the perspective of
the conquered Mexican population—Ruiz de Burton created a narrative
space for the counterhistory of the conquered Californio population, that
by 1870 was a marginalized national minority, precluded from agency,
and whose voice and history were effectively muzzled if not erased. A
writer who witnessed the disappearance of the old order and the disrup-
tion of everyday life with the disintegration of its political and economic
structures, shifts in power relations, and the rapid capitalist development
of the territory, Ruiz de Burton would seek to reconstruct a bracketed
history and to question a wide range of dominant Anglo-American ideological discourses. Unwilling to adopt a position of resignation or to en-
sconce herself in nostalgia for the past, Ruiz de Burton, through her
novels—and despite their contradictions—takes a forthright and vocal
stand, whether it be in denouncing the despoliation of the Californios or
satirizing the presumed superiority of the Anglo-Americans. At a moment
when the few histories narrated by Californios themselves remained in
manuscript form and were even then already collecting dust in archives,
the very act of writing and publishing her historical romances was a call
to action and at the same time a form of empowerment for the collectiv-
ity. So, too, the recovery of these texts today has an important role to
play in tracing back the literary and ideological historiography of the
Southwest and its inhabitants and highlighting issues that are still very
much with us.

Aside from her fiction writing, Ruiz de Burton would, throughout her
life in the United States, correspond with a number of important
Californio, Mexican, and U.S. individuals, mostly men. Although only a
relatively small number of her letters are available to us today, these have
been recently collected and published.[6] These letters, like her novels, bear
witness to her ongoing criticism of the United States and her admonish-
ments as to the short- and long-term dangers of "Manifest Destiny" and
its corollaries. The letters also provide us with important information on
her life and difficulties as a Latina, as a woman, and as a single head of
household after 1869, faced as she was with numerous legal entanglements
and financial problems.

It would be her fight to retain the Rancho Jamul and later her major
legal and public battle for her claim of Ensenada in Baja California that
would lead Ruiz de Burton to write and publish several articles and letters
in San Diego newspapers. Though in both cases she ultimately lost the
land, she marshaled her substantial legal and writing skills to put up a

valiant fight. These struggles, which were at heart personal battles for economic survival, are recorded in court briefs, newspaper accounts, legal documents, and letters, as well as in her novels; taken together they serve to delineate the situation of Californios in general and of women in particular in their common fight for redress on a number of fronts throughout the nineteenth century.

A woman of many projects, Ruiz de Burton was quite busy not only with her writing but also with the various enterprises at her San Diego County Jamul Ranch, which included a cement plant, commercial-scale castor bean production, and the construction of a reservoir. She also had mining interests in Baja California. But her most ambitious undertaking was her claim to the whole of the Ensenada tract of land in Baja California, which she tried for many years to have recognized as her own, envisioning a large-scale colonization and development project. This long and convoluted story reveals that, although she was a U.S. citizen after 1848, Ruiz de Burton identified herself as Mexican against the foreign investors, backed by U.S. businessmen, who sought to colonize the Baja California area. Her efforts—and the machinations involved—would turn her mother and brother against her, lead her to write newspaper articles against the colonization companies, and eventually take her to Mexico to fight the foreign (both U.S. and British) companies in court. At the time of her death in Chicago in 1895, she was preparing new legal appeals in both U.S. and Mexican courts. In the end, Ruiz de Burton died in poverty, like countless other Californios; she was, however, very much the individual entrepreneur with a strong sense of her "Latina" roots and the willingness and energy to do battle even with giants all too willing to crush anyone and anything that got in their way. Ruiz de Burton was by all rights an exceptional woman, as M. G. Vallejo recognized in the prologue to his five-volume memoirs: "*erudita y culta dama, celosa de la honra y tradiciones de su patria, valiosa esposa, cariñosa madre y leal amiga* [a learned and cultured lady, concerned with the honor and traditions of her land, worthy wife, loving mother and loyal friend]." She was, moreover, the only woman mentioned as having been instrumental in the writing of his history of California.[7]

In all her work, what is perhaps most striking is Ruiz de Burton's ambivalent sense of identification and nationality, her sense of displacement, her contradictory accommodation to and disidentification with the United States, her sense of a "Latin" race beyond national identity and citizenship, and her strong sense of herself as a woman challenged by gender constraints. These are all traits that reveal Ruiz de Burton as an intriguing, multitalented, and multifaceted woman and as a Latina writer who used her pen to indict wrongs. Her work remains worth studying with an admiring and yet simultaneously critical eye.

NOTES

1. María Amparo Ruiz de Burton, *Who Would Have Thought It?* (Philadelphia: J. B. Lippincott, 1872; rpt., with an introduction and notes by Rosaura Sánchez and Beatrice Pita, Houston: Arte Público Press, 1995); María Amparo Ruiz de Burton, *The Squatter and the Don: A Novel Descriptive of Contemporary Occurrences in California*, pseud. C. Loyal (San Francisco: Samuel Carson and Co., 1885; rpt., with an introduction and notes by Rosaura Sánchez and Beatrice Pita, 2d ed., Houston: Arte Público Press, 1997).

2. María Amparo Ruiz de Burton, *Don Quixote de la Mancha: A Comedy in Five Acts, Taken from Cervantes' Novel of That Name* (San Francisco: J. H. Carmany and Co., 1876).

3. Ruiz de Burton, *The Squatter and the Don*, 366.

4. Frank Norris, *The Octopus* (Boston: Houghton-Mifflin Co., 1958), 15.

5. Ruiz de Burton, *The Squatter and the Don*, 366.

6. María Amparo Ruiz de Burton, *Conflicts of Interest: The Letters of María Amparo Ruiz de Burton*, ed. Rosaura Sánchez and Beatrice Pita (Houston: Arte Público Press, 2001).

7. Mariano Guadalupe Vallejo, *Recuerdos Históricos y Personales Tocante a la Alta California*, Vols. I–II, 1875. Manuscript available at the Bancroft Library, University of California, Berkeley.

Material adapted by Rosaura Sánchez and Beatrice Pita is from *The Squatter and the Don* by María Amparo Ruiz de Burton. Reprinted with permission from the publisher of *The Squatter and the Don* (Houston: Arte Público Press—University of Houston, 1992).

5

LOLA RODRÍGUEZ DE TIÓ AND THE PUERTO RICAN STRUGGLE FOR FREEDOM

Edna Acosta-Belén

I carry the Motherland within me

Lola Rodríguez de Tió

Nation-building is not usually associated with women. The process of engendering nations and nationalizing women in historical research is just beginning to take root, perhaps a long overdue recognition of women's historical agency even during periods when they were not emancipated and did not have full citizenship rights. Until recently, scant attention was paid to the ways in which patriarchal societies limited the access of women to public life, or the ways in which many women challenged those limitations. In a broad sense, life for women in nineteenth-century Puerto Rico was not that much different than that for many other women in other parts of the Americas. They were mostly to be seen and not heard, largely left out of public life, and denied the societal privileges accorded to men. This is the world that surrounded one of the most prominent female figures of nineteenth-century Puerto Rico, María de los Dolores (Lola) Rodríguez de Tió.

Born in the western municipality of San Germán, Puerto Rico, known as "la ciudad de las lomas" (the city of hills), on September 14, 1843, Lola Rodríguez was the daughter of Sebastián Rodríguez, a prominent lawyer and one of the founders of the Colegio de Abogados (Lawyers Bar Association) of Puerto Rico, and Carmen Ponce de León, a descendant of the famous conquistador who had initiated the colonization of the island in 1508. From a family of the creole privileged class, Lola was educated by private tutors and her parents, unlike most Puerto Rican women of her time. Over the years she became familiar with some of the classics of world literature, including the literature of the Romantic movement, which was popular in the island's creole intellectual circles. Romantic writers such as the Spaniards José de Espronceda and Gustavo Adolfo Bécquer, Frenchman Alfred de Musset, and the German Henrick Heine, in particular, would influence Lola's sentimental and melancholy tone, her longing for freedom, the rebellious spirit that shaped her poetry, and the political and cultural activities she pursued during most of her adult life. Her ability to improvise verses at will was notorious, and while some of her poetry was written for an educated audience, many of her poems have popular appeal and are influenced by Puerto Rican folkloric traditions and nationalist sentiments.[1]

The poet was far from the feminine ideal expected in her class in Puerto Rico's patriarchal society. Most of her photographs from her youth and adult years show not a glamorous or frail woman, but a corpulent and resolute matriarch—a woman in charge of her own destiny, who seems ready to overcome any barriers that limit her individuality or sense of purpose. In Lola's case, her destiny was defined by a strong devotion to her family, a love of writing, and her commitment to freeing the Puerto Rican motherland from the chains of Spanish colonial rule.

Although other Spanish colonies in the Americas had achieved independence by the late 1820s, Puerto Rico and Cuba remained under the yoke of an unresponsive colonial government that allowed few civil liberties and limited the possibilities for island creoles to take charge of their own affairs. Freedom of expression was absent from public life, and those creoles who advocated reforms or liberal ideals took the risk of facing imprisonment or exile.

In 1865, when she was only twenty years old, Lola married Bonocío Tió Segarra, a prominent liberal Puerto Rican journalist. He had studied in Barcelona, where he absorbed the fundamentals of the European liberal ideas that had inspired independence movements in the Americas and engaged in political discussions with other young creoles about freedom, individual rights, and nation-building. When he returned to Puerto Rico and after he married Lola, Bonocío Tió's journalistic career, particularly in light of the dream he and his wife shared of an independent Puerto Rico, was carefully followed by the colonial authorities. To be a liberal journalist or a poet on the island during those years was to hold a precarious professional position, but both occupations played a crucial role in the process of imagining a sovereign Puerto Rican nation. It was in part through newspapers and the work of printer-journalists and creative writers that a notion of a *patria* (motherland)—separate and distinct from the Spanish mother country—began to be disseminated among Puerto Rican creoles.

It was clear from the beginning of their relationship that Bonoció Tió and Lola shared many passions: for each other, for writing, and for Puerto Rico's freedom. From their extensive travels and contacts throughout Europe and the Americas emerged longtime friendships with other liberal intellectuals of many different nationalities. The couple also amassed an impressive home library that reflected their love of learning and their basic intellectual and creative compatibility. They were completely devoted to each other. The letters and poems Lola wrote to Bonoció when they were forced apart by political circumstances or by his work capture the deep love they shared, the mutual respect and admiration for their respective creative endeavors, and the anguish of separation. She used to call him *mi Sajón* (my Saxon) because of his unusually Nordic appearance for a Puerto Rican man.

At their residences in the towns of San Germán and Mayagüez, the couple's intimate family life centered around their two daughters and a niece they raised as an adoptive daughter. Their lives were also enriched by a circle of prominent friends who attended their frequent and celebrated literary *tertulias*—gatherings that allowed for unguarded political discussions about the future of Puerto Rico, as well as a display of artistic and intellectual talent. Writers, journalists, politicians, and musicians all relished these exceptional opportunities for enlightened exchange and enjoyment.

At a time when most other women led lives out of public view, Rodríguez de Tió could not stay away from her country's struggle for political reforms and independence. Her opinions were broadcast in the front pages of the few newspapers that Spanish authorities allowed, her poetry inspired readers, and her provocative articles that advocated the education and intellectual development of women challenged traditional views. One of those early articles was "La influencia de la mujer en la civilización" ("The Influence of Women on Civilization") which appeared in the San Germán newspaper, *El eco de las Lomas* (*Echo of the City of Hills*) in 1875. In it, Rodríguez de Tió calls for educating women and engaging them in the nation-building process:

The woman is ready, she does not appear to be opposed to progress; why is it then that some want to condemn her to stay permanently engulfed in the eternal shadows of ignorance? Why not break the obstacles against the development of her intelligence and the elevation of her spirit? Why use frivolous language against her that humiliates and relegates her to ineptitude? It is necessary for a woman to receive solid liberal instruction that develops her intelligence so that on the day she can join her intellectual efforts to those of men, the result would be the complete wholeness that many great thinkers are fruitlessly searching for.[2]

Rodríguez de Tió refused to accept that other Puerto Rican women had to be socially confined by marriage and motherhood. Despite the fact that in her verses she often comes across as a woman with the nurturing and passionate sentimentality of a mother and wife, her poetry also conveys the unrestrained impetuosity of a concerned, informed citizen and fearless patriot. It is no coincidence that she nicknamed her first-born daughter "Patria" (the Spanish word for motherland), for Lola always claimed to carry her beloved Puerto Rico in her womb.[3] Most of her life came to be defined by the events that were shaping the political destiny of the Puerto Rican motherland. Major historical events such as the September 23, 1868, *Grito de Lares* (Cry of Lares) revolt, which marked Puerto Rico's first armed struggle for independence from Spain; the 1887 period of political persecution and repression against island autonomists known as the *Compontes* (literally, the "Behave Yourself" regime); the Antillean separatist movement in exile; and Cuba's wars of independence against Spain were all to play a deciding role in the lives of the Tió-Rodríguez family. These events not only solidified the couple's liberal views and commitment to the separatist cause, but they also contributed to the decision of the colonial authorities to condemn Bonoció and Lola to exile on three separate occasions.

Despite the failure of the Grito de Lares revolt to fuel a larger uprising throughout the island, the event was an inspiration for some island separatists to continue the struggle initiated by their fallen or imprisoned comrades. Lola's initial encounter with colonial authorities came less than a year before, when she wrote the verses of "La borinqueña" ("Song of Borinquen") in 1867 to incite her fellow compatriots to take up arms against the Spanish oppressor. The lyrics of "La borinqueña" were soon adapted to the melody of a popular *danza* by Félix Astol, a well-known Spanish musician, turning the poem into an anthem of revolution:[4]

Awake, Borinqueños,
for the signal has been given!
Awake, from your sleep
for its time to fight!

* * *

We don't want any more despots!
Let the tyrant fall!
Supportive women
also will know how to fight![5]

From this point on Lola's verses became one of her most powerful weapons, not only in the clamor for Puerto Rico's freedom, but also in her expression of her patriotic love and nostalgia for the island during the years she lived in exile. Out of the frequent gatherings and communications with other political expatriates, Lola became one of the creators of the Puerto Rican flag, which was inspired by its Cuban counterpart, but with inverted colors. The Puerto Rican flag has a white single star set on a blue background and red and white stripes, while the Cuban flag sets its star in a field of red and has blue and white stripes.[6]

Rodríguez de Tió's first published book of poems, *Mis cantares* (*My Songs*) (1876), was so successful that the edition sold out in a short period of time. Her poetic sensibility and the combative spirit reflected in many of her writings led Spanish intellectual Carlos Peñaranda, who wrote the preface to her second collection of poetry, *Claros y nieblas* (*Clarities and Mists*) (1885), to describe her as a woman with "a Roman heart and an Athenian spirit," a phrase befitting a woman with the valor and strength of a soldier and the gift of a poetic Muse.[7] In addition to her poetry, Lola was a fervent advocate for women's education and their involvement in public life. She continued to write articles occasionally on this and other topics for island newspapers:

Let us not have any doubts, ladies and gentlemen, that one of the main engines of moral progress in this essentially civilized era we have reached, is the education of women.

Her ignorance or enlightenment will always determine the lesser or greater glory of societies, the blessings or misfortunes of the home, the ruin or ascent of the motherland.

We should know once and for all: Ignorance only engenders slaves. Enlightenment forms workers of the intellect and citizens of the motherland.[8]

Like many other liberals and separatists, Lola and Bonoció's political inclinations and standing within the Puerto Rican creole intellectual community made them targets of the Spanish colonial authorities. Thus exile became an unwelcome but regular part of their lives. Their first exile (1877–1880) took them to Caracas, Venezuela. There, they continued to host their celebrated tertulias for the intellectuals and artists that came through the Latin American capital.

In Venezuela the couple developed a friendship with Eugenio María de Hostos, another Puerto Rican intellectual and freedom fighter residing there. Lola was invited to be the matron of honor at his wedding, and over the years they maintained a personal correspondence that gives testimony to their friendship and political concerns for the destiny of their motherland. She also knew and corresponded with Ramón Emeterio Betances, the leader of the Puerto Rican separatist movement in exile. The political affinities among these three separatist expatriates were so strong that they, among others, have been called "the pilgrims of freedom."[9] While in exile, all three pursued from afar lives dedicated to supporting the independence cause and a shared vision of an Antillean federation of free republics that would include Cuba and Puerto Rico. Rodríguez de Tió reaffirmed this ideal in her poetry, echoing the sense of Antillean unity and solidarity that Betances and Hostos discussed in more detail in some of their essays and correspondence. The common political destiny of both islands is the essence of Lola's celebrated poem, "A Cuba" ("To Cuba"):

> Cuba and Puerto Rico are
> two wings of one bird.
> They receive blows or bullets
> in the same heart. . . .
> What a great feeling if in the illusion
> that glows red in a thousand tones
> With fervent fantasy,
> Lola's muse dreams
> Of this land and mine
> becoming a single motherland![10]

Lola and her husband were able to return to Puerto Rico from Venezuela in 1880, when a more liberal shift in the colonial administration led the Spanish to relax some of their repressive measures. In 1887, when the Puerto Rican Autonomist Party was constituted as the major creole political force in the emerging nation's claims for self-government, the Spanish rulers decided, once again, to limit freedom of expression and severely curtailed the activities of creole liberals. Repression intensified to the extent that this period is recorded in Puerto Rican history as the "terrible year of 1887."[11]

This was the year of the infamous regime of the Compontes, implemented by Spanish governor Romualdo Palacio in a desperate attempt to crush the liberalist currents that riled up a creole population against a despotic colonial government. Within a few months, the frequent imprisonment and exile of autonomists and separatists under the Compontes regime reminded Puerto Rican creoles that Spain was far from ready to relinquish control over the island to its colonial subjects. Undeterred, Lola protested the imprisonment of fourteen of the most prominent autonomist leaders. Outraged by the incarceration of journalists Román Baldorioty de Castro, Ramón Marín, Samuel R. Palmer, and others, she wrote a letter to the Spanish Overseas Minister that contributed, along with others' expressions of protest, to the prompt removal of Governor Palacio from his position. She also requested an audience with the newly appointed Governor Contreras in order to plead for the prisoners' release. With great courage and indignation, she denounced the injustices perpetuated against her journalist friends: "There is mockery, insult, harassment, and physical mistreatment of dignified journalists; the infamous *componte* has been applied to honest and defenseless peasants; a multitude of families are forced to ruin even when they do not carry the weight of any guilt on their conscience, except being liberal! . . . Send to Puerto Rico intelligent and enlightened men with wide political horizons and that way you will save from ruin this piece of land, as unfortunate as it is loved."[12] In response to the public outcry, the prisoners were released by the new Spanish governor. Despite the abuses and persecution perpetrated by Spanish authorities and Lola's defiant attitude, she always upheld that she was not an enemy of Spain, "only the foolish Spaniards who want to rule us with an iron hand."[13]

The cumulative consequences of Lola's and Bonoció's patriotism and opposition to the government resulted in another exile, however. In 1889 the family was again forced to leave Puerto Rico. This time they went to Havana, Cuba, where they stayed until 1895. No matter where the family was driven, Lola carried her beloved Puerto Rico within her. These feelings are expressed in "Autógrafo" ("Autograph"), her most memorable verses about the perils of exile:

> I never feel like a foreigner:
> I find home and shelter everywhere.

The blue sphere offers me amplitude;
My graying temples always find a friendly bosom
in this or that shore
Because I carry the Motherland within me.[14]

Over the years, Cuba became the family's adoptive home; however, in 1895 the Spanish authorities in Cuba asked them to leave the island, and they were forced into exile once more. They found a new destination in New York. Since the early decades of the nineteenth century, many Cuban and Puerto Rican expatriates had settled in New York City. The *Sociedad Republicana de Cuba y Puerto Rico* (Republican Society of Cuba and Puerto Rico), founded in 1865, was one of the Antillean expatriates' first political organizations. Upon their arrival in New York, Lola and Bonoció joined other separatist émigrés and continued to work for the revolutionary cause. Rodríguez de Tió became vice president and later honorary president of the *Club Hermanas de Ríus Rivera* (Sisters of Ríus Rivera Club), the first women's club of the *Sección de Puerto Rico* (Puerto Rican Section) of the *Partido Revolucionario Cubano* (PRC, Cuban Revolutionary Party). The PRC had been founded in 1892 by Cuban patriot and celebrated writer José Martí. The club was named after the prominent Puerto Rican general of the Cuban revolutionary army and veteran of both Cuban wars of independence, Juan Ríus Rivera. Along with club president Inocencia Martínez Santaella, wife of Puerto Rican separatist printer-journalist Sotero Figueroa, and other women members, Lola helped organize fundraising activities (such as cultural events, picnics, dances, and bazaars) and the collection of clothing and medicine to support the fighting troops in Cuba. Antonio Maceo, the commanding general of the Cuban revolutionary army once stated, "With women like Lola you can carry on revolutions."[15]

One of Rodríguez de Tió's best-known poems from her New York years is "Octubre 10" ("Ode to October 10"), read at a public function of Antillean émigrés in 1896. The poem uses the popular *décima* poetic stanza to convey the significance of the date that commemorates the Grito de Yara (Cry of Yara) uprising, which marked the beginning of the first Cuban Ten Years' War of independence (1868–1878) against Spain:

There is another country . . . mine!
Which with an arduous effort
Awakens from the heavy sleep
Prolonged by tyranny.

Perhaps the day will come
—In the not too distant future—
That she will follow in virtue and valor
the Cuban motherland,
since in the great pain they share
God himself has made them sisters!
* * *
Very soon beautiful Cuba,
the liberty you've wanted
will bring a thousand sources of life
to your generous land!
Once your sword is again idle
and the rude tyrant defeated,
you will forget how to hate,
and on your glorious shores
you will cover with your flag
both the victor and the vanquished![16]

The Tió-Rodríguez family lived in New York from 1895 to 1899, but it was Cuba and not Puerto Rico to which they decided to return after the Spanish-Cuban-American War of 1898 changed the political destinies of both countries. After the U.S. occupation, Cuba and Puerto Rico were forced by the United States onto different political paths. While Cuba was granted independence in 1902, Puerto Rico was designated an "unincorporated" territory of the United States. It was clear that in Puerto Rico's case colonial rule was transferred from Spanish to North American jurisdiction. Lola and Bonoció remained in the new republic of Cuba, where Lola was appointed to the Academy of Arts and Letters and worked for many years for the Ministry of Education, in charge of supervising the curriculum of private schools. After the uprooted nature of living so many years away from Puerto Rico, and the unresolved nature of their homeland's political status, the family made Cuba their permanent home.

Rodríguez de Tió's collection *Mi libro de Cuba* (*My Book about Cuba*) (1893), of all of her other books, is the one that best describes the loneliness and anguish of being away from her cherished Puerto Rico, her swelling love for her adoptive Cuba, and her dreams of redemption and unity for both islands:

I live far away from the land
that rocked my white cradle

where my memories are kept alive
and where lie the graves of those I cannot forget
and that I may never see again.[17]

The weight of so many years of exile eventually transformed Lola Rodríguez de Tió into "the daughter of two islands."[18] She enjoyed her prominent role as an educator of younger generations in Cuba, and these endeavors occupied the last few decades of her public life. She used to say that being in contact with children and young people was a way of keeping herself young. She wrote incessantly for children—poems, nursery rhymes, folkloric stories, many of which were selected for public and private school textbooks, both in Cuba and Puerto Rico.

The poet's visits to Puerto Rico during the last decades of her life were sporadic. She made briefs trips to the island in 1912, 1915, 1919, and, for the last time, in 1923. In addition to visiting with relatives, she maintained relationships with her artistic and intellectual peers, who celebrated her many literary and civic accomplishments. She was honored at the Ateneo Puertorriqueño, Puerto Rico's main intellectual academy, and at the University of Puerto Rico in 1915.

She rarely expressed in public her feelings about the island's new political condition under the U.S. regime, perhaps because of her ambivalent views about the North American nation. She deplored the lack of self-government for Puerto Rico under the new rulers, but she also saw the United States as a symbol of democracy and civilized progress, especially after its decisive role in ending World War I. These sentiments were shared by many other former separatists, who welcomed some of the benefits of Puerto Rico's association with the United States, even though they also claimed for self-government. Lola conveyed her admiration for the United States in her poem, "A la América" ("To America"), written to celebrate the peace treaty that ended the World War I:

America is to the world
the great nation sublime!
America is the noble one,
America is the good one!
* * *

Cheers, cheers America,
display your flag,
so that the light of your stars
can illuminate the whole world![19]

The few times that Lola ventured to express her political opinions, they were misconstrued as tacit support for the U.S. presence on the island, and thus as a betrayal of her former separatist ideals. She tried to clarify her position in a 1920 interview with the newspaper *La Democracia*:

> I have never been an autonomist. My most fervent wish is to see my compatriots united under a common ideal; in a spirit of harmony for the triumph of liberty and progress. . . . The thesis is this: Can we prove that we are capable of governing ourselves? Because a people who can govern themselves have the legitimate right to enjoy absolute freedom. This we have to justify with our own acts. If the United States would put us to the test, the triumph of freedom of Puerto Rico would be a reality.[20]

Another interview, conducted shortly before her death, made it clear that independence was always her ultimate dream: "I love Puerto Rico, I admire the United States, but I want Cuba to be Cuba; I believe the United States should be the leader of nations, but they should help them to be free; I am always on the side of the oppressed and weak."[21]

Some of the correspondence that Rodríguez de Tió exchanged with her friends during the last year of her life corroborates that despite her admiration for the United States, she still held many of the ideals that she struggled for during her younger years and hoped that the political status of her homeland would change. In a letter written from Cuba to a Puerto Rican friend, shortly after her last visit to the island, she reflected upon the criticism she had received for staying at the margins of Puerto Rico's political debates and away from the growing feminist movement:

> My life always has been "constant labor," intellectually and politically in my own way, without realizing that I was engaged in politics because what truly impelled me in all of my actions was the love for the highest ideals of progress, "home, the motherland, humanity," and I defended them with all the energy of my moral character, always rebellious against any infraction of duty and rights, as much for women as for men; for me men and women are one single idea and sentiment, both aware of their mission on earth: teaching to love the highest ideals of the spirit: truth and "compassionate justice." . . . I am ill and cannot prolong these considerations, but I am sorry for not seeing the

women of my country united under a single flag, the one I love the most, the one I defended and will always defend, the flag of my motherland . . . .[22]

Lola Rodríguez de Tió died in Cuba on November 10, 1924, at the age of eighty-one. It was the end of a long and productive life for "the daughter of two islands." She was buried in Cuba, but years later her remains were moved to her native San Germán. Her legacy, which included many unpublished poems and documents, was initially left in the hands of her daughter Patria. Like her parents before her, Patria Tió was a poet and writer in her own right. She held a doctoral degree in philosophy and letters from the Universidad de la Habana and dedicated her life to many literary and pedagogical endeavors. But her main labor of love was to begin the task of collecting and organizing the writings and personal documents of her mother's prolific career, particularly her unpublished poems. After Patria Tió's death, the task was continued by Lola's niece Laura Nazario de Tió and her son Félix E. Tió Nazario.[23] Their collective efforts culminated in the publication of Lola Rodríguez de Tió's four-volume *Obras completas* (*Complete Works*) (1968–1971) by the Institute for Puerto Rican Culture. However, there are still many neglected documents, especially personal correspondence, in the archives on the island of Cuba that could enhance our knowledge of Lola's political views and relationships with other intellectuals and political figures of her time.

NOTES

1. For information about Lola Rodríguez de Tió's life and her literary contributions, see Josefina Rivera de Alvarez, *Diccionario de literatura puertorriqueña, Vol. II* (San Juan: Instituto de Cultura Puertorriqueña, 1974), 1384–88. Also see Concha Meléndez's study of Rodríguez de Tió's poetry, "Nuevo verdor florece: Homenaje a Lola Rodríguez de Tió," *La Torre* 2.8 (1954): 55–79; and Aurelio Tió's prologue to Vol. I of Lola Rodríguez de Tió, *Obras completas* (San Juan: Instituto de Cultura Puertorriqueña, 1968).

2. Rodríguez de Tió, *Obras completas*, Vol. IV (1971), 82–83.

3. Although she was known to most as Patria, she was baptized María Dolores Elena Patricia Tió Rodríguez. See Patria Tió de Sánchez Fuentes (Elsa), *Autógrafos* (San Juan: Colección Hipatia, 1979).

4. For a detailed account of the origin of the lyrics and music of "La borinqueña," see the introduction to Vol. IV of *Obras completas*, 7–8.

5. Rodríguez de Tió, *Obras completas*, Vol. II (1971), 5. All English translations of the cited poems and excerpts are my own, unless otherwise specified.

6. Historian Aurelio Tió states that Rodríguez de Tió took credit for promoting the idea of a Puerto Rican flag similar to the Cuban flag, but with inverted colors. Prologue to Vol. I, *Obras completas*, x.

7. See Carlos Peñaranda's prologue to *Claros y nieblas*, in Rodríguez de Tió, *Obras completas*, Vol. I, 119.

8. Rodríguez de Tió, *Obras completas*, Vol. IV, 135. This article, first published in *El comercial*, was originally a speech given by Rodríguez de Tió in 1886 at the inauguration of a women's institute in the city of Mayagüez, which was to be directed by her friend Clementina Albéniz de Ruiz. Rodríguez de Tió's daughter Patria was a teacher at the institute.

9. The appellative was used by Félix Ojeda Reyes in his book, *Peregrinos de la libertad* (San Juan: Editorial de la Universidad de Puerto Rico, 1992).

10. Rodríguez de Tió, *Obras completas*, Vol. I, 321.

11. See Antonio S. Pedreira, *El año terrible del 87: Sus antecedentes y sus consecuencias* (San Juan, 1937). Also in *Obras de Antonio S. Pedreira* (San Juan: Instituto de Cultura Puertorriqueña, 1970).

12. Quoted in Ojeda Reyes, *Peregrinos de la libertad*, 99.

13. Rodríguez de Tió, *Obras completas*, Vol. I, xiv.

14. Ibid., Vol. I, 317.

15. Quoted in ibid., Vol. I, xi.

16. Ibid., Vol. I, 450.

17. "Lejos," ibid., Vol. I, 395–96.

18. The appellative "the daughter of two islands" was, according to Josefina Rodríguez de Alvarez (1974), attributed to Rodríguez de Tió by the prominent Nicaraguan poet, Rubén Darío. Quote is from Josefina Rivera de Alvarez, Diccionario de literatura puertorriqueña, Vol. II (San Juan: Instituto de Cultura Puertorriqueña, 1974), 1386.

19. Rodríguez de Tió, *Obras completas*, Vol. II, 95–96.

20. Ibid., Vol. IV, 338.

21. Ibid., Vol. IV, 311.

22. Ibid., Vol. IV, 277.

23. Ibid., Vol. IV, 3.

6

TERESA URREA

Curandera and Folk Saint

Marian Perales

God is the spirit of love; that we in the world must love one another and
live in peace; otherwise we offend God.

Teresa Urrea

Teresa Urrea's fame as a folk saint and *curandera* (folk healer) preceded
her. She dedicated her life to providing medical and spiritual sustenance
to those in need. Her reputation, like the fluid and permeable nature of
the border, crossed over international boundaries. It began in northwest
Mexico in the 1880s, and in the early 1900s it spread into the United States.
Notoriety accompanied her as she journeyed from the interior of Sonora
to Nogales, Arizona, and later to El Paso, Texas. The *Porfiriato,* or the
Porfirio Diaz presidency, was in full swing by the time she came of age.
In the name of "order and progress," Diaz's governmental policies dis-
placed indigenous peoples, pushed small farmers out of business, and
created a disaffected, politically minded, middle class. As the daughter of
a middle-class farmer and an indigenous mother, Urrea identified with
the social plights that surrounded her. Although political exile partially
removed her from the spotlight of the Mexican government, it seemingly
enabled her to remain a public figure. In Sonora, she was a spiritual heroine much sought after, glorified, and admired by the borderland indigenous, dislocated mestizos, and anti-Diaz politicos alike. In the United
States, she became a media darling overnight. Local journalists in Arizona

publicized the forced exile of a young woman whose only outward wrong-doing was a commitment to *curanderismo*, Mexican folk healing. The media never seemed to entirely understand her; accounts ranged from judiciously rendered stories that sympathized with her healing to sensationalized accounts that connected her to a spate of ongoing border rebellions.

Teresa Urrea's youth, although shrouded in mystery, illustrates her sense of adventure. Raised primarily in a *criada/criado* settlement, a detachment of crude huts that lay on the periphery of the rancho and housed the local rancho servants, she demonstrated a certain lack of respect for both authority and girlish behavior. According to her biographer William Holden, Urrea seemed more content riding horseback with nearby *vaqueros* (cowboys) than with cultivating her feminine talents. Even during her adolescence, she remained unrestrained by expectations of womanhood appropriate for a patron's daughter.[1]

Teresa's father, Tomás Urrea, led a randy lifestyle as a ranchero. Frequently separated from his legal wife, Loreto Esceverría, Urrea regularly interacted with other neighboring women. Although repeated serial monogamy, despite a legal marriage, was not uncommon among men of Urrea's economic status, his constant womanizing threatened to dissolve his union with Esceverría, a descendant of a distinguished Sinaloan family and the mother of their ten children. The marriage, however, was never officially ended. Instead, Esceverría distanced herself from the Cabora, which was a spacious ranch where Urrea lived. She resided in the western rancho in the Alamos district. Meanwhile, her husband continued to father children out of wedlock.

By late 1872 or early 1873, Tomás Urrea cast his attention toward Cayetana Chávez; a young Tehuecan woman employed as a domestic servant (*criada*) in the home of Miguel Urrea, Tomás's uncle. The details of their relationship remain unclear, but their daughter Teresa would not be the first or the last child whom Urrea fathered with someone other than Esceverría. Teresa was, however, the only child he bore with Chávez.

The Urrea-Chávez relationship is representative of the sexual relationships between employers and employees that were common in rural western Mexico during this period. Commenting on mid-nineteenth-century Mexico City, Silvia Arrom has noted that domestic servitude entailed a virtual twenty-four-hour enslavement for Mexicanas. The intensive round-the-clock duties of domestic servants ranged from household chores to overseeing cooking and laundering and serving as wet nurses to the patron's children.[2] Unwanted sexual advances were often exacted upon criadas as an extension of their vows of "submission, obedience, and respect" to their patrons. The *casa chica* union between loftier-status men and "unattached women of lower social status than the males' wives" has been well documented by anthropologists Larissa Adler-Lomnitz and Marisol Pérez-Lizaur.[3] Often, the children born of those unions remained concealed from the man's legitimate family members. It seems likely that the elder Tomás Urrea pursued (or raped) Chávez when she was only fourteen years old. Still, as other scholars have suggested of parallel circumstances, this relationship might have allowed Chávez to curry favor or to lighten her circumstances.[4]

Teresa Urrea, born in October 1872 or 1873, lived within the confines of the meager criada quarters, a half mile from the main Santa Ana rancho, with her maternal relatives. She was baptized under the name Maria Rebecca Chávez in the nearby parish of Sinaloa Leyna. Urrea's early spiritual journey is sketchy. In all likelihood, her childhood was steeped in Roman Catholicism, which she later repudiated (or at least softened). In spite of her given name Maria Rebecca, Urrea assumed the name Teresa, which was used widely in Sinaloa and notably within indigenous communities.[5]

The extended family typified the dynamics of indigenous rural communities. Cayetana Chávez, Urrea's mother, resided with her sister, also an employee of the Urrea family, within the servant quarters. The Chávez household was not unique to indigenous family economies. Nineteenth-century women, often uncounted in the local census, contributed informally to the family economy. The veritable leisure time associated with upper- and middle-class Mexican women was nonexistent for lower-class women like the Chávez sisters. They worked as domestic servants as a matter of economic necessity. Moreover, lower-class women frequently worked throughout the various stages of the life cycle.

In 1885 Teresa's social position changed drastically. That year she was installed as one of Tomás Urrea's respectable, legitimate children. Instead of performing domestic duties with the other female members of her household, she socialized with vaqueros.. Meanwhile, another young woman captured Don Tomás's attention: Gabriela Cantúa, a fifteen-year-old mestiza, who lived in a nearby rancho.

Gabriela Cantúa, who doted on her ranchero father, Ramon Cantúa, carried out many of the responsibilities of the woman of the household. Tomás Urrea began frequenting the Cantúa rancho regularly, and within weeks Gabriela Cantúa relocated to the Urreas' Cabora estate. Although never legally wed to Urrea, Cantúa was recognized as his common-law wife until his death. Cantúa and Teresa Urrea developed a lifelong friendship, more like sisters than mother-daughter.

The transition from a criada child born out of wedlock to a member of a ranchero's legitimate family brought a host of radical changes for Teresa. In all likelihood, Tomás Urrea summoned his daughter to his home after securing permission from Cayetana Chávez. Some have suggested that Chávez died or inexplicably disappeared from Cabora, but evidence suggests that Chávez played an active role in the adoption of Teresa's daughters years later.[6] Whatever the emotional turmoil caused by leaving her mother's home, Urrea found a surrogate mother-sister in Gabriela Cantúa.

Unlike Teresa Urrea, Gabriela Cantúa epitomized the idealized nineteenth-century woman, who extolled a single-minded focus on domesticity and motherhood, regardless of class status. Despite the growing ranks of female factory workers and domestic workers, working women, like Cayetana Chávez, were thought to have simply refused their "place" in "*el hogar domestico*" (the conjugal home) and were stigmatized. Julia Tunon has delineated this contradiction between the *idealization* and *realization* of womanhood. Prescriptive literature, according to Tunon, provided one avenue to expound upon the meaning of Mexican womanhood. As noted in popular Mexican literature of the era, motherhood was the heart of womanhood. Or, as Francisco Zarco put it in 1851, "Mothers form the hearts of their sons, and they perpetuate the impressions of virtue and of order. If women were only good spouses, good mothers, their homes would be happy, their men organized, and society excellent."[7] Like the chasm separating idealized and realized women's roles, middle-class status gave Gabriela Cantúa and the teenaged Teresa Urrea the luxury of the domestic arena, whereas Cayetana Chávez remained working class despite her intimate relationship with Tomás Urrea. Cantúa assumed the role as mother and wife, but Teresa Urrea became a *curandera,* or a folk healer, which gave her a legitimate way to defy rigid gender expectations. She drew on characteristically "womanly" qualities, but she used them to serve a larger purpose as a healer.

Shortly after her relocation to the Cabora estate, Urrea developed a life-altering friendship with a local curandera, Huila. Besides serving as a curandera to the isolated Cabora rancho, Huila, a widowed mestiza, held an important position in the Urrea household overseeing the domestic workers. She dispensed home remedies and assisted pregnant women in labor. The opportunity to apprentice with this gifted healer appealed to Teresa. Accompanying Huila to treat patients, Urrea learned the various herbs used to treat internal disorders. Although Urrea learned the bulk of her craft from Huila, several key characteristics distinguished the two women.

One of the first healings in which Urrea played an integral part involved the treatment of a vaquero, Simón Salcido, with a broken leg. Both women approached Salcido where he fell from his horse. Huila set Salcido's leg using a makeshift cast and applied a poultice of leaves and herbs to counteract the swelling and infection. Meanwhile, Urrea called on her ability to heal while in a trance-state. The trance calmed Salcido while Huila rendered treatment. The elder curandera marveled at Urrea's gift.[8]

The apprenticeship continued through the fall of 1889, although Urrea remained a relatively obscure curandera until she experienced a near-fatal illness. The pivotal moment in Urrea's life occurred on October 22, 1889. Urrea heard a strange voice that instructed her to go outside, and she followed the voice to the opposite side of the house, where she reportedly saw a bright light that enveloped her body. Subsequently, Urrea lapsed into the first of a series of trance-like states she experienced during the rest of her life. This initial trance, likely the most deleterious, lasted two weeks.[9]

Certain that his daughter would never regain consciousness, Tomás Urrea instructed the household to begin preparing for Teresa's funeral. Following Tomás Urrea's instructions, the Cabora women readied the body for burial. According to Mexican pre-burial rituals, the women prepared the body for the *velorio* (wake), bathing her and clothing her in white garments. Next, she was placed atop a table covered with a white sheet. Four lit candles were positioned around her to resemble a cross pattern. After carefully positioning the body, the Cabora women began a twenty-four-hour prayer vigil. However, the velorio was disbanded when Teresa regained consciousness. Although the lapse of consciousness frightened Urrea's family, it was only the beginning of a three-month bout of seizures and catatonic states.

During that period, Cabora family members and friends worried incessantly about Urrea's mental health. She exhibited particularly bizarre behavior, first noticed as changes in her personality. Once an outgoing, optimistic young woman, Teresa became seemingly introverted and moody after her illness. She appeared to enjoy solitary activities more than the hubbub of the Cabora estate. She began openly preaching about God to her family and friends. According to Lauro Aguirre, she spoke frequently of things "completely incomprehensible to those who surrounded her. For this reason, they thought she had lost her mind."[10] Later, Teresa contended that she had experienced a "vision" from the Virgin Mary during her illness. In exchange for renewed health, Urrea promised to devote her energies to the desires expressed by the Virgin. The *manda* (promise) she made included offering her healing treatments to the sick and attempting to "heal humanity" of its wounds. Tomás Urrea, an avowed skeptic, derided his daughter's newfound faith.

In addition to this personality change, Teresa Urrea exhibited a bevy of uncharacteristic traits. She stopped eating, required assistance dressing and bathing, and continued lapsing into trance-like and catatonic states even while maintaining consciousness. In spite of these trance states, Urrea continued healing the sick. The patients she attended noted a strange perfume-like odor emanating from her body. That aura would become one of Urrea's hallmark symbols.

Understandably, the period following Urrea's illness proved volatile for all. She appeared to have relied significantly on the Cabora women. Her surrogate mother became a vital confidante. She also relished the brief moments spent with her healing mentor, Huila. According to biographer William Holden, upon regaining consciousness, Urrea predicted the death of a Cabora resident. Little did she know that death would strike her beloved Huila, a woman much advanced in age when the apprenticeship commenced.[11] Teresa's healing ventures continued unabated, despite the loss of her mentor.

Treating a well-known woman residing in the Cabora community, Rosario Bajo, lent credence to Urrea's growing reputation as an extraordinary healer. Suffering from what was referred to as a "pulmonary hemorrhage," Bajo sought Urrea's assistance. It seems likely that Bajo may have suffered from a tumor, bronchitis, pneumonia, or a type of cardiovascular disorder, as vomiting blood is a consistent symptom of all of those disorders. After recognizing the internal nature of the illness, Teresa Urrea responded, "I am going to cure with the blood from my heart." Urrea concocted a salve from her own saliva, mixed with a drop of blood and some dirt. After Urrea applied this to the small of Bajo's back, the hemorrhage immediately subsided.[12]

By December 1889, Teresa Urrea had amassed a considerable following at the local, regional, and national levels. Those waiting to see her created a makeshift encampment outside the walls of Tomás Urrea's estate. *El Monitor Republicano*, a daily Mexico City newspaper, noted, "Cabora had been transformed into a market place due to the miracles of Teresa Urrea."[13] Informal eateries and public altars erected to the Virgin of Guadalupe transformed Cabora from an insulated rancho into a thriving cultural and religious center of activity. Contained as a local, or even regional center of folk Catholicism, Cabora posed little threat to the Catholic Church. However, the very existence of an unrecognized folk saint dubbed

La Santa de Cabora caused the Catholic hierarchy to begin to reevaluate its initial disregard of this local spirituality.

According to coverage in *El Monitor Republicano*, the Catholic Church criticized Urrea's words and actions. In her sermons, Urrea openly criticized clerical abuses, including almsgiving and the divine mediation. Common themes of equality and love peppered her informal speeches. Her rejection of the sacraments, including confession and matrimony, raised the ire of the clergy. Perhaps clergy saw in Urrea's criticism of divine mediation an erosion of their real power.

The existence of popular religion was not uncommon during the late 1800s in Mexico. The northern state of Sonora, far removed from the center of the Catholic Church in Mexico City, was especially vulnerable to popular proselytizers like Urrea. In many northern Mexican communities, a shortage of clergy made servicing rural Catholics nearly impossible. Thus, for many nominal Catholics, Teresa Urrea became a reasonable alternative.

In December 1889, as Urrea's following grew, the popular press began reporting on these events in Cabora. In fact, by that time her following had grown so significantly that Teresa Urrea began issuing statements herself to blunt the attention. Some had already taken to calling her La Santa de Cabora, calling into question the legitimacy of Catholic sainthood. In fact, men and women outside of Cabora had taken to kneeling before her after she cured them. That action prompted her to affirm, "I do not demand anything ceremonial. God is who we ought to venerate." She also recognized her unique spirituality, stating: "My body is like yours but my soul is much different."[13] By April 1890, she had begun a renegade style of sacramental dispensation, baptizing nearby Yaqui children. Yet it was the ubiquitous veneration of her as La Santa de Cabora that most deeply disturbed the Catholic Church. To test the validity of her claims of sainthood, the church dispatched several nuns to her home. According to Aguirre, Teresa drove several hatpins through her leg, pulled them out without drawing blood, and told the nuns to report back to their priest the actions they had witnessed.[14]

By the 1890, Urrea's appeal had reached great heights, just as political and economic unrest characterized much of rural Mexico. In the eastern state of Chihuahua, the village of Tomochic experienced increased tension when the federal government sought to buy up its communal land. Far-removed from the nearest Chihuahuan Catholic Church, Tomochitecos practiced a form of folk Catholicism that included veneration of "La Santa de Cabora." As veneration of "Santa Teresa" increased, the

Catholic Church dispatched an itinerant priest, Miguel Castelo, who urged the community to abandon the form of sacrilege. The Tomochitecos rebuffed him and continued to venerate Teresa Urrea.

In addition to this battle over religious freedom, Tomochic experienced a host of economic, political, and ecological problems. Subsistence agriculture had been the mainstay of the local economy, but increasingly communal lands were stripped and purchased by the federal government. Drought conditions made farming tenuous at best. Additionally, foreign investment in gold and silver mining appeared in the 1870s and 1880s. Although mining provided Tomochitecos with opportunities for wage labor at a time of diminished returns in farming, it also created economic dependency on international companies. Political change also affected the community, as a recent pro-Diaz village appointee threatened to tear apart the social fabric of the community.

Between December 1891 and October 1892, community disaffection reached a high point, and a disgruntled group of community activists decided to seek out the counsel of Teresa Urrea in Sonora. When they reached Cabora in the spring of 1892, they found the rancho deserted. Unbeknownst to neighboring local communities, the Urreas had already been sequestered and deported by the federal government. As the Tomochitecos returned to their community, they met a contingent of Chihuahuan *rurales* (federally organized militia). Though small in numbers, the Tomochitecos managed to fight off the better-equipped rurales. Despite their failed attempts to enlist the aid of Teresa Urrea, the Tomochitecos reportedly could be heard defending their land in her name. By year's end, more than three hundred residents had been massacred; only a small number of local women and children survived the slaughter.[15]

Political and social unrest continued to characterize much of Chihuahua. Although the Tomochic rebellion remains a touchstone of pre-Revolutionary disaffection, it was not an isolated occurrence. In April 1893 uprisings transpired in Chihuahua among the survivors of Tomochic. In the neighboring village of Temosachic, "Viva La Santa de Cabora" *gritos*, or shouts, rang out. Groups of rebel guerrillas continued marauding the Sierra Madre Mountains throughout 1894; however, Diaz employed any means necessary to stifle the uprisings.

Although seemingly detached from Teresa Urrea's experiences in Cabora, the Tomochic rebellion illustrates that chasm between the symbolic "Santa de Cabora" and the actual Teresa Urrea. In the span of less than two years, Urrea had gone from a local healer to a symbol of resistance and liberation. Yet no evidence corroborates her participation at

Tomochic or in other border disputes. When events were becoming heated in Chihuahua, the federal government deported the Urrea family. Tomás Urrea may have maintained his connections to anti-Diaz activism, but Teresa Urrea quietly pursued healing in southern Arizona.

How, then, did Teresa Urrea become a symbol of resistance? No simple explanation exists; however, women have played symbolic roles throughout Mexican history. Ideals of liberation have long been associated with the Virgin of Guadalupe symbol, which represented the melding of a specifically indigenous goddess, Tonantzin, with a decidedly Catholicized Mary icon. From the 1660s to the 1810s, New Spain strove to appropriate Tonantzin and to recast her as a Catholic Mary who symbolized liberation from colonization. Similar to the ways in which an emphasis on millennialism fitted well with an indigenous belief system of "hope and apocalyptic history," the Virgin of Guadalupe represented those notions during the struggle for Mexican independence.

With rapid modernization at the end of the nineteenth century, including the advent of the railroad, the increase in foreign investments, and the shift from agrarianism to capitalism, the Tomochitecos witnessed the physical, emotional, and spiritual displacement of their localized community and economy. Whereas they were once ignored by the state government and Catholic clerics, their religious practices, once deemed acceptable, became taboo. Gradually, "La Santa de Cabora," in the shadow of the Virgin of Guadalupe, was appropriated to represent liberation from increasing economic exploitation, religious censure, and political repression.

Even without evidence directly linking Teresa Urrea to the events in Tomochic, the federal government, by the spring of 1892, moved swiftly to curb her activities. Correspondence between the federal and state governments suggests that the Urrea family had been monitored for some time prior to their deportation. The government may not have fretted over healing, but it seems likely that they disapproved of the fanaticism surrounding Teresa's cult worship. Her homilies, which stressed equality, justice, and love of humanity, seemed dangerous to the federal government, especially when her followers were largely indigenous and mestizo, and they clung to communal landholding and subsistence agriculture, which threatened the economic policies of the federal government. It seems that folk religion may have suggested cultural revitalization.

Perhaps challenged by Teresa Urrea's widespread following, the central government moved to undercut her support. Dispatched by the Mexican secretary of war, General Abraham Bandala, leading the Eleventh Regiment and the Twelfth Battalion, was instructed to marshal the Urrea family from their home to the coastal port city, Guaymas, that served as a way station for future deportation cases. When Bandala reached the area on May 17, he instructed the Urreas to leave their home. In addition to the family's capture, Bandala called for the persecution of the countless indigenous peoples who had sought Urrea's counsel. According to a telegram sent from General Bandala to the secretary of war, Cabora was a place rife with political conspirers: "this is where the fanatical uprisings of the Mayo Indians began."[16] Fearing incarceration, the Urreas agreed to relocate to the United States.

Even after crossing the border, controversy followed the Urreas. Arriving in Nogales, Arizona, by train in June 1892, Urrea became a cause célèbre. Hordes of Nogales residents met her at the train station. A police escort from the train station to a local hotel only highlighted her public exile. The Mexican government, embittered (and perhaps embarrassed) by the notoriety Urrea had gained, continued to investigate her. The Sonoran government sent Manuel Mascarenas, the president of Nogales Sonora, who encouraged the family to move further northward. Mascarenas gently reminded them that residing away from the United States–Mexico border was part of the terms of their exile, and by flouting this agreement, they risked deportation.

In response to the visit, Tomás and Teresa Urrea went to Tucson to apply for United States citizenship. Mr. Urrea believed that without citizenship, the Mexican government might be able to convince the United States to extradite them back to Mexico. No public record exists that shows they obtained citizenship; however, it seems likely that the Urreas began but failed to complete the process. Meanwhile, mounting pressure from the Mexican government forced them to relocate to the rural community of El Bosque, outside of Nogales. Reuniting with his common-law wife, Gabriela Cantúa, and their children, Tomás and Teresa Urrea lived quietly in El Bosque. Out of the gaze of the Mexican government, Urrea renewed her healing. Although record of Urrea's time in El Bosque is lost, she resurfaced in Solomonville, Arizona, in November 1895, where there was an outpouring of support from the small farming community.

By 1896, four years after entering the United States, Teresa Urrea found herself at the center of political controversy. Solomonville, Arizona, became the site of a fledgling anti-Diaz newspaper, *El Independiente*, under the direction of Lauro Aguirre and Flores Chapa, Mexican liberals with whom Tomás Urrea associated. Porfirio Diaz had promoted policies including dispossessing indigenous peoples, pushing out middle-sized farmers like Urrea, censoring opposing viewpoints, and quelling public opposition movements. Aguirre and Flores Chapa, who were outspoken critics of the Diaz regime, wasted little time drafting a political treatise that criticized Diaz's political, economic, and social policies. Published on February 5, 1896, *Plan Restaurador de Constitución y Reformista* outlined the atrocities committed by the Diaz government and called for institutional reform. Using the Tomochic rebellion as a touchstone, the *Plan Restaurador* stated that the 1857 Constitution had been violated by electoral fraud, property violations (especially with respect to communal lands), agricultural monopoly, exploitation of mine workers, and censorship of freedom of expression. The circular called for free and open elections, a radical reorganization of the military, and civic equality. To fulfill those aims, it advocated an armed revolution to overthrow the Porfirian government.[17]

Many scholars have speculated about Teresa Urrea's participation in the fledgling revolutionary movement. Signed by twenty-three men and women, the *Plan Restaurador* circulated throughout southern Arizona. Mexican scholars have pointed out two unusual signatures on the document. One was that of Mariana Avendano, Teresa Urrea's comadre from Cabora, who had become a close friend in 1890 when she sought Teresa's treatment. Avendano accompanied the Urrea family to the United States and remained a lifelong friend. Additionally, a signature by Tomás Esceverri appears on the document. Some have wondered whether this signature was that of Tomás Urrea, just using the surname of his legal wife, Loreto Esceverría. Although Teresa Urrea's name did not appear on the document, her critics assumed her political participation. Indeed, she may have agreed with the governmental oppression noted in *Plan Restaurador*, yet her family and friends may have counseled her not to publicly sign the document. Given her personal politics, it is hard to completely divorce her from those activities.

The local Solomonville authorities, sensing a political firestorm brewing, were quick to forward the document to the Chihuahuan governor. In response, the governor enlisted the aid of the Mexican consulate in El Paso, Texas. Aguirre and Chapa were watched closely. A month later, the two men were charged with committing "subversive acts" and tried in an El Paso court. During the trial, attention began to focus on Teresa Urrea's involvement in the alleged "conspiracy." The court, finding no real evidence of any wrongdoing beyond exercising freedom of speech, released Aguirre and Chapa after they served two weeks in jail.

Perhaps trying to avoid the political climate associated with Solomonville, the Urreas moved to El Paso in June 1896. Then, as in Cabora, an impromptu encampment was erected at Teresa's El Paso home, which was located across the street from the local courthouse. When covering Urrea in the local press, reporters commonly interviewed outgoing courthouse patrons. Those seeking her treatment cut across all socioeconomic classes and included local Mexicans/Mexican-Americans, Mexicans from Chihuahua and Sonora, and local Euro-Americans.

Urrea treated a host of ailments using a wide range of methods, like the laying on of hands; poultices; herbs, including Yerba Negra, Yerba Blanca, and Yerba del Indio; massage; and the application of oils. Several paralyzed individuals who sought her healing reportedly walked easily after receiving treatment. Skeptics became believers as their lifelong ailments disappeared. Many recipients tried to compensate Urrea, who refused most monetary compensation and gave away what money she did accept. By representing Teresa Urrea as an apolitical spiritual healer, the El Paso press helped her to stay outside the political fray, that is, until an outbreak of border rebellions in August 1896.

Hearkening back to the political symbolism used six years earlier in Tomochic, the residents of Nogales, Arizona, took La Santa de Cabora as a sign of liberation. Early on the morning of August 12, 1896, at least seventy Mexicans, Yaquis, and Pimas, many of whom were laborers for the Southern Pacific Railroad, stormed the Nogales customhouse in search of money and contraband. To quell the melee, the Mexican consulate, Manuel Mascarena, enlisted the aid of the American military forces. A makeshift group of American civilians also banded together to subdue the Mexican intruders. In all, at least three people were killed and countless were wounded.[18]

The Nogales uprising is best understood as a local protest movement against anti-agrarian and anti-indigenous Mexican land policies. To better accommodate urbanization, foreign-backed mining, and commercial agriculture, Diaz had indigenous peoples, notably Yaquis, transported far south to the Yucatan. Many did not go quietly, and that forced migration has become a sore spot in the annals of Mexican history.

The casualties of the Nogales uprising provide the best direct evidence of the role that Teresa Urrea played in the border conflict. The American and Mexican press wasted little time broadcasting the events, suggesting that the Mexican rebels carried copies of Lauro Aguirre's *El Independiente* and photos of Teresa Urrea. Perhaps emboldened by the success of *Plan Restaurador*, Aguirre began printing *El Independiente* from El Paso. The newspaper took the liberty of glorifying Teresa Urrea as a visionary woman advocating an apocalyptic revolution.

References to "Viva La Santa de Cabora" resurfaced in the customhouse raid. The connection to Tomochic was one that deepened the chasm between the historical Teresa Urrea and the mythical La Santa de Cabora. During the mid 1890s, while Teresa Urrea practiced her craft as a curandera and distanced herself, at least publicly, from the border uprisings, La Santa de Cabora grew to mythic proportions. Well schooled in the power of cultural iconography, Lauro Aguirre capitalized on the opportunity to reinvent Urrea as a symbol of liberation and to foster the renewal of La Santa de Cabora. He only needed a captive audience, which he found in the border peasantry. In the midst of radical upheaval, Yaquis, Mayas, Pimas, and mestizos believed La Santa de Cabora would usher in a simpler era that defied modernization.

Meanwhile, Urrea distanced herself from the ensuing events. In an article in the *El Paso Herald*, Urrea stated:

> The press generally in these days has occupied itself with my humble person in terms unfavorable in the highest degree, since in a fashion most unjust—the fashion in the republic of Mexico; they refer to me as participating in political matters; they connect me with the events which have happened in Nogales, Sonora in Coyame and Presidio del Norte, Chihuahua where people have risen in arms against the government of Sr. General Don Porfirio Diaz. . . . I have noticed with much pain that the persons who have taken up arms in Mexican territory have invoked my name in aid of the schemes they are carrying through. But I repeat I am not one who authorizes or at same time interferes with these proceedings. Decidedly I am a victim since in the most unjust way have I been expatriated from my country since May 19, 1892.[19]

It is entirely possible that the Urreas played a part in initiating the customhouse raid. It is also likely that Lauro Aguirre could have helped to craft this public apology defending Urrea's political apathy. Whatever the motives, this very public statement may have bought the Urreas some time out of the eye of the Mexican government. Perhaps realizing the gravity of the situation, in 1897 the family moved to Clifton, Arizona.

In light of persistent media scrutiny of Teresa Urrea's politics, Clifton proved to be a mining community insulated from the controversies that plagued such political charged communities as El Paso. Although the natural landscape was a treasure trove for mining companies, which included Longfellow, Arizona Copper Company, and later Phelps Dodge, it was disastrous for the laborers, who were predominantly Mexicanos.

Several factors created a separate but unequal community. In the town's racial composition, most nonwhites lived in the Chase Creek and Shannon Hills areas, in proximity to the mines, while whites made their home in southeastern Clifton. The stratified residential pattern was thus forged along economic and racial lines. Restrictive covenants barred nonwhites from registering land claims. Consequently, persons of color who resided in southeast Clifton relied on land leased from the Shannon Hills or Arizona Copper Companies, as did the Urrea family. The Chase Creek and Shannon Hills areas, located at a significantly lower altitude, suffered disastrous flooding whenever torrential rainfall occurred.

In addition, a dual system of wage labor created a fixed economy. Whites occupied higher class positions as skilled laborers, mine owners, business owners, and professionals, whereas persons of color, including Mexicanos and to a lesser extent Chinese, occupied lower strata mining positions. Moreover, persons of color were paid significantly lower wages, usually in limited amounts of cash and vouchers, which could only be redeemed at the overpriced company store.

The Urrea family occupied a middling economic position in the Clifton socioeconomic hierarchy. Neither miners nor owners, they labored as "auxiliary" workers: as mule drivers, woodchoppers, and common laborers.[20] Tomás Urrea quickly started a wood lot business and dairy, but restrictive covenants barred him from owning property. Therefore, he leased land from the Arizona Copper Company and erected a moderate-sized adobe home for his family.

In the late 1890s, Clifton displayed all the hallmark characteristics of mining "company towns." The Arizona Copper Company was thriving, while Mexican laborers struggled to carve out a meager existence and suffered from the toxic conditions caused by the mining caverns and smelters. Tuberculosis ran rampant. Dr. Lacy, the company doctor in the 1880s, was so horrified by the environmental conditions that he abandoned his responsibilities. His replacement, Dr. Lewis Burtch, developed an influential and important bond with the Urreas. Though little evidence exists, Teresa Urrea likely continued healing, and perhaps that accounts for Burtch's interest in the family. The style of healing that Urrea brought to Clifton may not have been considered so exotic to intermarried Anglo and Mexican families.

In Clifton, Urrea began to exert her own autonomy. First, she wed a local miner, Lupe Rodríguez, on June 22, 1900. The marriage seemed troubled from the start. The popularized version of the story casts Teresa Urrea as a forlorn lover who uncharacteristically made a bad decision. Some observers repeatedly highlighted the different social and economic classes that the two occupied. Rodríguez was a Yaqui who appeared to have moved to Clifton to find work as a miner; Urrea, on the other hand, was perceived to be in a higher social category because of her father's middling business ventures. According to this popular account of the marriage, Urrea blindly fell in love with Rodríguez. The ill-fated marriage dissolved in Metcalf, a community several miles from Clifton, where the two were informally celebrating with family and friends. By early morning, Rodríguez brandished a rifle and tried to coerce Urrea onto a southbound train headed for Mexico. An angry group of Metcalf residents assisted authorities in separating the couple. The local press seized on the opportunity to present Rodríguez as "demented" and "delusional" and Urrea as a "forlorn lover." In this way, the mythologized version of Urrea as "la Santa"—wholly pure, maternal, and altruistic—is reified.[21]

Other possible narratives consider Teresa's decision to wed as an attempt to break filial ties with her father. At twenty-seven years old, she may have sought an independent life that she was unable to achieve as an unmarried woman (*soltera*). Upholding all the expectations of the patron's daughter may have grown tiresome for Teresa Urrea. She could heal independently, but still that suggested degrees of maternalism and domesticity. Marrying a miner, conversely, might have created greater possibilities for her; at least it freed her from her father's supervision. In any event, the couple quickly separated twenty-four hours after the wedding.

Soon thereafter, encouraged by local Clifton business leaders, including banker Charles Rosencranz and mine owner Charlie Shannon, Urrea traveled to San Jose, California, to treat an ill young boy named Alvin Fessler. Doctors had been unable to cure the boy, who had become blind and completely immobile. After enduring a ninety-minute treatment by Urrea, including a plasterlike poultice applied directly to the spine and the laying on of hands, Alvin Fessler completely recovered six weeks later.[22]

In September 1900, Urrea embarked on a medical tour, likely with the assistance of Shannon and Rosencranz. Soon, a manager, John H. Suits, a fledgling San Francisco publisher, was hired to oversee her tour. Surprisingly, Urrea agreed to a contract under which she would earn $10,000 per year. It was an odd decision because Urrea had always healed with minimal compensation. In a curious move, Urrea took on the role of a theatrical folk healer, although her *curanderismo* had never been about theatrics and spectacle. Her general discomfort may illustrate the different perspectives on her skills; she recognized her actions as viable medical treatment, whereas her manager and entourage perceived her healings solely as a form of entertainment. The differing perspectives eventually resulted in Urrea severing her legal contract.

The medical tour that commenced in San Francisco in September 1900, moreover, was riddled with internal problems. From the beginning, Urrea experienced isolation and deceit. Adelaida Fessler, who was Alvin Fessler's mother, had accompanied her to serve as interpreter, yet Urrea longed for her Clifton friends. In addition, her manager assured Urrea that patients would not have to pay for her services, yet he hid from her that he charged all recipients who sought healing.

The Metropolitan Hall, with a capacity of 2,500, served as the site for all of Urrea's healing exhibitions in San Francisco. Originally built as a Baptist church in 1877, its main purpose by the early 1880s was to house vaudevillian and other cultural presentations. Urrea's first healing exhibition drew more than a thousand spectators. Some were Mexicans, others were Euro-Americans; some sought treatments, others spectacle; all were from a working-class background.

The healing tour officially began as a truck driver approached the stage for treatment. P. J. Hennelly, who transported whiskey barrels, suffered from a paralyzed back and legs. After submerging her hands in a bowl of fluid, Urrea made several passes over Hennelly's injured back and feet. After the treatment, Hennelly walked from the stage to his seat without using his cane. Despite such successes, newspaper articles suggested that Urrea was often uncomfortable healing in front of crowds of onlookers.[23]

Yet if she appeared uneasy during healings, during interviews she displayed maturity and wisdom. The interviews she granted to the California press provide the best clues about her personal beliefs. She told one reporter in July 1900 that she valued honesty, integrity, and justice: "Truth is everything; of truth I have no fear; in truth I see no shame." Moreover, she pointed to a notable change in her own beliefs after she endured her month-long coma. Although she did not subscribe to a religion, she believed that "God is the spirit of love; that we who are in the world must love one another and live in peace; otherwise we offend God."[24] Lifted out of context, these words reflect little beyond a humanist worldview. Yet expressed to discontented indigenous and mestizo peoples a decade earlier, they may have tacitly encouraged rebellion and resistance.

By the end of September, the tour had stalled in San Francisco. Realizing Suits's unscrupulous business practices, Urrea sued for breach of contract. Nearly a month into the tour, she had been paid only $50, instead of the promised $832 per month. The court sided with Urrea, who formally broke her contract. In addition, Urrea seemed lonely and bitterly at odds even with the San Jose entourage who admired and supported her. She did not wish to make curanderismo a public spectacle, but she had been hired to entertain audiences. This sort of unease and discord plagued Urrea.

The tour regrouped without J. H. Suits and Adelaida Fessler, and departed for St. Louis in December 1900. Susie Crimman, who had befriended Teresa in San Francisco, now served as her interpreter, but this working relationship proved untenable. Sometime in early 1901, Urrea wrote to her longtime Clifton friend, Juana Van Order, asking her to send one of her sons as an interpreter in exchange for Urrea's assistance with Van Order's sons' schooling. John, the older son, who was eighteen years old, was sent to St. Louis. John Van Order and Teresa Urrea developed a working relationship that turned to a sexual relationship by spring.

The tour trudged on to New York, though it remained largely outside the headlines. Once the nature of the Urrea–Van Order relationship moved beyond business, it seems that Van Order pushed his way into her finances. In New York, Urrea continued healing, but she frequently disagreed with Van Order about financial compensation. She frequently gave money away to the needy, and those acts of altruism angered Van Order, who believed they could attain unprecedented wealth.

Two pivotal events may have influenced Urrea's desire to return west. First, she gave birth to a daughter, Laura Urrea Van Order, on February 15, 1902. Although little is known about Laura Van Order's infancy, the isolation that Urrea experienced in New York may have been too difficult for her. Second, Teresa Urrea's father died on September 22, 1902. The death of her father may have prompted a return to more familiar surroundings. She decided to move to East Los Angeles with Van Order.

Urrea's tenure in Los Angeles reflects a renewed commitment to social justice activism. Urrea found her home in the heart of the barrio at the corner of Brooklyn Avenue and State Street. With its influx of Mexicans from Sonora, the neighborhood was dubbed "Sonoratown" and likely felt comfortable to Urrea. At the beginning of the twentieth century, Los Angeles experienced extraordinary growth in the transportation and agribusiness industries, with Mexicans and other persons of color providing much of the labor force for both. The development of interurban railways that linked the east and west sides of Los Angeles gave the newly arriving Mexicans jobs. Mexicans who lived in East Los

Angeles were adjacent to their work site and crowded into dilapidated housing courts.

Perhaps recognizing a parallel between the exploitation of the railroad laborers in Los Angeles and the disfranchised indigenous and mestizos in Sonora, Urrea rallied to the fledgling union cause. In April 1903, the Mexican laborers had organized as *Union Federal Mexicanos* (UFM). The wages paid to the Mexicans ($1.00–$1.25) were considerably less than those paid to Greeks ($1.60) and Japanese ($1.45).[25] In addition, whites occupied higher strata jobs, as engineers and conductors, and Mexicans were isolated in the lowest skilled and paying jobs. Seemingly reaching a breaking point, UFM planned a strike, which began in earnest on April 25, 1903, with the backing of the Los Angeles and San Francisco American Federation of Labor (AFL) unions. On the first day, over seven hundred Mexican laborers walked off the job site. They were replaced largely by African American, Chinese, and Japanese laborers. Although the UFM never received a broad base of support, it was supported by the local Sonoran community, including Teresa Urrea.[26]

The extent of Urrea's participation in union activism, however, has been difficult to uncover. It seems that she spoke at several key labor sites, urging the men to abandon their work. On at least one occasion, she spoke at a meeting of UFM members. By now, Urrea, firmly committed to the rights of disfranchised laborers, probably recognized the power of the created La Santa de Cabora. Although the historical Teresa Urrea remains shadowy, Santa Teresa lived on in headline articles that described the fledgling strike. Although the strike was not a success, many of the striking Pacific Electric Railway workers relocated to Oxnard, supported by local union activists. Drawing on social justice activism and a powerful iconographic presence, Teresa Urrea played an important role in this chapter of Los Angeles labor history. Those efforts hearkened back to her days of social activism both in Sonora and later in Arizona. Yet throughout her life, Urrea never strayed from proclaiming that spirituality was the cornerstone of her seemingly political activism. Although the arena might have changed, her message remained the same: an egalitarian vision of social harmony and economic justice based on spiritual values.

After the failed UFM activities, Urrea may have watched as the local Mexican laboring community deteriorated. Mysteriously, her home burned down in August 1903. We can only speculate about the episode, although newspaper accounts suggest that it burned down while she was in the

Ventura area. The fire may have been purely accidental, but its cause may have been arson. Whatever the cause, after losing nearly all of her personal belongings, Urrea returned to Clifton by the early fall of 1903.

Never swerving from her devotion to the poor, oppressed, and infirm, Urrea continued her healing activities in Clifton. Teresa and John Van Order returned to the San Jose ranch outside of Solomonville. In June 1904, Urrea bore a second daughter, Magdalena. Although the healing tour had challenged Urrea, her pay enabled her to purchase a sizable family home. Unlike the restrictive covenants that barred her father from freely purchasing land ten years earlier, Teresa Urrea purchased a large, eight-room home in southeastern Clifton in Hills Addition. She continued healing and frequently assisted neighboring Mexican children with written Spanish lessons.

By late 1905, Urrea's health had deteriorated significantly. In December, a significant flood struck Clifton. Some have speculated that Teresa's wading in waist-deep floodwaters caused her to contract a serious illness. The heroic tale told about Urrea rescuing Mexican women and children further fuels the legend of La Santa de Cabora. More likely, Urrea contracted tuberculosis.

Urrea sensed that her health was weakening, and she made efforts to secure guardianship for her two young daughters. Curiously, the historical records suggest that John Van Order was frequently absent from the family home. She summoned her biological mother, Cayetana Chávez, and her surrogate mother, Gabriela Cantúa, to her side. Yet it was the presence of her lifelong friend and comadre, Mariana Avendano, that seemed to bring Urrea most peace, and she entrusted her daughters to Avendano and her husband, Fortunato.[27]

Surrounded by family and friends, Teresa Urrea died peacefully on Friday, January 12, 1906. A wake was held later that evening, followed by a funeral service at the family home. Clifton residents lined the street that ran along the perimeter of Hills Addition. Over four hundred people attended the funeral, which ended with a long horse-drawn carriage procession from the family residence to the local Catholic cemetery. In a curious move, never entirely understood or well documented, Urrea's eight-room home was donated to the Phelps Dodge Company, who converted it to the local company hospital. In life, as in death, Teresa Urrea's commitment to healing persisted.

The body of existing biographical literature has overwhelmingly shaped perceptions of Teresa Urrea as the quaint "Teresita" or as La Santa de

Cabora, creating a gulf between the mythical and the historical Teresa Urrea. The historical Teresa Urrea should be viewed as a woman well connected to pre-Revolutionary social justice activism in Mexico and deeply embedded in local indigenous communities. She emerged from modest, yet complex circumstances, straddling two worlds as the daughter of a domestic servant and a middle-class ranchero. Becoming a curandera allowed her to achieve some level of independence while simultaneously upholding womanly qualities like domesticity and maternalism, enabling her to negotiate rigid gender roles in her traditional community.

Moreover, Teresa Urrea needs to be understood within the nexus of borderlands social activism. Some have suggested that she directly participated, or even led borderland uprisings, while others suggest that Urrea was never directly implicated in those actions. Certainly, Teresa Urrea's significance lies in her craft as a curandera. Yet to truly understand Urrea, one needs to recognize that social justice mattered most to her. Indeed, it may be that her very symbolic presence has generated depictions of her as a revolutionary activist. It is likely that Urrea created some distance from the outbreak of repeated border activism, yet that does not mean that she did not endorse such actions. If one listens closely to Urrea's spoken messages of justice, equity, and social harmony, there is little doubt that she believed in the anti-Diaz activism that many of her family and friends supported, and it is clear why she became such an important symbol to activists.

In the United States, Teresa Urrea's life as a curandera became increasingly complex. Friendships forged with intermarried Anglo-Mexicans may have provided a unique opportunity to merge western medicine and curanderismo. The company physician appeared enthralled by her unique methods, which relied on equal doses of herbal medicine, pure faith, and external massaging techniques. Assuming the role of a theatrical folk healer highlighted the contested meaning of her healing. She saw healing as a cultural tradition that melded assisting the infirm and social activism; her managers saw it as entertainment devoid of cultural meaning or social commentary.

Recognizing this difference in perceptions of the meaning of curanderismo helps us to better understand the multiple frames of interpretation of Urrea nearly a century later. Through the beginning of the twentieth century, Teresa Urrea seemed to be a forgotten historical figure; however, the Chicano movement rescued her from the historical dustbin. Indeed, it was the period of the mid- to late-1970s that her history was retold.

However, many of those depictions seemed more interested in extolling her as a Chicana warrior woman, than in recounting the actual story.[28] To some extent, that sort of nostalgia did little to strengthen Urrea's credibility.

In the mid-1980s, the town of Clifton, after surviving a protracted and sometimes violent mining strike, sought to resurrect the importance of Teresa Urrea. Many Clifton elders remembered hearing stories about the mysterious Santa Teresa, so the town planned a fiesta in her honor, slated for April 9, 1994.[29] According to one resident, if anyone could heal the fractured community, it was Santa Teresa.[30] Throngs of people came to Clifton for the event. At least momentarily, Teresa Urrea seemed to take on an iconic role as she had a century earlier.

Certainly the origins of curanderismo in Latino communities cannot and should not be attributed solely to Urrea. Respected elders relied on herbs and other *remedios caseros* (home remedies) before her arrival and after her death. Unsurprisingly, Teresa Urrea has wended her way into the annals of Chicano/Chicana history. That fact is not hard to comprehend. She was a woman committed to social justice for Latinos, whether that meant speaking out against anti-agrarian land policies or oppressive labor conditions. She was a woman who acted selflessly on behalf of the greater good of her community. Yet she used qualities like domesticity and maternalism to mask her deep commitment to social justice. Indeed, Teresa Urrea's comadre Josefa Félix from Ocoroni, Sinaloa, may have said it best when she quipped of Urrea's healing: "She is gentle as a dove; but energetic when necessary."[31]

NOTES

1. William Holden, *Teresita* (Owings Mills, Md.: Stemmer House, 1978), 38–39.

2. Silvia Arrom, *The Women of Mexico City, 1757–1821* (Stanford, Calif.: Stanford University Press, 1991), 187–88.

3. Larissa Adler-Lomnitz and Marisol Pérez-Lizaur, *A Mexican Elite Family, 1820–1980* (Princeton, N.J.: Princeton University Press, 1987), 142.

4. Ibid.,142; see also Deborah Gray White, *Ar'n't I a Woman: Female Slaves in the Plantation South* (New York: W. W. Norton, 1985), 98–102.

5. Angel Santini to William Curry Holden, January 10, 1963, Correspondence file, Box 51, William Curry Holden Papers (hereinafter cited as WCH), Southwest Collection, Texas Tech University, Lubbock, Texas.

6. Gabriela Cantúa affidavit, July 17, 1906, Graham County Courthouse, Safford, Arizona; L. A. W. Burtch affidavit, July 17, 1906, Graham County Courthouse, Safford, Arizona.

7. Francisco Zarco, "Consejos a las Señoritas," quoted in Julia Tunon, *El Album de Mujer, Vol. III* (Mexico, D.F.: Instituto Nacional Antropologia e Historia, 1991), 89.

8. Holden, *Teresita*, 62.

9. Lauro Aguirre, "Tomochic! Redención!" in *Tomochic: La Revolución Adelantada, Vol. II*, ed. Jesus Vargas Váldez (Ciudad Juarez: Universidad Autonoma de Ciudad Juarez, 1994), 108.

10. Ibid.

11. Holden, *Teresita*, 58.

12. Aguirre, "Tomochic! Rendención!"109.

13. *El Tiempo*, April 4, 1890.

14. Holden, *Teresita*, 160; Anita Treviño interview, November 23, 1961, Folder 18, Box 53, Interview with Anita Treviño, November 25, 1961, conducted by William Holden, Box 53, Folder 18, WCH.

15. Paul Vanderwood, *The Power of God Against the Guns of the Government: Religious Upheaval in Mexico at the Turn of the Nineteenth Century* (Stanford, Calif.: Stanford University Press, 1998), 67–131.

16. Telegram from General Bandala to secretary of war, May 24, 1892, *Teresita* Research Notes, Box 54, WCH.

17. Brianda Domecq, "La Santa de Cabora," in *Tomochic: La Revolución Adelantada, Vol. II*, ed. Vargas Váldez, 36; Lilian Aguiar Illades, "La Santa de Cabora," in ibid., 76–78.

18. "Santa Teresa and the Nogales Insurrection," *Arizona Silver Belt*, August 27, 1896.

19. *El Paso Herald,* September 11, 1896.

20. Andrea Yvette Huginnie, "'Strikitos': Race, Class, and Work in the Arizona Copper Industry, 1870–1920" (Ph.D. dissertation, Yale University, 1991), 98.

21. *Arizona Range News*, July 4, 1900.

22. Helen Dare, "Santa Teresa, Celebrated Mexican Healer," *San Francisco Examiner*, July 27, 1900.

23. *San Francisco Bulletin*, September 9, 1900; "Santa Teresa Whom the Yaquis Revere," *San Francisco Chronicle*, September 9, 1900; "Santa Teresa the Yaqui Idol," *San Francisco Examiner*, September 9, 1900; "Santa Teresa Uses Her Healing Powers," *San Francisco Morning-Call*, September 13, 1900.

24. Dare, "Santa Teresa, Celebrated Mexican Healer."

25. Charles Wollenberg, "Working on El Traque: The Pacific Electric Strike of 1903," in *The Chicano*, ed. Norris Hundley (Santa Barbara, Calif.: ABC-Clio, 1975), 100.

26. Ibid., 99.

27. Gabriela Cantúa affidavit, July 17, 1906; L. A. W. Burtch affidavit, July 17, 1906.

28. For example, see Carlos Larralde, "Santa Teresa, a Chicana Mystic," *Grito del Sol* 3 (April-June 1978): 9–114.

29. Vanderwood, *Power of God Against the Guns of the Government*, 323–29.

30. Personal interview with Walter Mares conducted by the author, August 19, 1998, Clifton, Arizona.

31. *El Tiempo*, April 4, 1890.

7

LUISA CAPETILLO

Feminist of the Working Class

Nancy A. Hewitt

Tyranny, like freedom, has no country, any more than do exploiters

or workers.

Luisa Capetillo

Luisa Capetillo, a fiery labor organizer and feminist in early twentieth-century Puerto Rico, was a prolific writer who expressed her vision of liberated workers, emancipated women, and a free society through essays, books, and plays. Committed to living her ideals, Capetillo bore three children but refused to marry, embraced "natural" forms of healthcare, exchanged skirts for pants as she pursued a public career, and supported herself and her family on the proceeds of her labor. Yet she did not value ideological purity over practical needs. Dedicated to the principles of anarcho-syndicalism, which rejected the state as an oppressive institution, she nonetheless advocated woman suffrage. Intensely anticlerical in response to the Catholic Church's support of repressive political regimes, she remained deeply spiritual. Part of a growing circle of working-class feminists in Puerto Rico, Capetillo defined a broad and humanistic agenda for social change that echoed across the Caribbean and reached into immigrant enclaves in New York City and South Florida. Recognized in her own time as both an effective organizer and a radical visionary, Luisa Capetillo has only recently begun to receive the attention she deserves among present-day activists and scholars.[1]

Luisa Capetillo was born on October 28, 1879. Her French mother, Margarita Péron, lived through the Revolution of 1848 and absorbed lessons of revolutionary romanticism and women's rights despite the rebellion's failure. Her father, Luis Capetillo Echevarría, was raised in northern Spain, a region fraught with conflicts between peasants, landlords, and the Catholic Church. As young people, both moved with their families to Puerto Rico in hopes of improving their economic circumstances, but neither escaped their class origins. Margarita sought work as a governess, but she labored instead as a laundress in the homes of affluent local families. Luis worked a variety of jobs in construction and agriculture and along the docks, his employment changing with the seasons.

Margarita and Luis met in the town of Arecibo, fell in love, and established a household, but they never sought legal or church sanction for their union. Luisa, a precocious reader, was their only child. Her parents doted on her and introduced her at a young age to the writings of revolutionary thinkers, women's rights advocates, and progressive educators. Although Luisa attended school, it was the informal education she received at home—reading works by Victor Hugo, Leo Tolstoy, George Sands, Emile Zola, Peter Kropotkin, and John Stuart Mill and discussing anarcho-syndicalism, religion, and workers' rights with her parents—that formed her political consciousness. At some point during Luisa's adolescence, her father left the family and did not return. Luisa never mentioned him in her writings, although years later, she would name her third child for him. Her mother remained a critical figure in her life, who encouraged her to think and live freely.

While still a young woman, Luisa sometimes accompanied her mother to work, including to the estate of Don Gregorio Ledesma, the Marqués de Arecibo. Don Gregorio was one of the most powerful political figures in the region and a man of great wealth. Manuel Ledesma, the Don's son, was enchanted by Luisa, and the two became lovers. In 1897, the year that Manuel inherited his father's property and title, Luisa bore their first child, Manuela. Two years later, at age twenty, Luisa gave birth to a son, Gregorio. Both children lived with Luisa's mother while Luisa moved between her household and that of the Ledesmas. The affair appears to have been fairly public and might have been tolerated in a less volatile period. Instead, it unfolded in the midst of the War of 1898, the end of Spain's rule over Puerto Rico, and the entrance, in its stead, of United States troops, officials, and corporations. Under the Foraker Act of 1900, the United States government claimed political and economic control of the island as a nonincorporated territory. Given these upheavals, island elites were perhaps less tolerant of challenges to social convention. Manuel was censored by his family and by Arecibo society more generally for his serious involvement with a daughter of the working class. Although the couple appeared to be very much in love and he recognized the children as his own, the relationship ended. Manuel embraced a more conventional life and became Alcalde of Arecibo, but he continued to provide financial support for the children and offered assistance to Margarita Péron. Although it is not clear whether Luisa wanted to marry Manuel, she was clearly disappointed and disillusioned by his embrace of social propriety, and she refused any economic help for herself. Instead, she used her experiences in this relationship to fuel her feminist critiques of traditional forms of marriage, motherhood, and the family.

Left to her own devices at a time of political ferment, Luisa soon carved out a career in the burgeoning labor movement. *La Federación Libre de Trabajadores de Puerto Rico* (the Free Federation of Workers, or FLT) was established in 1902 and began organizing workers in both the agricultural and industrial sectors. The organization espoused anarcho-syndicalist principles. Although some anarchists in this period advocated the violent overthrow of the state, anarcho-syndicalists focused instead on the organization of mass trade unions as the foundation of civic and political life. In the ideal society, local and individual interests would be subordinated to collective needs and desires, which would be expressed through an international network of labor organizations. The unions would necessarily make decisions in the best interests of the majority of the world's citizens, who were workers. At the same time, individuals and communities could protect their own priorities through direct action, such as strikes, when local concerns were at odds with policies established by broader coalitions of workers, or when workers in a particular community were at odds with union leaders.

Despite the radical cast of most anarcho-syndicalist groups and the anti-imperialist tenor of their vision, the FLT did not reject U.S. intervention in Puerto Rico. Indeed, union leaders sought to work with U.S. corporations to improve wages and working conditions. The decision to seek reform within, rather than the overthrow of, colonial relations was fueled in large part by labor leaders' distrust of local capitalists and landowners, who had long been allies of Spain and the Catholic Church. These local elites served as leaders of the Union Party, which sought independence from the United States. The FLT believed that workers would be better served under U.S. authority than under the control of the island's traditional power brokers.[2]

Luisa Capetillo joined the FLT via one of its strongest affiliates, *La Federación de Torcedores de Tabaco* (FTT), the tobacco workers' union. Hired as a *lectora*, that is, a reader, in a cigar factory in Arecibo, Capetillo joined the FTT and became immersed in the radical politics embraced by its members in Puerto Rico and their counterparts throughout the Caribbean. Luisa's mother enabled her daughter to establish her career as a reader and, later, as an itinerant organizer and lecturer by caring for her children for extended periods.

Los lectores held pride of place within the cigar industry. Hired and paid by the workers themselves, readers entertained and educated workers on the shop floor. Seated on a raised platform, surrounded by men and women at the rolling benches, Luisa Capetillo began the day by reading selections from a variety of newspapers, translating those in French into Spanish and emphasizing stories about workers and labor movements around the world. She might follow with classic essays on anarcho-syndicalist or socialist politics by Peter Kropotkin, Pierre-Joseph Proudhon, Mikhail Bakunin, and others. After a midday break, she would spend the afternoon presenting, with some dramatic flair, chapters from a novel selected by the workers and read serially over several days.

In addition to her duties as a reader, Capetillo contributed articles to progressive periodicals, including the FLT's newspaper, *Unión Obrera*. She made her debut as a labor organizer in 1905 during a strike by Arecibo sugar workers, many of whom were familiar with her ideas through her work as a lectora and journalist. With a strong voice and a passionate belief in workers' right to a decent living, Capetillo was as successful at rallying *campesinos* (farmers) in the cane fields as she was inspiring factory workers on the rolling benches. From this point on, she expanded her activities, combining organizing efforts and strikes in specific industries with broader writings and lectures on anarcho-syndicalist politics, workers' rights, women's rights, and collective emancipation.

Capetillo rose into the leadership of the male-dominated FLT and traveled throughout the island, rallying local labor leaders and ordinary workers to the cause. She believed that syndicalism was "the only method that could combat the injustices committed against the producing class" because it replaced the self-interest that drove capitalists with collaboration and collective action. A prolific writer, Capetillo published her first book, *Ensayos libertarios*, in 1907, which was "dedicated to the workers of both sexes."[3] The collected essays presented life as a moral drama, in which virtue, labor, and communal effort among the workers were pitted against the parasitic greed, exploitation, and rampant individualism of capitalists.

Although the book was fervently anticlerical, the struggle of impoverished workers against wealthy employers was posed as a sort of religious crusade in which the individual liberty of the oppressed was expressed most fully through their voluntary cooperation in advancing collective, and collectivist, interests.

In the early 1900s, Capetillo was probably the best-known woman labor organizer in Arecibo, but she was not the only one. The city was home to many militant FLT affiliates, including an all-female local of coffee workers. Many of the woman union members supported bread-and-butter issues—increased wages, shorter hours, and improved working conditions, for example—but they struggled as well on behalf of a variety of social concerns, such as the education of workers' children. Several also advocated woman suffrage, arguing that votes for their sex would aid the working class as a whole. Some middle-class and affluent woman reformers in Puerto Rico had also spoken out for suffrage, but they proposed that the vote be granted only to literate, educated women. Capetillo and her coworkers argued instead for universal suffrage, a demand that received the approval of the FLT at its 1908 congress. Indeed, the union remained one of the staunchest supporters of universal woman suffrage throughout the early twentieth century.

The primary goal of the FLT was to organize workers throughout the island, across all occupations and skill levels, and in rural and urban areas. Launching *la Cruzada del Ideal* in 1909, the union sent its most effective speakers to Puerto Rico's factories and workshops and to its sugar and coffee plantations. Capetillo traveled widely, lecturing on behalf of the FLT and writing articles for labor papers on the conditions of workers and their need for organization. At the same time, under union auspices, she began publication of *La Mujer* in an effort to reach female workers and working-class wives more directly. During her journeys, Capetillo began to formulate an even broader political agenda, one that linked better wages and working conditions to a just and decent life. The year following the FLT crusade, she published her vision of the ideal society in *La humanidad en el futuro (Humanity in the Future)*. Emphasizing the importance of sustaining "natural" relations in the family, in the workplace, and among humans more generally, she advocated free love and vegetarianism, progressive health reform and education, communal responsibility for social services such as child care, and the anarcho-syndicalist organization of labor.

During this same period, Luisa began a relationship with a local pharmacist in Arecibo, and in 1911 she gave birth to her third child, Luis. The father, who was already married, refused to recognize the child as his own, and Luis joined his older brother and sister in the household of Margarita Péron. Manuela and Gregorio remained close with their father as well as their mother, and they often felt torn between loyalty to parents with very different visions of their future. Luis had no such conflicts since his father did not acknowledge his existence. He thus followed closely in his mother's footsteps, accompanying her on many of her travels and later joining her as a labor activist.

Capetillo viewed motherhood as central to a woman's existence, one of the functions naturally reserved for the female sex. Yet she believed that the role of mothers extended far beyond the domestic sphere. Sounding at times like a middle-class maternalist, Capetillo claimed, "The mother is the first one who teaches, who leads the future monarch, as well as the minister and the president; the useful laborer and the intelligent educator. She forms, carefully molds, although sometimes equivocally because of her lack of education, future teachers and revolutionaries. If women were properly enlightened, educated and emancipated from traditional routines, the politics of nations would be different."[4] Yet she saw the role of working-class mothers not only in terms of child rearing, but also of wage earning, and demanded the kind of education and social services that would allow women to act effectively in public as well as private spheres. Indeed, she insisted that women, whether affluent or poor, were already active outside the home, and she noted that elite women's participation in social and cultural events and organizations *depended* on the paid work of poorer women. Far from being relegated to the domestic sphere, women had always worked, had always performed public roles, and yet were denied sufficient support—economic and social—to carry out their functions properly. True social advancement was only possible when workingmen recognized women's centrality to class struggle and affluent women realized their responsibility to their poorer sisters.

By the time she had borne her third child, Capetillo had developed a comprehensive feminist analysis. Her collection of essays, *Mi opinión, sobre las libertades, derechos y deberes de la mujer, como compañera, madre y ser independiente (My Opinion on the Liberties, Rights, and Duties of Woman, as Companion, Mother and Independent Being)*, published in 1911, brought her ideas together in a single volume. One of the most powerful feminist treatises of the era and the first published in Puerto Rico, Capetillo addressed a wide range of issues from prostitution and sexual oppression in marriage to domestic labor, religious tyranny, education, women's work, politics, and motherhood. Convinced that education was critical to securing woman's emancipation, she demanded that they be taught the

sciences, mathematics, geography, and literature in addition to basic reading, writing, and domestic or ornamental skills. This would allow women
not only to be better mothers but also better companions to men. Arguing that adult relationships must be built on love and mutual respect rather
than legal or church bonds, Capetillo insisted that women must share the
social, political, and cultural concerns of their partners. Yet knowing that
many relationships would end and leave women responsible for the care
of children, she also sought expanded job opportunities for women to
enable them to support families. Ultimately, she argued that both the
possibility of committed loving relationships and of satisfying, remunera-
tive labor depended on progressive education and the syndicalist organization of society.

Like many anarchist feminists of her day, most notably Emma
Goldman, Capetillo advocated free love and sex education for women and
men and condemned conventional marriage as a form of prostitution.[5]
Many anarchist men supported these beliefs as well, but for the most part,
it was women who delved most deeply into the consequences of such
"natural" relations for women, for children, and for society as a whole.
Building on the ideas of Madeleine Vernet, a French advocate of women's
rights and progressive education, Capetillo claimed that women needed
to learn about their sexuality so that they could distinguish between mere
desire and true love. Although she considered both worth satisfying, only
the latter could form the basis for a long-term union. Moreover, unless
women were knowledgeable about their own sexuality, they were likely
to subordinate their needs to those of men.

Capetillo echoed the vision of other anarchist feminists on issues of
free love, women's education, and syndicalist organization, but she did
break with this group in one significant area: suffrage. As opponents of
the state, most anarchists viewed electoral participation as anathema for
women and men. Emma Goldman's famous essay critiquing the U.S.
woman suffrage movement synthesized the basic arguments against what
was considered a bourgeois effort to strengthen the state and further obscure its militaristic and capitalistic goals.[6] In contrast, Capetillo advocated
a view shared by many socialists, who saw voting rights as an additional
weapon in workers' struggle. Capetillo, other Puerto Rican working-class
feminists, and the FLT more generally argued that if the ballot was valuable, then it should be wielded by women as well as men. Yet neither
Capetillo nor her coworkers allied themselves with middle-class suffrage
organizations on the island, which promoted voting rights only for educated women. Instead, anarchist feminists and FLT leaders advocated

women's voting rights as part of a broader working-class agenda, through which they sought to improve the position of labor vis-à-vis both the United States government and local and foreign capitalists. Capetillo also stood out in this period because she traded in her skirts for pantaloons, and later pants, allowing her to move much more freely through tobacco factories, cane fields, and union halls and, perhaps, to blend more easily into the male-dominated ranks of the FLT leadership.

Despite her commitment to the workers' struggle in Puerto Rico, Capetillo decided in 1912 to visit the United States and Cuba. During extended sojourns in New York City, Tampa, Florida, and Havana, Cuba, she interacted with anarchists and socialists and worked as a reader, writer, and labor organizer. It was in New York City that she first experienced the excitement generated by an international community of anarchist and socialist labor activists. Immersed in the Spanish-speaking environs of the city's cigar centers, Capetillo wrote for local newspapers and joined the circles of Cuban, Puerto Rican, and Spanish radicals and writers.

Indeed, upon settling in New York City in 1912, she was immediately welcomed into a vibrant world of exiles, émigrés, and immigrants. Some had arrived in the 1870s and 1880s, fleeing the first, failed effort to overthrow Spanish rule in Cuba and Puerto Rico; others had moved to the U.S. mainland more recently, seeking out the cultural, political, and social excitement created by a pan-Caribbean community of activists. These intellectual and political circles were augmented and nurtured by large numbers of workers who moved to New York City from Puerto Rico, Cuba, or other parts of the Caribbean in hopes of finding jobs and camaraderie. In his memoirs, Bernardo Vega, who arrived from Cayey, Puerto Rico, a few years after Capetillo, described the desperate working conditions, animated cultural and political exchanges, and rich traditions of Cuban and Puerto Rican radicalism that inspired Caribbean labor organizers to settle in the city. He met Capetillo on a number of occasions and described her as "the first woman suffragist in the Antilles." He noted that although she worked tirelessly "to propound her revolutionary and strongly anarchist ideas," she combined "her enthusiasm for the revolution" with "a great love for cooking" and fed all who came to her door. Vega also commented on Capetillo's commitment to transnationalism. Writing in New York's *La Prensa* in 1919, for instance, she proclaimed, "Tyranny, like freedom, has no country, any more than do exploiters or workers."[7]

During Capetillo's first visit to New York City in 1912, she wrote articles for various anarchist and labor papers in the city, including *Brazo y Cerebro, Fuerza Consciente,* and *Cultura Obrera.* For the last, she penned an essay, "La Mujer," which was later included in an Argentine collection, *Voces de liberación*. The anthology gathered together articles by the most influential socialist and anarchist women around the world, including Louise Michel, Rosa Luxemburg, Emma Goldman, Clara Zetkin, and a number of their Latin American and Caribbean counterparts.

Although Capetillo planned to return to Puerto Rico and her children eventually, when she left New York City in late 1912 or early 1913, she traveled to South Florida. There she worked as a lectora and journalist and immersed herself in the working-class life of Ybor City, the Latin enclave of Tampa.[8] For at least part of the time, she roomed with the family of a German machinist in an area bordered by downtown Tampa on the south, Ybor City on the east, and the city's black business district on the west. During her stay, she penned short sketches of Latin life and longer essays on political and social issues. Several of these essays were incorporated into a revised edition of *Mi opinión*; others were included in her final book, *Influencia de las ideas modernas* (*Influence of Modern Ideas*), which she began writing in Ybor City in July 1913. Given her previous experience, Capetillo sought work as a reader in a local cigar factory, and she was soon hired. She was, however, the only woman reader working in Ybor City and one of only two hired for the position in the entire history of the industry there. Although all male, her fellow lectores were a diverse group in other ways. A number of longtime residents, mostly older white Cubans, represented a range of political ideologies and reading styles. But local readers also included the Afro-Cuban Facundo Acción, president of a local mutual aid society, and a number of Spaniards, including a young immigrant, Maximiliano Olay. Olay had arrived as a teenager in 1908, having traveled first from Spain to Havana and then on to South Florida. When arrested for vagrancy in 1913, Olay identified himself as a cigar maker and reader and admitted to being an anarchist. He was among a group of anarchists residing in Ybor City at the time who were being investigated by the Tampa police, the Spanish and Mexican consuls, and the U.S. Department of Justice.

Since the establishment of the cigar industry in Ybor City in 1886, large numbers of Cuban, Spanish, and Italian radicals had settled in the community, along with smaller circles of Puerto Rican and Mexican anarchists and socialists. During the 1890s, South Florida cigar workers provided critical support for anticolonial struggles against Spain. By 1912–13, anarchist agitation in the ethnic enclave had become a major concern of domestic and foreign security forces. Over the previous decade, Ybor City had attracted leaders of the Industrial Workers of the World, including

Elizabeth Gurley Flynn and Carlo Tresca, and anarchist organizers from Mexico, Spain, Italy, Puerto Rico, and other parts of the United States. During Capetillo's sojourn in the city, other visiting radicals included Jaime Vidal of the Maritime Workers Union; Manuel Salinas, who was involved in a plot to assassinate the Mexican president; and Francisco Martines, who headed a plot against the president of Argentina. They gathered around them a circle of young anarchists who met at the coffee shops and restaurants interspersed among the cigar factories.

Civic authorities and factory owners were convinced that the lectores were the instigators of radical activism in Ybor City. And the readers, who held sway throughout the industry in South Florida and flourished in Cuba, Puerto Rico, and New York, did present workers with a range of radical ideas and international perspectives on labor politics. Manufacturers had long been hostile to the institution, which allowed an individual complete freedom from employer control to proselytize among workers throughout the day on the shop floor. Yet cigar workers made it clear they would fight as vehemently for their right to employ readers as they did for higher wages, better working conditions, and union recognition; and by the 1910s, the institution had become entrenched.

Despite the accusations, the revolutionary politics embraced by residents of Ybor City and other cigar centers did not originate with Capetillo and her fellow readers. Rather, cigar workers employed readers who could extend and revitalize views the workers themselves already held. Capetillo probably introduced more feminist ideas on the reader's platform than other lectores, but even this perspective was not entirely new. During a massive industry-wide strike in Tampa in 1910, women cigar workers from Key West had published a manifesto of support. Twenty-eight women, half Cuban and half Italian, had signed the appeal. Calling on the legacies of religious martyr Joan of Arc, French communard Louise Michel, and Spanish labor radicals Belén de Sárraga, Teresa Claramunt, and Soledad Gustavo, they proclaimed: "It is our duty to protest" against those "who degrade our sons," for degradation to them is "degradation to us."[9]

The heroines chosen by the Key West women illustrated both the global reach and local knowledge of anarchist feminists. They also suggest the connections between Capetillo and her counterparts in other parts of the Spanish- and French-speaking world. Teresa Claramunt carved out a path in Barcelona that Luisa Capetillo would later follow in Puerto Rico. At age twenty-two, in 1884, Claramunt co-founded an anarchist collective within the Spanish Federation of Workers. She participated in a number of textile strikes, organized anarchist circles in several Spanish cities, traveled through France and England, founded the newspaper *El Productor,* and published *La mujer: Consideraciones generales sobre su estado ante las prerrogativas del hombre* (*Woman: Considerations about Her Condition in Comparison with the Privileges of Man*). Belén de Sárraga echoed Capetillo's anticlerical concerns as she campaigned against the church in late nineteenth-century Spain before traveling to the Americas in the early 1900s. There Sárraga continued to do battle with the conservative politics of the Catholic Church, organizing meetings and demonstrations in Chile and Mexico. Louise Michel was the foremother of all of these women, an international hero among anarcho-syndicalists for her efforts during the 1871 Paris Commune. And Joan of Arc, though perhaps an unlikely model for radical Latin workers, was continually maligned by conservative church officials into the twentieth century as more progressive Catholics agitated for her canonization. Her inclusion in this pantheon suggests that, like Capetillo, anarchist women in South Florida combined virulent anticlericalism with deep spirituality.

Luisa Capetillo was easily incorporated into the radical networks and revolutionary influences that shaped South Florida's cigar centers, although she no doubt stood out among local women by choosing to dress in men's pants, shirt, and tie. This made her less conspicuous, however, among union leaders in Ybor City, who like their counterparts in Puerto Rico, were primarily men. Capetillo developed close working relations with several of her new male colleagues. When she completed a second edition of *Mi opinión* in 1913, it was published by Jorge Mascuñana, a radical editor in Ybor City; the preface was written by Jaime Vidal. Signed copies were placed in the libraries of local mutual aid societies, such as *El Centro Asturiano,* one of several ethnic clubs founded by immigrants to Ybor City.

As a reader, speaker, and journalist in South Florida, Capetillo proclaimed the benefits of vegetarianism and cold water baths; the dangers of religious orthodoxy; the transformative power of progressive education; the struggles of labor in Spain, France, and Puerto Rico; the significance of modern drama, dress reform, free love, and woman suffrage to workers' emancipation; and the importance of cooperatives to working-class self-sufficiency. Although some of her views—vegetarianism and suffrage, for example—may have seemed peculiar to Ybor City residents, most were readily embraced. From their first years in South Florida, cigar workers had established mutual aid societies that provided a wide range of health services for members; they filled opera houses and theaters; they opened schools and supported a variety of progressive educational programs; denounced the Catholic Church as part of the campaign for Cuban inde-

pendence in the 1890s; they formed food and child care cooperatives; they organized and joined anarcho-syndicalist unions in large numbers; and they had sustained several months-long industry-wide strikes.[10]

The political and cultural environment of Ybor City spurred Capetillo to think and write more broadly than ever before. She benefited especially from her contact with the rich traditions of Spanish, Cuban, and Italian theater, opera, dance, and music in Ybor City. A number of the essays collected in *Influencia de las ideas modernas* were shaped by her experiences in South Florida. The influences flowed both ways, however. In the aftermath of her stay, local women workers struck out on their own more often, staging a wildcat cigar strike in 1916 and demanding that their issues be addressed by union leaders as well as by employers. And women and men worked together during the 1910s in forming food and child care cooperatives.[11]

By 1915, Capetillo had left Tampa, moving to Cuba where she continued her organizing efforts. She lived in Havana and Cárdenas and joined in the activities of *La Federacíon Anarquista de Cuba* (the Anarchist Federation of Cuba). She assisted sugarcane workers during a 1915 strike, lectured on the establishment of cooperatives, and supported an anarchist manifesto that denounced the actions of the government in its attempts to suppress labor uprisings. In response, President Mario G. Menocal ordered her deportation as a dangerous alien. Before his order was carried out, however, Capetillo was arrested in Havana for provoking a scandal by dressing as a man in public. Although most of the daily papers used the occasion to ridicule Capetillo and anarchists more generally, the Havana-based *La Lucha*, along with more radical publications in Puerto Rico, supported her right to dress as she chose. In combining political and stylistic subversion, however, Capetillo assured her deportation from Cuba. By 1916, she was back in Puerto Rico.

Inspired by her interactions with radical labor organizers in the United States and Cuba, Capetillo once again threw herself into campaigns in her homeland. Shortly after her return, she published *Influencia de las ideas modernas*, most of which was written during her travels abroad. She quickly reconnected with her coworkers in the FLT and was soon back in the thick of class struggle. She helped to direct a strike by some 30,000 agricultural laborers in the Ceiba area, as well as smaller walkouts in Vieques and other parts of the island. In 1918, while leading a protest march in Ceiba, she was accused of inciting a riot, arrested, and imprisoned. She was found guilty and fined $400; workers and political supporters raised the funds to pay the fine.

In 1919, Capetillo once again traveled the Caribbean-U.S. circuit as an organizer and agitator. She was invited to Santo Domingo that year to reinvigorate striking workers there. She also commuted back and forth between Puerto Rico and New York City in 1919–1920. Bernardo Vega recalled that while in the city, she ran a boardinghouse, serving vegetarian meals to the residents, engaging in public political debates, and devoting her free time and her scarce resources to various radical causes. By 1921, however, she was back in Puerto Rico and at least briefly campaigned for candidates of the Socialist Workers' Party. The party supported universal suffrage for women and men and required that one-third of the members of all committees be women. Throughout this period, she also sought to raise funds—from American Federation of Labor leaders in the United States as well as comrades in Puerto Rico—for a school for the children of agricultural workers.

At some point in her travels, Luisa Capetillo had contracted tuberculosis, and by 1921, she was increasingly debilitated by the disease. She moved into a small duplex that had recently been constructed as part of a workers' barrio in Río Piedras, Puerto Rico. On April 10, 1922, her younger son, Luis, took her to the municipal hospital, where she died at the age of forty-two. Capetillo's body was then taken to her home, accompanied by local FLT organizers, and was buried the next day in the municipal cemetery. Members of the FLT, the Socialist Workers' Party, and a group of striking workers from Río Piedras escorted the casket to the burial site and joined her children at the simple graveside ceremony.

Coworkers throughout the Caribbean eulogized Capetillo. The secretary of the FLT in Santo Domingo dedicated that year's celebration of May 1, the traditional workers' holiday, to "the strongest woman combatant" in the struggle for a better life for workers and the disfranchised. A comrade in Puerto Rico called her "a fighting apostle for the great causes of humanity."[12] An obituary in Unión Obrera noted that Capetillo "spoke from the platform and directed strikes of rural workers and traveled long distances by foot and rose to the head of public demonstrations" at the same time as she expressed workers' and women's grievances through books, articles, and her own newspaper.[13] Although Capetillo died young, she had left her mark on campaigns for workers' and women's rights. Stories of her efforts were handed down from generation to generation in Puerto Rico and Ybor City; and labor newspapers, the memoirs of other radicals, and her own publications provided accounts of her labor and feminist activities. In recent years, she has attracted the attention of numerous scholars and is currently the subject of several dissertations and master's theses.[14] Yet Capetillo never sought fame for herself, but rather she sought advances for the community as a whole.

Capetillo both worked alongside and inspired other women in the labor movement. Although she is often portrayed as the lone woman among a cohort of male union leaders, she was in fact part of a wave of female organizers and agitators in early twentieth-century Puerto Rico. Few gained her stature within the movement at home or abroad, but together they created a powerful legacy of Latina labor feminism. Josefa Pérez, Concha Torres, Paca Escabí de Peña, Francisca Andújar, Rafaela López Negrón, and Isabell Gatell joined Capetillo in organizing women workers and fighting for women's rights at FLT conventions in the early 1900s. Tobacco workers like Emilia Vásquez, Paula Dávila, Ana Delgado, Tomasa Yumart, Raymunda Otero, and Luisa Torres represented their locals at FLT meetings during the 1910s and 1920s. They were joined by Emilia Hernández, Genara Pagán, Juana Colón, Elvira Matos, Amparo Miranda, María Orta, Ricarda Bruno y Rivera, Julia Infante, and María L. De Jesús, all of whom spoke out and campaigned for the special concerns of women workers. Through her extensive travels and writings, Capetillo linked the activities of these women to their sisters elsewhere in the Caribbean, the United States, Latin America, and Europe. She was the lynchpin in a vast network of Latina anarchist and socialist feminists who sought to advance the interests of workers and women internationally. Capetillo's books and articles, the record of her participation in strikes and demonstrations, and the images that remain of her powerful public presence allow us to enter a dialogue with the past that speaks to critical issues around women, work, transnational organizing, and feminist agendas today.

NOTES

1. The two most important works to date are Yamila Azize, *La mujer en la lucha* (Río Piedras: Editorial Cultural, 1985); and Norma Valle Ferrer, *Luisa Capetillo: Historia de una mujer proscrita* (San Juan: Editorial Cultural, 1990). See also Felix V. Matos and Linda C. Delgado, eds., *Puerto Rican Women's History: New Perspectives* (New York: M. E. Sharpe, 1998); and Julio Ramos, ed., *Amor y anarquía: Los escritos de Luisa Capetillo* (Río Piedras: Ediciones Huracán, 1992). No book-length study of Luisa Capetillo's life and work has yet been published in English.

2. Ivette M. Rivera-Giusti, "Feminism, Colonialism, and Working-Class Politics in Puerto Rico: The Writings of Luisa Capetillo, 1904–1911" (1999), unpublished paper in author's possession.

3. Luisa Capetillo, *Ensayos libertarios* (Arecibo: Imprenta Unión Obrera, 1907), 23. Original in Spanish. All translations are by the author unless otherwise noted.

4. Luisa Capetillo, *Mi opinión, sobre las libertades, derechos, y deberes de la mujer como compañera, madre, y ser independiente* (San Juan: The Times Company, 1911), 10. Original in Spanish.

5. There is no evidence that Capetillo and Goldman ever met, or even that they were familiar with each other's work. Of course, it is likely that Capetillo would have heard of Goldman's activities in the United States, but it is less likely that Goldman, who could not read Spanish and did not travel to the Caribbean, was aware of Capetillo's efforts. Articles by the two were reprinted in *Voces de liberación,* a collection published in Argentina in 1921, shortly before Capetillo's death.

6. Emma Goldman, "Woman Suffrage," in *Anarchism and Other Essays,* introduction by Richard Drinnon (New York: Dover Publications, 1969), 195–211.

7. Bernardo Vega, *Memoirs of Bernardo Vega,* ed. César Andreu Inglesias, trans. Juan Flores (New York: Monthly Review Press, 1984), 106–7.

8. On Capetillo's experiences in Tampa, see Nancy A. Hewitt, *Southern Discomfort: Women's Activism in Tampa, Florida, 1880s–1920s* (Urbana: University of Illinois Press, 2001), 1–7, 214–16, 223.

9. "A Los Trabajadores de Tampa" (1910), *La Federación* and Labor Manifestos, Microfilm, Reel 1, University of South Florida Library, Tampa, Florida. Original in Spanish.

10. On the activities of local mutual aid societies, see Gary R. Mormino and George E. Pozzetta, *The Immigrant World of Ybor City: Italians and their Latin Neighbors in Tampa, 1885–1985* (Urbana: University of Illinois Press, 1987), chap. 6.

11. See Hewitt, *Southern Discomfort,* chap. 8.

12. Valle Ferrer, *Luisa Capetillo,* 93, 96. Original in Spanish.

13. *Unión Obrera,* April 15, 1922. Original in Spanish.

14. I first learned of Luisa Capetillo's activities in Ybor City during an interview with playwright Jose Yglesias and Dalia Corro on December 19, 1989, in Tampa, Florida. They had grown up in a cigar-making family in Ybor City and had heard tales of the radical woman reader. On recent work by doctoral students in the United States, see Rivera-Guisti, "Feminism, Colonialism, and Working-Class Politics in Puerto Rico"; and Rivera-Guisti, "'Rebellious Women' and 'Bitter Bread': Feminism and Women Tobacco Workers, 1910–1921," paper presented at 2002 Southern Labor Studies Conference, Miami, Florida. In 1993, a documentary of Capetillo's life was produced. See Sonia Fritz, *Luisa Capetillo: Pasión de justicia* (New York: Isla Films with Cinema Guild, 1993).

8

ADELINA OTERO WARREN

Rural Aristocrat and Modern Feminist

Elizabeth Salas

New Mexican babies grow up with politics and their mother's milk.

New Mexico proverb

Suffragist, education reformer, and writer, Adelina Otero Warren was the first Latina to run for Congress. In 1922, she was the Republican candidate for a seat in the U.S. House of Representatives for her native New Mexico. Born in 1881, María Adelina Isabel Emilia (Nina) Otero was a member of the Hispanic (commonly known as Hispano/a) elite of New Mexico. She came from a family of landowners with political connections to the United States that were enhanced after the 1848 Treaty of Guadalupe Hidalgo because of the family's successful "sheep drives" to California during the gold rush. Even as a young teenager, Adelina Otero Warren was determined to succeed. Family members remembered, "Nina wanted to be the boss. She took it upon herself to be in charge. She showed leadership qualities early on and she had the brains of the family."[1]

Otero Warren made the transition from the traditional life of an upper-class Hispana in the territory of New Mexico to that of an educated, geographically mobile, financially successful woman who left a legacy of civic service in New Mexico. Her life demonstrates how quickly Hispanas adapted after they were thrown into the vortex of American life, three decades after the signing of the Treaty of Guadalupe Hidalgo and the Seneca Falls Women's Rights Convention in 1848, and how well they responded to the challenge of maintaining Hispana values as village matriarchs.

Otero Warren's story is one of privilege, tragedy, challenge, politics, and activism. Tragedy began early for Adelina; in 1883, when she was a baby, her father, Manuel B. Otero, was murdered by a Euro-American over land rights. Her English stepfather, A. M. Bergere, was highly educated but a relatively poor man in comparison with Adelina's mother, Eloisa Luna, a member of the landed gentry of New Mexico. In addition to her two older brothers, Adelina had seven half sisters and two half brothers. A child of privilege, she grew up at the Luna Mansion, modeled after a plantation mansion of the American South. The adobe-brick structure was built in 1881 by the Santa Fe Railroad in exchange for the right of way through the Luna land grant, in what is now the town of Las Lunas. Adelina's Irish governess, Mary Elizabeth Doyle, stayed with the family from 1884 until her death in 1947. In 1892, eleven-year-old Adelina was sent to boarding school (now known as Maryville College) in St. Louis, making her one of the first Hispanas to receive a Catholic school education in the Midwest. Her education seemed typical for upper-class Catholic women. She learned that women had two choices: to get married or to remain single and pursue careers as teachers and community leaders. Her schooling ended in 1894 at the age of thirteen, as was the custom in the education of wealthy Hispanas. Adelina taught her many siblings what she had learned in St. Louis. To increase her own sense of independence, she insisted that her male relatives teach her about pistols and other firearms for her own protection.

Adelina married Lieutenant Rawson Warren, U.S. Army, on June 25, 1908. He was stationed at Fort Wingate, New Mexico. She did not like army life, and in 1910, she finally decided to leave him after learning that he had a common-law wife and two children in the Philippines. Adelina did decide, however, to keep Warren as her last name. Rather than admit publicly that she was divorced, she preferred to call herself a widow, claiming that her husband had died shortly after their marriage. She forbade anyone in her family from ever mentioning her husband's name. Shortly after the divorce, Otero Warren ventured to New York, ostensibly to care for her brother Luna Bergere, who attended medical school at Columbia University. While in New York, she volunteered her time at a local settlement house, organizing arts and crafts programs.

Adelina's role model was her mother, Eloisa Luna Otero Bergere, who as a youngster had attended boarding school in New York. In 1897, Eloisa, at that time only twenty-three years old, wrote out her will, in which she bequeathed her first husband's lands to her two sons by that marriage and bequeathed her Luna family landholdings to her daughter Adelina.[2]

Eloisa thus followed a long tradition of Hispanas' bequeathing the lands they brought into a marriage to their daughters in accordance with Spanish/Mexican precepts and customs.

In Santa Fe, Eloisa assumed the roles of "town matriarch" and "big mother heart." Elite Hispanas were part of the "informal" political force that offered their homes as gathering places for Hispano and Euro-American politicians to wine, dine, and discuss politics with the women. She particularly took up the cause of fighting poverty among Hispanos and also seemed especially concerned about improving local schools. Written in 1910, the New Mexico state constitution contained provisions defending the ethnic, cultural, and linguistic rights of Hispanic New Mexicans. However, Article VII, which proclaimed these rights, also limited the rights of women to the holding of school offices such as superintendent, director, or member of boards of education. Spanish/Mexican law had given women a legal identity and many rights. Some of these rights consisted of maintaining one's maiden name after marriage, property ownership within the marriage, and community property in case of divorce. Hispanas could buy and sell crops, animals, and material goods, as well as operate stores, enter into contracts, and file lawsuits in court as well as testify. While the state's constitution defended Hispano rights in general, Hispanas were circumscribed in terms of direct, public political participation. Her eldest daughter Adelina had convinced Eloisa to put her lands and other holdings into a trust fund for all her children. Adelina believed that her stepfather would mismanage the family income.

When Eloisa died at the age of fifty, she had given birth to fifteen children (three died in infancy) and raised three children from her first marriage and nine from her second. As the town matriarch, her influence reached beyond informal social services and civic charities. Eloisa had been elected to the Santa Fe Board of Education and served as its chair for less than a year.

The death of Eloisa in 1914 brought Adelina back from New York and another daughter, Anita, home from a religious vocation in a convent to help raise the younger siblings. In preparation for taking her mother's place as matriarch of the family, Adelina insisted that the family remain financially solvent. With her mother's passing, Adelina took on the role of surrogate mother for her siblings; however, she delegated to her sister Anita and to Elizabeth Doyle, the governess, the day-to-day tasks of child rearing.

Though thrown into raising her siblings, Adelina focused her efforts not on becoming a school board member like her mother, but rather on becoming a professional career woman. Although her education had ended at the age of thirteen, she served as the superintendent of public schools for Santa Fe County for the next twelve years. Hispano Democrat governor Ezequiel Cabeza de Baca first appointed her to the position. She ran for the post in 1918 in Santa Fe, easily winning her election, and she continued to be reelected until 1929. She was committed to the education of New Mexico's children, especially Hispanos and Native Americans. During her tenure as superintendent, she emphasized education for students in rural areas surrounding Santa Fe. In addition to repairing old and inadequate school buildings, she increased the school term to nine months of the year, founded a county high school and adult education programs, and raised teacher standards and salaries. The curriculum she created provided a blended education for Hispano children, including English language instruction in the classroom, teacher sensitivity to different cultures, Spanish instruction through the arts, no punishment for speaking Spanish in the classroom or in the schoolyard, and parent-teacher instruction of artisan trades.[3]

This blended education was unique in educating Spanish-speaking children in the Southwest. In other schools in other locales, children were punished for speaking Spanish and were taught by apathetic, insensitive teachers who had low expectations for their charges. Teachers generally practiced Americanization with humiliation, as schoolchildren would routinely have their tongues "soaped" for speaking Spanish. While Otero Warren agreed in principle that all students should speak English at school and on the playground, she did not believe in punishing children for speaking Spanish. Once, while visiting a village school in her district, she heard the schoolchildren sing "My Country, 'Tis of Thee," and then "a little chap, with eager brown eyes," asked her if they could sing a song in Spanish. Otero Warren "smiled and their voices rang out with real feeling in the rhythmical music of La Golondrina."[4] Otero Warren, by her actions, believed in Americanization with kindness.

Another issue of concern for Otero Warren was Catholic Archbishop Jean Baptiste Lamy's condemnation of Hispano Catholics who refused to send their children to Catholic schools. She defended public schools from what she considered narrow, self-interested criticism. While many Hispanos believed that secular public schools represented a threat to their religion and culture, others, like Adelina Otero Warren, did not subscribe to these conservative sentiments. She knew that the only route available in a Catholic educational system for women's leadership positions was through the convent; thus, she considered the Catholic Church an institution that set up barriers to women's full political and civic potential.

Otero Warren became deeply involved in woman suffrage politics and served as the head of many state committees concerned with social welfare issues. She was often appointed to head social welfare organizations. Otero Warren was a confirmed suffragist determined to work with women's groups and to lobby state legislators for votes for women. The national suffrage group, Congressional Union (CU), recognized that in New Mexico, organizers needed to incorporate Hispanas in their plans to secure the state's ratification of the Nineteenth Amendment, which extended the franchise to women. Because of her leadership skills and her appointments to state welfare groups, she was selected to take charge of the CU chapter in New Mexico. Due to her political skills and reputation, Otero Warren was also selected as the chair of legislative committees for the Republican Party and the New Mexico Federation of Women's Clubs. Her influence in the state legislature was considerable because her uncle and other Hispano relatives were powerful elected politicians at the local level who found her arguments for woman suffrage convincing. Indeed, Alice Paul, the head of the CU and later the National Woman's Party, credited Otero Warren with securing New Mexico's passage of the Nineteenth Amendment, which officially became part of the U.S. Constitution in 1920.

Otero Warren served on many committees focusing on social welfare. In April 1919, Governor Octaviano A. Larrazolo appointed her to the state Board of Health, and then she was promptly elected its chair. She was then appointed to the state Board of Public Welfare, and again, her colleagues on the committee elected her chair. When she tried to resign from the post in 1921, the new governor, Merritt C. Mechem, refused her resignation, saying that her retirement "would serve seriously to impair the public service." She reconsidered her decision.[5]

Given her record and high political visibility, Otero Warren believed that if she were elected to a national office, she could do more on behalf of Hispanics, especially in the area of education. She decided to run for the U.S. House of Representatives as a Republican. Representing the numerical majority of residents in New Mexico until the 1940s, Hispanos held different and at times competing views about how to succeed in American New Mexico. Many Hispanos valued the preservation of the Spanish language, as well as New Mexican traditions, while simultaneously seeking the rewards of the U.S. market economy, including consumer culture and education. Hispanos rarely presented a united front on political, educational, and linguistic issues. Almost every prominent Latino in New Mexico has served in public office, especially at the local level. Hispanics have envisioned public service as one way to be both Hispano and Americano at the same time. An old proverb or *dicho* sums it up nicely: "New Mexican babies grow up with politics and their mother's milk."

In the 1920s, New Mexico, because of the small size of its population, had only one member of the House of Representatives. Therefore, when Adelina Otero Warren decided to run for Congress in 1922, she sought a prized and influential position. Her opponent was Nestor Montoya, the Republican incumbent. In contrast to Montoya's mild-mannered personality, the charismatic Otero Warren was known for "her ease of manner, for her vivid personality to say nothing of her [red] hair and for the sweet graciousness of manner seldom found except in convent-bred women." In the Republican primary, she trounced Montoya; she received 466½ votes to Montoya's 99½ votes.[6]

As a "progressive" Republican, she vowed that if elected, she would try to get New Mexico's communal land grants returned to their Hispano owners. She thought that if New Mexicans owned their own lands, the people would have the money to support education, child welfare reform, and pensions for teachers. Otero Warren advanced the fairly radical idea for the time that the federal government should contribute to the support of public schools. As a "conservative" Republican, she favored protective tariffs high enough to protect the wool and livestock producers of New Mexico. In her campaign, Otero Warren emphasized her Hispano heritage when she spoke in Spanish to New Mexicans. She called herself "a native daughter," reminding voters that Hispanos were the earliest settlers of New Mexico. With one foot in the traditional Hispano way of life and another in the modern world of the 1920s, Adelina Otero Warren's campaign promises called for the preservation of Hispanic culture and heritage while promoting the need to bolster forward-looking education, health care, and child welfare initiatives. New Mexico poet Felipe Maximiliano Chacón wrote a poem in celebration of her campaign, entitled, "To Mrs. Adelina Otero-Warren, Republican Candidate for Congress, 1922." A portion follows:

> Born in suffrage equal to man
> but spiritually, more elevated,
> In moral purity she carves her name
> And the earth benefits from her journey.

This very meritorious evolution
Marking the noble path of Progress
Will cover New Mexico with glory
by putting a woman in Congress.
Able, competent, honorable
With a gentle soul and a sincere heart
There she is, proclaimed by the people,
The typical lady, Adelina Otero!
Noble offspring of Spanish lineage
And what is more, pure American.[7]

Other Hispanos were more critical. For example, a group of angry Hispano voters confronted her, furious that she had removed a popular Hispana second grade teacher from their school. When they informed her that they would vote for her opponent, Otero Warren stated simply that they could vote "as they pleased," but that as a superintendent of schools she had an obligation to "get the best teacher I can send you just the same."[8] The issue of Spanish language instruction and Hispana teachers became hot-button issues throughout the campaign and probably cost her much needed votes. She did not remove other Hispana teachers because she did not want to face more confrontations that would result in negative press coverage in the Spanish-language newspapers. She also had to fight the perception among the Hispano elite that schooling was a class privilege not to be shared with the common people. Folk wisdom had it that "to educate a boy is to lose a good shepherd."

Adelina Otero Warren ran a campaign infused with Progressive ideals in vogue nationally a decade earlier, which seemed out of step with the mood of the Roaring Twenties. She detailed her record on education, temperance, and other social issues. But it was an old family feud between her and her cousin, the former governor Miguel Otero, that brought calamity to her campaign. He revealed that she was not a "widow" but a divorcée. Her brother Eduardo, incensed over the revelation, inflicted a severe beating upon his older cousin Miguel Otero, garnering even more negative publicity for the campaign. News of her divorce rocked the election, although in that year Democrats were swept into office across the state. Otero Warren lost the election to her Democrat opponent, John Morrow, a lawyer, rancher, and educator from Raton, New Mexico. The official results of the election were 59,254 to 49,635, a difference of 9,619 votes. However, Otero Warren did carry four of the five Hispano counties, despite the fact that only a year earlier, in 1921, all five counties had voted against a woman's right to hold office.[9] She never sought elective public office again, primarily because of the revelations about her past but partially because during the course of campaign she met a woman who would become her partner for over thirty years.

Born in Arkansas and a graduate of the University of Arkansas, Mamie Meadors journeyed to Santa Fe in 1918 to seek relief from tuberculosis, like many new Euro-American residents of the Southwest. The salubrious climate did the trick, and in 1922 she served as a volunteer in Otero Warren's congressional campaign. After the failed election, Otero Warren, in addition to her duties as school superintendent for Santa Fe, was appointed for a short term as an inspector of Indian schools and hired Meadors as her assistant. The women lived in Santa Fe at different residences, but they were always seen together and were referred to as "Las Dos" (The Two). Otero Warren's relationship with Meadors never became a public issue among Hispanos probably because she belonged to the landed elite and thus had more privacy and flexibility in her personal life, in addition to her considerable standing in the community as a reformer and local government official.

As an inspector of Indian schools, Otero Warren's purview included the education of Native Americans, and she proved a staunch opponent of separating Indian children from their families in order to send them to nonreservation boarding schools, a popular federal policy since the 1880s. In speeches about Native American education, Otero Warren emphasized, "the Indians are not a vanishing race, as many suppose." Changes in Native American education that Otero Warren sponsored included special attention to education for mothers and closer cooperation between the school and home. Her efforts to "Americanize" the Native Americans were balanced by her view that students should "be taught to appreciate the history and traditions" of their people and should be encouraged to continue the "native arts" of their "race," as well "as acquire a new type of learning."[10]

Otero Warren's career as a school superintendent was threatened in 1927 as a result of a dispute with the state superintendent of schools, Lois Randolph. Randolph had heard that Otero Warren was the local sales representative of the Houghton Mifflin Company, an activity banned by Section 1415 of the 1925 New Mexico School Code, which stated that a county superintendent could not represent any firm dealing in books, equipment, or school supplies. On May 6, 1927, Randolph wrote to Otero Warren to inform her that she was in violation of the New Mexico School Code and to summon her to a meeting where she would be given a full hearing and the opportunity to "controvert or defend" her dealings with the publisher. In response, Otero Warren argued that prior to entering such employment, she had asked the opinion of John J. Kenney, her brother-in-law and a district attorney, as to the legality of her representation of the book company and had been advised that there was "nothing in the law to prevent her accepting such work." Otero Warren had also sought the advice of two members of the state Board of Education, and they had offered no objection. Further, she did not keep her business relationship with Houghton Mifflin a secret. On the legal advice of both a local judge and attorney, she decided after being brought before the board to sever her connection with the publishing company. Upon hearing the testimony, the state Board of Education exonerated Otero Warren from "any wrong or intentional violation of the law by reason of the said representation."[11]

Rather than seek reelection for a twelfth term as Santa Fe school superintendent, Otero Warren decided to retire from running for elected public office. She did, however, want the position to remain in the family, so she and the conservative old guard Republicans of Santa Fe sponsored her half sister Anita Bergere for the post. Bergere won the election but held the office for just one term.

Otero Warren's concern about the education of Hispanos/as was undiminished. The problems "Spanish Americans" faced in New Mexico were not as much about discrimination as poverty and educational and vocational neglect. Otero Warren sought funding from the Laura Spelman Rockefeller Foundation, a national foundation dedicated to educational reform efforts. Before submitting her application, she wrote a letter in 1930 to Dr. Hermon M. Bumpus, an educational consultant. Otero Warren noted, "In an effort to preserve the Spanish-American people and their culture I feel this can best be accomplished through education. Heretofore, there has been a neglect of the great opportunity to incorporate the culture of these people—their arts, crafts and literature—in our educational work throughout the country. Therefore, with the combination of the most progressive American educational methods, together with the stimulus to preserve their culture, the Spanish-Americans can be put on a sound economic basis."[12]

Otero Warren believed that public school curricula for New Mexico needed to incorporate the ethnic cultures and languages of that region. While progressive educators incorporated industrial education into the curriculum to train citizens and workers, Otero Warren wanted to emphasize literacy and artisan training. Teaching Hispano arts and crafts would provide a link between modern New Mexicans and their artisan ancestors, Spanish/Mexican settlers who arrived in the 1700s. While Otero Warren agreed with the progressive emphasis on industrial training in the schools, she also held forth the idea that the answer to the economic needs of working-class Hispanos rested in retaining (or re-learning) their artisan crafts of weaving, furniture making, and leather goods.

Otero Warren's efforts to protect and promote the culture of Hispanos, while important, reflected her belief in a "Spanish American" identity, typically held by Hispanos in New Mexico and Colorado. However, this Spanish American identity did not reflect the true historical mixture of Native American, African, and European ancestry of the Spanish-speaking settlers who founded New Mexico, the settlers whom New Mexicans had whitewashed into pure-blood Spaniards. During the 1930s, the term "Spanish" was the polite term, the respectful term, a marker of class distinction, in contrast to the term "Mexican." New Mexicans continue to embrace a Spanish identity, one rooted in a pioneer past separate from later Mexican immigrants. Perhaps this Spanish heritage facilitated a group identity that led to the Hispano elite's extensive participation in local and state politics and community organizations.

Between 1932 and 1935, Otero Warren and Meadors focused their energies on their homestead, a 1,257–acre parcel about twelve miles northwest of Santa Fe. The lands were part of the Homestead Act, and the criterion for gaining its purchase was to live on the land for three years. The women did not live in the same house but had two adobe houses built side by side. They moved into their homes in 1932 and remained there until 1935, when they gained full title to the land. During this time at "Las Dos Ranch," Otero Warren wrote a number of folk stories, as well as a book of folklore, *Old Spain in Our Southwest*, published in 1936. *Old Spain in Our Southwest* continues to generate debate among scholars. Critics claim that the stories "romanticize" life in Hispano New Mexico and ignore the class conflicts between the elite Hispano families and the majority of Hispanos. However, distinguished Chicana literary critic Tey Diana Rebolledo characterizes *Old Spain* in *Our Southwest* as "narrative of resistance to the Anglocization of New Mexico."[13]

Certainly both class consciousness and Hispano cultural conservation mark Otero Warren's written work. Four years before her book was published, she recalled her trips to northern New Mexico to inspect rural schools in a story entitled "My People." She emphasized her strong urge to preserve the arts, customs, and traditions of New Spain "in an effort to save its charm which is its very life." Otero Warren reaffirmed the idea that a boy's education involved his work at the plow, herding the sheep, or in the tin shop making art objects, that a girl's education involved training in home economics, and that a parent's education focused on caring for young children and taking care of the home. Education curricula would be class-based. For members of the elite, children would receive a classical education in preparation for college. Vocational education should be promoted in rural villages. Although Otero Warren lived an unconventional life largely unfettered by constraints of gender, she emphasized traditional gender roles for village children: boys would inherit the farm, and girls needed to learn homemaking skills. She believed that rural schools should include in the curricula such artisan crafts as blanket weaving in the Chimayo/Rio Grande style, wood carving in the Santero tradition, tin work, and embroidery. She believed that students should receive credit for artisan crafts, in addition to grades for reading, writing, and arithmetic, so that schools "might then perpetuate for the people something of lasting educational value."[14]

Otero Warren's presence and influence in local education continued with her appointment as Director of Literacy Education for New Mexico's Civilian Conservation Corps as part of the 1930s New Deal. Literacy programs were crucial in a state where over 13 percent of the population in 1930 could neither read nor write. First, she keyed literacy to dual language acquisition, as she promoted bilingual opportunities to teach Hispanos in Spanish and English. In a 1938 report, Otero Warren also stressed the importance of literacy to civic education; by learning to read and write, she argued, Hispanos would become better citizens and seek solutions for health, social, economic, and civic problems.

In 1941, Otero Warren was appointed by the Work Progress Administration as Director of the Work Conference for Adult Teachers in Río Piedras, Puerto Rico. Often New Mexicans were appointed to government positions in Puerto Rico because they could speak Spanish. Otero Warren investigated school conditions and the work of adult education classes in Ponce, a city of 70,000 people. She discovered that 56 percent of the children of school age had no school facilities due to limited government funding. She submitted a proposal that would place 50,000 children in schools and create jobs for 1,000 teachers. Moreover, Otero Warren implemented a program in which all instruction until the fifth grade was in Spanish, with English taught as a foreign language. In the remainder of the lower grades, English and Spanish would be used together in a dual immersion program. In the high school curriculum, English was the language of instruction, with Spanish taught as a subject. She thought her

experiences in Puerto Rico would give her ideas in her efforts for addressing the language issue in New Mexico. Otero Warren also set up a language program for U.S. soldiers, sailors, airmen, and marines. At Borinquen
Field, about 250 officers attended Spanish-language classes taught by
teachers whom she had personally trained.[15]

Upon returning home to her native New Mexico, Otero Warren turned
her attention to her and Mamie's financial future. She received advice from
one of her family members, her brother-in-law Aldo Leopold. He convinced Otero Warren and Meadors to preserve the land on their "Las Dos
Ranch" by prohibiting grazing or cutting down trees for Christmas celebrations. In 1947, at the age of sixty-five, when many people's thoughts
turn toward retirement, Otero Warren decided to start a real estate business. She and Meadors opened the successful Los Dos Realty and Insurance Company in Santa Fe. Meadors wrote insurance policies, and Otero
Warren sold homes.

Always one to challenge conventions about respectable and unrespec-
table women, Otero Warren, a pillar of Santa Fe conservative society, held
a party in 1949 at the Magoffin House, a historic structure scheduled for
demolition. She arrived at the party "gaudily dressed" as Gertrudis Barceló,
"La Tules," a powerful Hispana saloon owner in Santa Fe during the period immediately following the U.S. conquest of New Mexico. The house
was decorated as a casino, and the guests were instructed to arrive in nineteenth-century costumes. With a poster on the wall encouraging party-
goers to "Try your luck with Doña Tules," Otero Warren spent the evening
as a gambling dealer. One could argue that, like "La Tules," Otero Warren's
private life was unconventional, and that as politicians she and "La Tules"
had sought power in their societies.[16]

Tragedy struck Otero Warren with the death of Mamie Meadors in 1951.
Working through her grief, she decided to continue their business. Generating considerable income from landholdings, stock portfolios, and the
real estate business, Otero Warren was known throughout Santa Fe as a
very gracious host for a wide variety of social occasions and charitable
causes. She also generously provided financial support to many relatives
and friends. At the age of eighty-three, Otero Warren was still attending
to her real estate business, when on January 3, 1965, she collapsed and
died. She was buried next to her mother Eloisa in the family plot at Rosario
Cemetery. Twenty-three years after her death, an elementary school was
named in her honor. On October 26, 1988, Otero Elementary School in
Colorado Springs, Colorado, opened its doors, a fitting tribute to this pioneering educator and suffragist.

NOTES

1. Vicki L. Ruiz, *From Out of the Shadows: Mexican Women in Twentieth-Century America* (New York: Oxford University Press, 1998), 91; Charlotte Whaley, *Nina Otero Warren of Santa Fe* (Albuquerque: University of New Mexico Press, 1991), 31.

2. Folder 13, A. M. Bergere Family Papers, Santa Fe State Records Center and Archives, Santa Fe, New Mexico.

3. Elizabeth Salas, "Ethnicity, Gender, and Divorce: Issues in the 1922 Campaign by Adelina Otero Warren for the U.S. House of Representatives," *New Mexico Historical Review* 70 (October 1995): 372.

4. Adelina Otero, "My People," *Albuquerque Journal*, May 3, 1931.

5. Joan M. Jensen, "'Disenfranchisement Is a Disgrace': Women and Politics in New Mexico, 1900–1940," *New Mexico Historical Review* 56 (January 1981): 5–36; *Albuquerque Morning Journal,* January 1, 1922.

6. "Stars of the G.O.P. Outline Their Platform" (undated newspaper clipping), Folder 122, Bergere Family Papers.

7. Mamie Meyer, "Felipe Maximiliano Chacón: A Forgotten Mexican-American Author," *New Scholar* 6 (1977): 112–26.

8. *Albuquerque Morning Journal*, October 1, 1922.

9. Salas, "Ethnicity, Gender, and Divorce," 375–80.

10. Elizabeth Salas, "Soledad Chávez Chacón, Adelina Otero-Warren, and Concha Ortiz y Pino: Three Hispana Politicians in New Mexico Politics, 1920–1940," in *We Have Come to Stay: American Women and Political Parties, 1880–1960*, ed. Melanie Gustafson, Kristie Miller, and Elisabeth I. Perry (Albuquerque: University of New Mexico Press, 1999), 166.

11. Letters from May 4–6, 1927, December 22, 1927, April 1928, and June 2, 1928, Exhibit 15, Folder 299, Justice Noble Papers, Santa Fe State Records Center and Archives.

12. Adelina Otero Warren to Hermon M. Bumpus, January 30, 1930, Folder 43, Bergere Family Papers.

13. Ruiz, *From Out of the Shadows,* 91.

14. Otero, "My People."

15. *Santa Fe New Mexican*, June 1941, clipping in Folder 55, Bergere Family Papers.

16. Deena J. González, *Refusing the Favor: Spanish-Mexican Women of Santa Fe, 1820–1880* (New York: Oxford University Press, 1999).

9

PURA BELPRÉ

The Children's Ambassador

Lisa Sánchez González

For a while at least, through the power of a story and the beauty of its language, the child escapes to a world of its own.

Pura Belpré

Pura Teresa Belpré, one of the most admired figures of twentieth-century Puerto Rican history, was a storyteller, folklorist, children's librarian, and advocate for low-income, Spanish-speaking children in New York City. During her lifetime, she traveled widely, performing stories, writing children's books, and contributing to the fields of library science and bilingual children's bibliography. Literary critics and historians have only recently recovered Belpré's body of work. In light of her contributions to children's literature, writing, researching, and translations of Puerto Rican legends and myths for bilingual audiences, she has been dubbed the island's folkloric "ambassador" to the United States.[1]

Pura Teresa Belpré was born in 1899, during the early years of the colonial transfer of power in Puerto Rico from Spain to the United States. During this period, Puerto Ricans experienced radical social turbulence and political upheaval. In the wake of the Spanish-American War of 1898, the United States military occupied the island and all but demolished its already weak insular economy, provoking a number of workers' protests and resulting in rampant unemployment and poverty. Furthermore, Puerto Rican women feared U.S. soldiers after many publicized incidents of sexual violence. The largely rural population of the island soon migrated to larger towns in search of work and security. During the first decade of occupation, many Puerto Ricans anxiously awaited the national independence that was promised but has never been granted by the United States government. In the world into which Belpré was born, most Puerto Rican families simply strived to eke out a decent living and to hold their families together under increasingly desperate circumstances.

Biographical information about Belpré's childhood and early adolescence on the island is scarce. However, one can infer that her experiences as a child were typical of migrant families of the period. In a 1977 essay, Belpré claimed Cidra, a small town in the southwest mountain range of Cayey, as her place of birth and hometown.[2] Her father, Felipe Nogueras, was a building contractor, so she may have spent much of her early childhood moving around the southwestern part of Puerto Rico as her father searched for itinerant jobs. She told of attending primary schools in Cayey, Arroyo, and Guayama. In 1919, she graduated from high school in Santurce, a historically free black neighborhood near the dock area of the capital, San Juan. Her mother probably died when Pura was a young child, since she was raised primarily by her stepmother and one of her grandmothers. During her lifetime, Belpré seemed exceptionally guarded about her youth, volunteering only snippets of information about her family history.

She migrated to the United States in 1920, at the age of twenty-one. For reasons unknown, she apparently did not use her father's surname. Belpré may have been her mother's maiden name, or perhaps her paternal grandmother's or her stepmother's surname. Like most Puerto Ricans, Belpré's physical appearance belied the U.S. racial grid; she was a very beautiful woman, with classic Afro-Mediterranean features. She noted that her father and stepmother were of mixed French extraction, and she herself spoke fluent French, which may suggest intergenerational familial ties in the French Caribbean. It seems that upon arrival in New York City she lived with her sister and brother-in-law somewhere within walking distance of 135th Street and Lexington Avenue in Harlem.

When Belpré arrived in New York City soon after World War I, she formed part of the first wave of post-1898 migration from Puerto Rico to the continental United States. Although she had become, like all Puerto Ricans, a U.S. citizen through congressional decree, the type of citizenship granted by the Jones Act of 1917 did not guarantee full citizenship free of prejudice or discrimination.[3] Like some of her public intellectual contemporaries—among them, Arturo Schomburg, Bernardo Vega, Luisa Capetillo, and Jesús Colón—Belpré experienced a rude awakening upon arrival to the mainland. She came into contact with the ignorance about and condescension toward Puerto Ricans that characterized *Boricua* (Puerto Rican) interactions with virtually all ethnic groups in New York City.

Like Jesús Colón and Arturo Schomburg—Puerto Ricans who shared Belpré's visibly multiracial background—Belpré also dealt squarely in her writings with the problem of racial prejudice. An untitled manuscript in her archival papers includes a discussion of a children's book she considered racist. She did not note the title of the book, but the substance of her critique concerned the politics of hair texture in the black community. With uncharacteristic vehemence, she argued in this essay that preschool and grade school textbooks should not indulge in racial stereotypes and clichés.

Belpré landed her first library job shortly after her arrival in the United States. In 1921 or 1922, she was hired as an assistant librarian at the 135th Street branch of the New York Public Library system in Harlem. In an interview conducted in the early 1970s, Belpré explained how much she had admired an African American woman, Catherine Allen Latimer. She first saw Latimer working at this library when, by chance, Pura went to study there one day with her sister. She repeatedly mentions in her archival papers that Latimer inspired her to become a public librarian. Belpré also credits her employment in the early 1920s to the recruitment efforts of 135th Street branch librarian, Ernestine Rose. In Belpré's words:

> [Rose,] noticing a "Bodega" (grocery store) and a "Barberia" (barber shop) suddenly appearing in the community, thought that the best thing to do was to secure the services of a Spanish-speaking assistant. One of the readers at the branch was a Puerto Rican teacher. To him she confided her thoughts. He said, "I have just the person you need." So home he came to offer the job to my recently married sister. "No," said her husband, "my wife is not going to work." My sister said to me, "Why don't you go and try it. You might like it." So I did, liked it, and a wonderful new world opened for me[.][4]

This position led to Belpré's enrollment at the New York Public Library's librarian school, where her coursework included a storytelling class taught by Mary Gould Davis. In this storytelling class, Pura wrote and performed her first children's story, "Perez and Martina." Throughout the late 1920s and early 1930s, Belpré increasingly gained a reputation for storytelling performances and puppet shows, community outreach, and bilingual programming. She credited a number of women for supporting her during these early years in the New York Public Library system, including Ann Carroll Moore, Maria Cimino, and Dr. Lillian López. In a 1968 essay, "Library Work with Bilingual Children," Belpré celebrated her colleagues' collaboration in creating the New York Public Library's first bilingual programs and events for children.

Belpré's cultural activities during the Great Depression were an important contribution to satisfying the cultural and educational needs of a Latino, largely Puerto Rican, community, which endured one of the highest poverty and unemployment rates in the country. To help serve the needs of the Spanish-speaking community in Upper Manhattan, East Harlem, and the South Bronx, Belpré was frequently transferred during the 1930s to different library branches, as the Puerto Rican, Cuban, Spanish, and other Latino neighborhoods grew and shifted locations. Those who knew Belpré at this time described her as a dynamic, charming, and affectionate woman, whose enthusiasm for her work was contagious, especially among neighborhood children, mothers, and grandmothers. Maria Cimino, who worked with Belpré on her first bilingual children's story hours at the 115th Street branch in the late 1920s, described Belpré in an interview as "affable, elegantly attired, vivacious, skillful, and extremely attentive to children."[5]

Belpré worked as a children's specialist for the New York Public Library until she married the African American concert violinist and conductor, Clarence Cameron White, in December 1943. From 1944 to 1960, while she accompanied her husband on his performance tours, Belpré continued to write, perform stories, participate in professional library science conferences, and compile bibliographies on children's literature. She mentions in her papers that the time she spent away from the library system afforded her the opportunity to concentrate on her creative writing as well. In addition, since her husband often performed in historically black colleges and universities, she learned a great deal about African American communities in the South during her travels. Although she devoted her life to children, she and her husband had no children of their own. After her husband's death in 1960, she returned to live permanently in New York City and began working again for the library system.

For over two decades, Belpré helped create and expand various bilingual education projects in New York City's schools, libraries, and community centers. Her life and work reflect both an engaged community activist and a gifted writer. Her institutional interventions as an advocate placed a special emphasis on mitigating the harrowing experiences of low-income, Spanish-speaking children in New York City as they adjusted to the language and cultures of their new environment. Her writing and storytelling performances were gauged to help educate both children and adults, including teachers and community workers, about the intrinsic value of cross-cultural knowledge and respect. In an unpublished and undated draft essay, "Writing for Bilingual Children," Belpré explained that her motive for researching, writing, and performing Puerto Rican tales was to foster cultural "belonging" and mutual intercultural awareness. "There is room for books," she wrote, "that would relate America to these children in stories where they can identify themselves." She continued, "This type of book is greatly needed, for it will give the child a sense of belonging. It will bring understanding between people of two different cultures and help [them] to see their similarities and values instead of [the] differences that tend to keep them apart." Throughout her life, Belpré strove to get these types of books on library shelves, even if it meant she had to write them herself.

When she began looking for children's books on Puerto Rican culture, Belpré realized she would have to start from scratch: "As I shelved books, I searched for the folktales I had heard at home, and had told my cousins and friends. To my amazement, I found not even one."[6] Explaining why she set out to commit some of the stories she had learned as a child to paper, she remarked that simply hearing those stories at the library story hours "does wonders" for the bicultural child. "Here is something he can identify himself with and share with his school friends. Here is part of his heritage come alive for him in a form that he can both read and tell." She continued, "Through this folklore, [Latina/o children] become one cultural family."[7]

Perez and Martina, Belpré's first and highly popular children's book, may be the first Puerto Rican folktale ever published in the mainland United States. The story is about courtship and marriage, a very common pair of themes in children's folklore. But characteristic of all of Belpré's fiction, the story is narrated and illustrated with a Puerto Rican audience in mind. The main characters, Perez the Mouse and Martina the Cockroach, could be considered parodies. The story describes Martina as a bit coquettish, house-proud, and self-absorbed. The plot progresses when Martina, for no apparent reason, suddenly decides to entertain suitors after she finds a gold coin while sweeping her patio. Perez, whom Belpré depicts as a trickster figure in other stories, has regal airs and mannerisms; he dresses like a courtier, speaks in an affected Spanish, and thus captures Martina's heart. After she refuses a number of other animal suitors, Martina marries Perez. But the marriage ends tragically, even gruesomely. Perez falls into a pot of rice that Martina is preparing for their Christmas supper and is cooked to death. The story ends with Martina's song of mourning for him.

In analyzing this tale, as well as other stories by Belpré as I have argued elsewhere, a subtle allegorical critique of Spanish colonial social stratification in Puerto Rico, calling attention to the possible linguistic and symbolic motifs of African and Andalusian folklore embedded within her writings; for example, certain "nonsense" incantations in the magical stories, trickster figures in the animal fables, and, throughout her corpus, the recurrence of wells and running water as supernatural forces.[8] Frederick F. Warne, the publishing house made famous by the picture books of Beatrix Potter, Kate Greenaway, and Randolph Caldecott (among others), published *Perez and Martina* in 1932. Belpré maintained a close professional relationship with Arthur Treble, the editor who had opened the New York office of Frederick Warne in 1920; for close to fifty years after the publication of *Perez and Martina*, Belpré published her stories almost exclusively with this press. Of her eight books, six were contracted with Frederick Warne: *Perez and Martina*, *Juan Bobo and the Queen's Necklace* (1962), *Santiago* (1969), *Dance of the Animals* (1972), *Once in Puerto Rico* (1973), and *The Rainbow-Colored Horse* (1978). Her other two books were published by larger houses; *The Tiger and the Rabbit and Other Tales* (1946) by Houghton Mifflin Company and *Oté* (1969) by Pantheon Books. In addition, Arte Público Press posthumously published her manuscript about a young girl's mysterious holiday adventures, *Firefly Summer*, in 1996. Unfortunately, children's books tend to go out of print quickly; all of Belpré texts, with the sole exception of *Firefly Summer*, are currently unavailable.[9]

Pura Belpré shared a larger commitment common to first- and second-wave generations of Boricua writers in New York. These writers made a concerted effort to improve the quality of daily life in their community by generating awareness, between the literate and semiliterate and among Puerto Ricans and non-Boricuas alike, of Puerto Rico's cultural, political, and literary histories. Belpré credited a wide variety of sources for her folktales. In "The Folklore of the Puerto Rican Child," she argued that Puerto Rican folktales resemble children's stories all over the world, which, she wrote, was "not surprising considering that Spain at one time or another was occupied by Arabs, Romans, Jews, Iberians, Celts, Phoenicians, Greeks, Carthaginians and others." Belpré thus advocated in theory and practice a multicultural approach and global historical context for Latino (and, indeed, all) children's literature. She generally cited Spain and Africa as the primary ethnic source material of Puerto Rican storytelling, but

Spanish traditions, she argued, also "had roots in the Orient, brought to Spain by Arab people." She added, in terms characteristic of her approach to Puerto Rico's African roots: "African people who had also been brought to the island had their own beloved tales. By constant retelling, and by creative additions of island storytellers, these stories now form the folklore background of Puerto Rico. So it is today a beautiful island, with a culture enriched by old, old stories gained from many people."[10]

Most of Belpré's published and unpublished work derives from Puerto Rican legends that she heard at home or researched in her later years. Some of her stories are translations of Spanish-language originals compiled and edited by island authors such as María Cadilla de Martínez. Interestingly, Belpré only briefly mentions Puerto Rico's most famous folklorist, Cayetano Coll y Toste, in her research notes and lectures, perhaps suggesting some tacit disagreement she might have had with this celebrated author's interpretations and reinventions of insular legends.

Evident in her two major collections of folktales, *The Tiger and the Rabbit and Other Tales* and *Once in Puerto Rico*, are allegorical functions akin to *Perez and Martina*. *The Tiger and the Rabbit and Other Tales* represents Belpré's first collection of animal fables. In these tales, originally published in 1946, and twice reissued (1965 and 1977), we find stock folkloric characters, plots, and stylistic devices: some of African origin, some from Spanish folktales, and still others borrowed from sundry folklore traditions available to her. *Once in Puerto Rico* is an important collection of tales that is explicitly concerned with Puerto Rico's colonial history, a text likely influenced by Belpré's community activism when she worked with the South Bronx Library Project during the 1960s.

Once in Puerto Rico relates a number of entertaining stories about Puerto Rico's multicultural social history. Many of these stories merge Belpré's interest in legends about Puerto Rico's indigenous peoples, the Taínos, with archetypal romances and tropes from classical and medieval literature. For example, "The Legend of the Hummingbird" might be described as "Romeo and Juliet" meets Ovid's *Metamorphoses* in the Caribbean world before the arrival of Christopher Columbus. The story is about Alida and Taroo, who belong to rival tribes of the islands (Alida is Taína, Taroo is Carib). Alida's father discovers that the two young lovers have been meeting in secret, and he threatens to marry her to someone else against her will. She therefore prays to the Taína goddess, Yukiyú, for help. Out of pity for her broken heart, Yukiyú turns Alida into a beautiful red flower. Afterward, the moon tells Taroo what has happened to his beloved, and he beseeches Yukiyú to tell him the name of the flower that Alida has become so he can find her. But only Alida knows her new name. Taroo is inconsolable, so Yukiyú turns him into "Colibrí"—a hummingbird—so that he can dart from flower to flower, kissing each until he finds Alida again. "Ever since then, the little many-colored bird has hovered over every flower he finds, but returns most often to the flowers that are red. He is still looking, always looking, for the one red flower that will be his lost Alida."[11] Like most of Belpré's romantic legends, "The Legend of the Hummingbird" represents a hybrid narrative, set in the remote past, that valorizes cultural understanding by underscoring the emotional anguish that results from intolerance.

Some of Belpré's most interesting creative work revolves around similar themes of cultural tolerance but are not based in legend and myth. One of her latest publications, Santiago, is set in a contemporary New York City neighborhood and deals with a Puerto Rican boy's efforts to earn acceptance among his African American schoolmates. The storybook, gorgeously illustrated by Symeon Shimin, opens with the main character, Santiago, feeling sad because he misses Selina, the pet hen he had to leave behind in Puerto Rico when he moved to New York. Santiago wants his new friend Ernie to stop poking fun at him and doubting his story about Selina. One day in school, Santiago convinces his teacher to take his class to a parking lot where he saw a stray hen so that he can show Ernie and the others what Selina looked like. The class discovers that this hen's best friend is the lot's night guard dog, and that the man who owns both encourages the animals' friendship by letting them play together during the daytime. By analogy, the children thus learn a lesson in how friendships can help individuals transcend preconceived differences. Ernie finally acknowledges the truth about Selina when the class makes an impromptu visit to Santiago's home, where his mother shows them a photo of the beloved hen. The illustrations of the children, teachers, and neighbors in the book represent the African American and Puerto Rican character of many New York neighborhoods. Belpré's implicit message thus centers on the value of cross-cultural understanding for black and Puerto Rican youth. In a later essay, Belpré explained that her motive for writing Santiago was her desire to teach children of various ethnic backgrounds to respect their common humanity and cultural differences.[12]

Pura Belpré's unpublished work includes nearly forty drafts of other stories, mostly written in English. These stories do not stray far from the types of stories she published as collections of legends, myths, fairy tales, and word plays. Her archival papers also contain a wealth of essays, manuscripts, and notes reflecting her contributions to, as well as the history of, alternative children's librarianship in New York City throughout most of the twentieth century.

Her work as a children's advocate spans the more than sixty years she lived in the continental United States. During her first two decades in the New York Public Library system, she helped to plan and institute the system's first bilingual story hours in Spanish, started reading groups for young adults, and established cooperative programs with dozens of Latino organizations, churches, and community centers. She also scheduled performances wherever young audiences might be convened, such as settlement houses, state orphanages, and hospitals. She gained wide recognition for the *Dia de los reyes* (Epiphany) events that she organized at the 115th Street branch during the late 1920s and at the Aguilar branch during the 1930s.

In the final decades of her career, from about 1960 until her death in 1982, Pura Belpré worked on behalf of various children's programs, including the South Bronx Library Project (SBLP). The federal Library Services and Constructions Act (Title I) allocated around $200,000 dollars to this program in June 1967, which provided resources for library services in the South Bronx community.[13] Belpré mentions a few of the SBLP's projects in her papers, which include details on how she and her colleagues compiled information for bilingual programs in the public school system and formed an award-winning traveling puppet show that visited schools, day care centers, hospitals, parks, and orphanages. The SBLP also published annotated bibliographical pamphlets, such as *Libros en Español: An Annotated List of Children's Books in Spanish* and *Puerto Rico in Children's Books*. From her writing on this experience as well as her publication record during these two decades, it appears that Belpré's professional accomplishments in New York City were more prodigious than were ever recognized during her lifetime.

Over the course of her sixty-three-year career as a writer, performer, researcher, and children's librarian, Pura Belpré profoundly inspired perhaps three full generations of children in New York City. A national children's book medal for authors and illustrators bears her name: the "Pura Belpré Honor Book." She also received lifetime achievement awards from two organizations: in 1978 from the first international Conference of Children's Books in Spanish and, on the eve of her death, from the New York Public Library. On July 1, 1982, she died quietly at home. Memory and word of mouth, more than formal recognition for her many accomplishments, have kept Pura Belpré's reputation alive. In the years to come, this stunning woman and her work will garner much more critical attention.

NOTES

1. Julio Hernández-Delgado, "Pura Teresa Belpré, Storyteller and Pioneer Puerto Rican Librarian," *Library Quarterly* 62.4 (1992): 425–40 (quotation on p. 426).

2. Pura Belpré, "I Wished to Be Like Johnny Appleseed," undated [1977], unpublished essay in Pura Belpré Papers, Centro de Estudios Puertorriqueños, Hunter College, New York, New York.

3. José Trías Monge, *Puerto Rico: The Trials of the Oldest Colony in the World* (New Haven: Yale University Press, 1997), 43.

4. Lillian López and Pura Belpré, "Reminiscences of Two Turned-On Puerto Rican Librarians," in *Puerto Rican Perspectives*, ed. Edward Mapp (Metuchen, N.J.: Scarecrow Press, 1974), 83–96.

5. Quoted in Hernández-Delgado, "Pura Teresa Belpré," 429.

6. Pura Belpré, "Writing for Bilingual Children" and "The Art of Writing for Children, " undated, unpublished essays, Belpré Papers.

7. Belpré, "Writing for Bilingual Children."

8. Lisa Sánchez González, *Boricua Literature: A Literary History of the Puerto Rican Diaspora* (New York: New York University Press, 2001), 84–91.

9. An anthology of Belpré's essays and stories, *Pura Belpré: Her Life and Writing*, edited and with an introduction by Lisa Sánchez González, is forthcoming with Arte Público Press (2004).

10. Belpré, "The Folklore of the Puerto Rican Child"; "I Wished to Be Like Johnny Appleseed."

11. Pura Belpré, *Once in Puerto Rico* (New York: F. Warne, 1973), 28.

12. Belpré, "I Wished to Be Like Johnny Appleseed"; Belpré, "Writing for Bilingual Children," (undated typescript).

13. Hernández-Delgado, "Pura Teresa Belpré," 433.

10

JOVITA GONZÁLEZ MIRELES

A Sense of History and Homeland

María Eugenia Cotera

Texas is ours. Texas is our home.

Mamá Ramoncita

In a thirteen-page memoir written near the end of her life, Jovita González recounted an incident that resonated throughout her career as a folklorist, historian, writer, and educator. In 1910, González's parents decided to relocate from the borderlands where she was born to San Antonio, in order to improve their children's educational prospects. Shortly before they made the move, González and her siblings traveled to Mier, a small town on the Mexican side of the Texas-Mexico border to pay a final visit to Mamá Ramoncita, their great-grandmother and the family matriarch. "I have a clear picture of her lying in a four-poster bed," wrote González, "her clear-cut ivory features contrasting with her dark, sharp eyes." González recalled the meeting so vividly that she recited her great-grandmother's words verbatim:

> "Come, get closer to me, children, so I can see you better," she said. "Your mother tells me you are moving to live in San Antonio. Did you know that land at one time belonged to us? But now the people living there don't like us. They say we don't belong there and must move away. Perhaps they will tell you to go to Mexico where you belong. Don't listen to them. Texas is ours. Texas is our home. Always remember these words: Texas is ours,

Texas is our home. I have always remembered the words and I
have always felt at home in Texas."[1]

Jovita González would not forget, nor would she allow her Anglo contemporaries to forget, what for her, was the *true* history of Texas.

In her academic research and in teaching, González remained committed to uncovering the vast historical legacy of Mexicans in Texas. In doing
so, she hoped to bring Anglos and Mexicans to heightened consciousness
of their shared history in North America and to educate young Mexicans
about their rich linguistic and cultural heritage. While González resisted
Anglo-centered and anti-Mexican visions of Texas history and culture, like
the other Mexican American intellectuals of her generation, she firmly
believed that "better ethnic and race relations began with human understanding" and consequently stressed "what Anglos and Mexicans held in
common rather than what divided them."[2] Though this pluralistic worldview would be constantly tested in the face of continued institutional
racism against Mexicanos in Texas and the American Southwest, González
continued to insist, in both her writing and her pedagogical politics, that
cross-cultural understanding was key to unraveling the knot of race relations in the United States. The political contours of her rhetoric generally took the shape of a call to reform rather than revolution, and thus
her writing has often been characterized as "assimilationist." In her life
and in her work, Jovita González challenged reductive readings of her
people and refused to accept the limitations placed upon her by individuals
and institutions unable to imagine that a Mexican American woman could
possess a distinctive political voice.

Jovita González was born near the Texas-Mexico border on January 18,
1904. González's father, a native of Mexico, came from a family of "educators and artisans." Her mother's family had long been present in Texas.
They had owned land on both sides of the border for over five generations, and, according to González, her maternal grandparents were direct
descendants of the colonizers who had established the first settlements
in Nuevo Santander (the Rio Grande region of Texas). Notwithstanding
their instrumental role in the founding of Texas, González's ancestors
were forced to flee from Texas shortly after the Treaty of Guadalupe
Hidalgo was signed in 1848, ending the war between Mexico and
the United States. The family reestablished itself in Texas after the Civil
War, when González's grandfather—with financial support from his
widowed mother, Ramona Guerra Hinojosa (Mamá Ramoncita)—repur-
chased some of the family land. On this acreage, located in Starr County

near Roma, Texas, he established Las Viboras, the ranch where González was born.

González's early life was filled with stories and legends told by the people who lived and worked in and around her grandfather's rancho. In her memoirs, González vividly recalled people from her childhood, many of whom reappear in her later writing:

> We went horseback riding to the pastures with my grandfather, took long walks with father, and visited the homes of the cowboys and the ranch hands. We enjoyed the last the most. There were Tio Patricio, the mystic; Chon, who was so ugly, poor fellow, he reminded us of a toad; Old Remigio who wielded the *metate* with the dexterity of peasant women and made wonderful *tortillas*. Tia Chita whose stories about ghosts and witches made our hair stand on end . . . one-eyed Manuelito, the ballad singer . . . all furnished ranch lore in our young lives.[3]

González remembered her Tia Lola with special fondness. Tia Lola was her mother's sister who came to live with them at Las Viboras as a young widow. The strong-willed Tia Lola taught González and her siblings about their family's heritage in Texas, and, González implied, it was Tia Lola who ensured that their early education was rounded out with plenty of information about important women in history. As young girls, Jovita and her sister Tula memorized a poem in Spanish, entitled "La Influencia de la Mujer," that charted a distinctly feminist historical heritage beginning with "Judith, the Old Testament heroine," and ending with "Doña Josefa Ortíz de Dominguez, the Mother of Mexico's Independence." The girls also learned about Sor Juana Inés de la Cruz and were familiar with her famous feminist poem "Hombres Necios" ("Foolish Men").

Despite the nostalgic tone of her reminiscences, the years that González and her family spent at Las Viboras were not easy ones for Mexicans in South Texas. Indeed, the year of Jovita González's birth also marked a turning point in the economic and political destiny of the border communities. On July 4, 1904, the rail line from Corpus Christi to Brownsville was completed. Financed largely by Anglo ranchers and businessmen, the St. Louis, Brownsville, and Mexico Railway opened up the Rio Grande Valley to massive land speculation. The establishment of the railroad brought South Texas firmly into the fold of the U.S. market economy, enabling wealthy Anglo ranchers to take part in the massive economic and social transformations taking place across the nation. As historian

David Montejano notes, "with the railroad came farmers, and behind them came land developers, irrigation engineers, and northern produce brokers. By 1907, the three-year-old railway was hauling about five hundred carloads of farm products from the Valley."[4]

The railway was also hauling hundreds of midwesterners into the region, latecomers to the promise of westward expansion, who were seeking to rebuild their lives in what was promoted as the "Magic Valley." These Anglo immigrants brought with them not only the hope for a new start in an unexploited territory, but also an understanding of race relations that was often at odds with the accommodative social relations that characterized the Anglo-Mexican ranching community of the late nineteenth century. The years immediately following the U.S.–Mexican War (1846–1848) were marked by somewhat normalized relations between Anglos and Mexicans due to the relatively small Anglo population and the region's isolation from the world beyond the Nueces River. However, the new racial order that accompanied massive Anglo immigration to the area supplanted these accommodative race relations with segregationist "Jim Crow" policies that regulated interracial contact and created a castelike system that separated Mexicans and Anglos in a variety of settings, including schools, theaters, and beaches. The anti-Mexican sentiments generated by the bitter experiences of the Texas battle for independence in 1836 and the U.S.–Mexico War were now bolstered by popular eugenicist and Anglo-Saxonist theories of racial difference. After the entry of the railroad and the attendant agricultural "boom," it became clear to Texas Mexicans that social, political, and economic relations in South Texas would never be the same. Within fifteen years of the construction of the railway system, the Texas Mexican people of the border region, with a few exceptions, had lost the world that Jovita González knew, "the world of cattle *hacendados* and *vaqueros*," and would come to live in "a world of commercial farmers and migrant laborers." By the mid-1920s, horses and carts had been replaced by automobiles and highways; segregated public parks, movie houses, and drugstores took precedence over the plazas, churches, and *haciendas* as places to meet and exchange news.[5]

In her memoirs, González recounted that her family moved away from the border region in 1910 so that she and her siblings might receive an "education in English," but there can be little doubt that the need for a more standardized education was precipitated by the dramatic economic and cultural changes taking place in the borderlands during this period. Despite the worsening conditions for Mexicanos in South Texas, things could not have been much better in San Antonio, where Anglos had come to dominate political and economic life some fifty years earlier. In the notes she made prior to writing her memoirs, González included the phrase "some unpleasant incidents" in the section dealing with her early years in San Antonio. In the final draft no mention of these "unpleasant incidents" was made, but it must have been difficult for a young Mexican girl from the borderlands to adjust to life in San Antonio, a fast-paced city controlled by Anglos and where English was the dominant language. Thanks to the informal ranch-house schooling in English that she had received at Las Viboras and her somewhat more thorough education in Spanish, González advanced to the fourth grade by the age of ten and, by attending school in the summer, finished her high school equivalency by the age of eighteen.

González's somewhat circuitous path through higher education in the early 1920s is testament to the financial and institutional barriers that limited the professional aspirations of Mexican American women of her generation. Her family, though solidly middle class, was in no position to finance an expensive education at the University of Texas at Austin, the school she ardently desired to attend. Consequently, upon graduation from high school, González decided to return to the borderlands to work as a teacher in order to save for her college fund. She enrolled in a summer normal school and earned a teaching certificate in two years, after which time she took a teaching position in Rio Grande City, where she lived with her aunt and uncle. This arrangement allowed her to save up enough money to enroll at the University of Texas in the fall of 1921.

After finishing her freshman year, majoring in Spanish, González was forced to return to her parents' home in San Antonio because of lack of funds. Again she turned to teaching to raise money, this time in Encinal, Texas, where she served as head teacher of a small school with only two teachers total. After two years of teaching, González decided to return to college, though she gave up on the University of Texas because it was too expensive. She enrolled instead in summer school at Our Lady of the Lake College in San Antonio, where she was offered a scholarship in exchange for her services as a Spanish teacher in its affiliated high school. The deal was too good to pass up: "For teaching two hours a day and a class of teachers on Saturday, I would get a private room, board, and tuition. My worries were over." Despite this ideal situation, González longed to return to the University of Texas, where a few years earlier she had begun studies in "advanced Spanish" under Lilia Casis, the eminent teacher of Spanish language and literature. So González added yet another job to her already cramped schedule: she began tutoring fellow students at Our

Lady of the Lake College in order to earn enough money to enroll in summer school at the University of Texas. Gonzalez's dedication eventually paid off. In the summer of 1925, her mentor, Lilia Casis, introduced her to J. Frank Dobie, the man who had put Texas folklore studies on the map. This introduction was a turning point in Jovita González's life. "Heretofore," she wrote, "the legends and stories of the border were interesting, so I thought, just to me. However, he made me see their importance and encouraged me to write them, which I did, publishing some in the *Folk-Lore Publications* and *Southwest Review*."[6] González is far too modest in this account. Her involvement with J. Frank Dobie and the Texas Folklore Society had far-reaching implications for the ways in which the dialogue over Texas culture and history would be played out over the rest of the century.

A native son of the Anglo ranching community, Dobie was fascinated by what he called a "vanishing" way of life. As a young adult (Dobie was born in 1888), he witnessed the wave of agricultural development that had consumed the open ranges of his childhood and transformed formerly sleepy Texas towns into booming mercantile centers. Like González, Dobie recognized that the rugged ranch life that had provided his informal education was quickly disappearing. His experiences as a young man working on his uncle's ranch in South Texas also reinforced a deep and abiding respect for the largely dispossessed Mexicano vaqueros who worked the ranch. However, Dobie was ultimately ambivalent about Mexicans: on the one hand, because he had grown up on a ranch worked almost entirely by Mexicans, he idolized vaqueros for their "simplicity," their understanding of and proximity to the land, and their unabashed masculinity; on the other hand, he was a son of the Anglo ranching elite, the very community that had (often violently) dispossessed the "freedom loving vaquero."

Dobie's contradictory nostalgia structured the pursuit of knowledge about the Mexican folk in Texas for over thirty years. Under his direction, the Texas Folklore Society turned increasingly to the collection of the folklore of the dispossessed, with special attention to the folk traditions of Mexicans in Texas. However, the society's renditions of folklore tended toward the ahistorical and apolitical—focusing, for example, on plant and animal lore, *curanderismo* (folk medicine), and legends of lost treasure—the forms of cultural poetics that, in Dobie's estimation, offered his general readership the true "flavor" of the folk. Thus, while Dobie's focus on Mexican folklore traditions during this period did promote general interest in Mexican culture, it rarely moved beyond the "appreciation" of Mexican arts, crafts, and narrative traditions. The "beauty" of

Mexican culture was celebrated, while the political and social valences at the heart of Mexican cultural poetics in Texas were left largely unexplored.

In spite of the contradictions at the center of its formation—or perhaps because of them—the brand of romantic folklore studies that Dobie created at the University of Texas in the 1920s and 1930s initiated "a liberating exploration of the boundaries which separated the various 'folk' of the Southwest." And, even though the Texas Folklore Society generally "kept racial and ethnic conflict conveniently in the romantic past," the very process of exploring culture across ethnic and racial lines brought increasing interaction between Anglos and Mexicans and a newfound respect for the cultural poetics of Mexican Americans in Texas. For the first time in the tradition of knowledge production about culture and history in Texas, Mexicans were a part of the conversation, and a new generation of Mexican American scholars entered into this dialogue. People like Carlos E. Castañeda, Lilia Casis, and Jovita González played instrumental roles in the organizational structure of the Texas Folklore Society and contributed significantly to the production of knowledge about their communities. Moreover, the flexibility that Dobie built into the research methodologies of the organization enabled a greater number of nonprofessional Mexican American folklorists (like Adina de Zavala) to collect material on the folk practices of the neighborhoods, towns, and ranches.[7]

For Dobie, González embodied the virtues of the ideal collector of folklore: her fine literary abilities in combination with her "authentic" insider knowledge of the intimate customs of ranch life granted her a certain degree of ethnographic authority within the field of Texas folklore studies. On the occasion of her first contribution to the *Publications of the Texas Folklore Society*, an article entitled "Folklore of the Texas-Mexican Vaquero" (1927), Dobie played up Jovita González's personal history, somewhat hyperbolically: "Her great-grandfather was the richest land owner on the Texas border. . . . Thus she has an unusual heritage of intimacy with her subject."[8] Dobie clearly believed that his readers would appreciate González's contributions more if they knew that she represented an "authentic" folk subject, someone who had actually lived among the rancheros and vaqueros of South Texas. Indeed, González's "authenticity" as a daughter of ranchero culture constituted the very foundation of her ethnographic authority, and Jovita González was not beyond capitalizing on this patina of authenticity to further her own position within the mostly white, largely male, world of folklore studies at the University of Texas. For Dobie, González might have represented a more "sanitized" version of his idealized vaquero. As an educated daughter of the ranchero elite, she was removed from the more violent contradictions of Anglo/Mexican ranching culture. Her gender relegated her to the feminized internal world of the rancho, the world of plant lore, legends, and folk remedies; and her presumably "elite" status brought her in line with Dobie's ideological vision.

In her writings, however, González refused to remain within the cloistered walls of the hacienda. Her first contributions to the *Publications of the Texas Folklore Society* focused on the songs and legends of the masculine world of the vaqueros, and though she sometimes adopted the "superior" tone of her Anglo colleagues with respect to the Mexican folk, her folklore writings also betrayed a clear sense of admiration for Mexican folk figures who offered open resistance to Anglo domination. Indeed, in spite of her generally friendly relations with Dobie and her other colleagues at the Texas Folklore Society, there are many indications that González did always agree with their version of Texas history. In a 1981 interview, González revealed that she avoided Dobie's folklore classes at the University of Texas because the two shared such disparate views on Texas history: "You see, it was an agreement that we made, that I would not go into one of his classes because I would be mad at many things. He would take the Anglo-Saxon side naturally. I would take the Spanish and Mexican side." González acknowledged that many of her Mexican American colleagues at the University of Texas were careful not to contest the "official history" promoted by Dobie and his cohort: "teachers couldn't afford to get involved in a controversy between Mexico and the University of Texas . . . but if the history of Texas were written the way it actually was . . . because things, some of those things that happened on both sides were very bitter. So we just didn't mention them. You just forget about it."[9] González's comments illustrate the limitations she experienced in speaking for the "Mexican side" in the public dialogue over Texas history.

However, there is at least one instance during this period when Jovita González *did* insert her voice rather forcefully into this public dialogue. In 1929, just two years after completing her undergraduate degree at Our Lady of the Lake, González, by now a full-time Spanish teacher at Our Lady of the Lake, was granted a Lapham Scholarship to take time off from teaching to conduct research along the border for a master's degree at the University of Texas. González spent the summer of 1929 traveling through the remote regions of the Texas-Mexican borderlands, collecting notes for what would become perhaps her most vocal native-born critique of ethnographic, sociological, and historical representations of Mexicans in

South Texas, her master's thesis, "Social Life in Cameron, Starr, and Zapata Counties" (submitted in 1930).

Although she is best known as an expert in Texas folklore, when Jovita González decided to pursue an advanced degree she did so in history, under the begrudging guidance of Eugene C. Barker. Although we may never know why she decided to pursue a master's degree in history as opposed to English (where she would have studied under her mentor, Dobie) or Spanish (under Lilia Casis), we do know that Barker was singularly unenthusiastic about the thesis she submitted to him for approval. According to González, he was "somewhat hesitant at first to approve the thesis," but he relented after the intervention of Carlos E. Castañeda, a family friend, who insisted that the thesis would be "used in years to come as source material." When Barker finally approved the thesis, he commented to González that it was "an interesting but somewhat odd piece of work."[10] Barker's reluctance to approve the thesis was not so unusual given the counterdiscursive tone of González's account of "social life" on the Texas-Mexico border, an account that focused on the lives of its Mexican inhabitants, resisted Anglo ethnological assessments of Mexican people, and offered a highly polemical, counterhegemonic narrative of Texas history. In this respect, "Social Life in Cameron, Starr, and Zapata Counties" represents perhaps the earliest attempt within the institutional discourse of Texas history to intervene against colonialist representations of the Mexican community on the lower Rio Grande.

After completing her M.A. in history, Jovita González dedicated herself to the business of promoting folklore studies in Texas, and it seems that at least in these early years of her involvement with Dobie and the Texas Folklore Society, González had faith that the new, more dialogic temper of folklore studies might lead to deeper racial understanding between Mexicans and Anglos in Texas. Judging from her correspondence with J. Frank Dobie during these years, González and her mentor shared a great friendship and an intense professional camaraderie. From the moment that they met and for the next twenty years, Dobie "nurtured and mentored her, soliciting and editing her manuscripts, engaging her in sustained evening discussions of the subject [of Mexican folklore] in his home, underwriting bank loans for her field trips."[11] He also encouraged her increasing level of involvement in the Texas Folklore Society. With Dobie's support, González assumed the vice presidency of the group in 1928 and was elected president in 1930 and again in 1931, an astounding achievement given that at the time the Texas Folklore Society was dominated by white male Texans. She was also a regular contributor to the *Publications of the Texas Folklore Society* and offered lively presentations of her research at the annual meetings. By the late 1930s, under Dobie's mentorship, and through her own considerable determination, González was considered a national expert on Mexican Americans of the Southwest.

In 1934, with the help of letters of recommendation from noted economist Paul S. Taylor and J. Frank Dobie, González was awarded a Rockefeller grant to complete a book-length manuscript on the folklore and culture of South Texas Mexicans at the turn of the century. The manuscript, which she entitled *Dew on the Thorn*, remained unpublished during González's lifetime, but it has recently been recovered by folklorist and literary critic José Limón and is now in print. *Dew on the Thorn* is basically a collection of folklore loosely woven together into a semi-autobiographical novel. This type of experimentation with narrative form was not unusual at the time. Just a few years earlier, J. Frank Dobie had written his own novel/folklore study *Tongues of the Monte*, and it had met with some critical acclaim. González was perhaps trying to replicate the success of Dobie's folklore study with her own compendium of folklore and fiction, which opens in 1904, the year of her birth, and documents the changing lives of rancheros, vaqueros, and *peones* (laborers) during a three-year period. That González chose to document the years between 1904 and 1907 in her folkloric treatment of Mexicano communities is significant for a number of reasons. First, the period correlates with her own childhood in South Texas and thus offered an almost autobiographical narrative of a world she knew well. The primary figures of her childhood, the goat herder Tio Patricio, the nursemaid Nana Chita, her father (as represented by the schoolmaster Don Alberto), and of course, Mamá Ramoncita, the great-grandmother who cautioned her great-grandchildren to "never forget that Texas is our home," all appear as central figures in the text. The period is also significant in that it marked the beginning of the final decline of Mexicano political and economic dominance in South Texas. González documented this process in her master's thesis and located its origins in the completion of the St. Louis, Brownsville, and Mexico Railway on July 4, 1904. Through accounts of folkloric stories and personal narratives, the protagonists of *Dew on the Thorn* chronicle the period in which Anglo Americans asserted economic and political authority over the region.

As José Limón has suggested, *Dew on the Thorn* should not simply be read as a literary rendition of the folkloric practices of the Mexican people on the border, but as a *political* text, in which the primary objective was to use folklore and history as a tool to influence the discourse on race relations between Anglos and Mexicans. In her grant application to the

Rockefeller foundation, González indicated as much, explaining that she hoped her research would help Anglo/Mexican race relations by clarifying dominant misconceptions about "Latin-Americans" among the Anglo community. She also believed that the manuscript would build pride within the Mexican American community regarding its long history and important cultural heritage in Texas. Through the literary use of folklore, González hoped to appeal to two political constituencies at once and thus to shape cultural politics both externally and internally. Her writings, from the start to the end, provided arguments against scientific and popular discourses, which had sought to describe, contain, and dispossess her people. In both "Social Life in Cameron, Starr, and Zapata Counties" and *Dew on the Thorn*, González virtually rewrote the master narratives of the discipline, offering a native-born response to the changing colonial imperatives of Texas folklore studies.

By the late 1930s, Jovita González increasingly distanced herself from her friends at the Texas Folklore Society. Her correspondence with Dobie dropped off precipitously after 1938, and her presentations at Texas Folklore Society meetings and scholarly contributions to the *Publications of the Texas Folklore Society* all but ended by 1940. This may be due to the fact that in 1935, at the rather advanced age of 31 (for the standards of the time), Jovita González finally decided to marry. She met her husband, Edmundo Mireles, when they were both students at the University of Texas, most likely through their mutual friend, Carlos E. Castañeda. Edmundo Mireles was a true citizen of the borderlands; his mother was a sister of the Mexican revolutionary leader, Venustiano Carranza, and while still an adolescent, Mireles had served with Carranza's revolutionary forces. Shortly before their marriage in 1935, Edmundo had been appointed the principal of a high school in the newly established San Felipe Independent School District in Del Rio, Texas, a small town on the U.S.–Mexico border, and was spending his evenings at a night school he had founded to train recently arrived Mexican immigrants in American citizenship and English. Mireles's educational activism would unavoidably shape Jovita González's politics and her career choices after their marriage.

Quite apart from her husband's influence, though, it appears that González's sanguine view of the Texas Folklore Society and their "revolution" in folklore could not withstand the realities of Anglo/Mexican relations in Texas. By 1937, though her relations with Dobie and the others were still cordial, González issued a very public critique of the Texas Folklore Society's politics of culture in "Latin Americans," her contribution to a collection entitled *Our Racial and National Minorities*. In this essay, González pointedly noted that while Anglos were willing to celebrate the cultural contributions of "Latin-Americans," they persisted in denying them equal rights: "When one sees the great sums of money spent to reconstruct the Spanish missions and other building of the Latin-American occupation in our country, one cannot help but wonder at the inconsistency of things in general. If Anglo-Americans accept their art and culture, why have they not also accepted the people? Why have not the Latin Americans been given the same opportunities that have been given other racial entities in the United States?"[12]

This transformation in González's thinking regarding the power of cultural appreciation to change racist sensibilities should be understood not simply as a result of her increasing involvement in the battle for educational equity for Mexicans that her husband championed, but also her own maturing understanding of the limits and possibilities of folklore studies itself. While Texas folklore studies offered Anglos an opportunity to "appreciate" certain contributions that Mexicans had made to Texas history and culture, it did little to address the wretched circumstances in which many Mexicans found themselves during the Depression. During this period, González struggled to find new ways of addressing the inequities of American culture through writing. She rightly sensed that the celebration of Mexican folklore was a one-sided affair that ultimately relegated Mexicans to a fixed, primitive, and highly romanticized past.

An unpublished short story that González wrote in 1935, on the eve of her marriage to Edmundo Mireles, provides evidence of the tentative creative steps that she had begun to take toward an ideology of pluralism that was not merely a celebration of multiculturalism or cultural "difference," but that constituted a model for race relations based on mutual respect, reciprocity, and understanding. In "Shades of the Tenth Muse," González narrates an imaginary conversation between two foundational figures in American letters: Sor Juana Inés de la Cruz and Anne Bradstreet. In this imaginary dialogue, set within the "close and smoky" confines of Jovita González's study, Sor Juana Inés de la Cruz and Anne Bradstreet (both of whom came to be known as the "Tenth Muse of the Americas") disagree on many points, but in the end, they are able to bridge the cultural gap that divides them by sharing their experiences and, more important, their poetry. The aesthetic interchange outlined in "Shades of the Tenth Muse" seems to suggest a collaborative model of cultural pluralism based on mutual understanding and respect, as opposed to one-sided "appreciation." This understanding of race relations came to dominate González's thinking in later years, structuring her approach to writing, educational activism, and her political outlook.[13]

After her marriage, Jovita González joined her husband in Del Rio, where she ran the English Department at San Felipe High School and worked intermittently on various writing projects. She and her husband had a tremendous impact on that small community; they "helped bring about a renaissance of language and culture and established a Latin Club, which put on *zarzuelas*, or operettas, as a reinforcement of high culture as well as part of the formal education of young people."[14] During this period (1938–39), González explored the possibility of applying to Ph.D. programs at Stanford, the University of California, Berkeley, or the University of New Mexico and even solicited letters of recommendation from J. Frank Dobie and Paul S. Taylor. Although she ultimately decided not to pursue a doctorate and chose instead to relocate with her husband to Corpus Christi, Texas, sometime during this period Jovita González embarked upon a project that would eventually lead to her most important work of fiction and her reemergence in the 1990s as an icon of Latina writing.

In 1936, González put together a special display of photographs, short biographical narratives, and material culture for the Texas Centennial celebration in Dallas. The historical display, entitled "Catholic Heroines of Texas," focused on the role of Mexicanas in the founding of Texas. It was perhaps her research on this subject, as well as the triumphalist mood of Anglos during the centennial year, that inspired González to begin working on *Caballero*, a historical novel that traced the lives of a group of ranchero families living on the border during the U.S.–Mexican War. Interestingly, González chose to write this novel in collaboration with an Anglo woman named Margaret Eimer. Not much is known about Eimer except that she, like González, lived in Del Rio and was probably a teacher who had most likely met González through informal social gatherings. In *Caballero*, González and Eimer offer a feminist exploration of the politics of collaboration that recasts collaboration not as "betrayal," but as a mode of understanding and coping with the complexities of living in the borderlands. To this end, the novel traces a number of different kinds of collaborations: from the romantic love that binds its hero and heroine, Captain Warrener, the dashing southern gentleman, and Susanita, daughter of the ranchero; to the rather more pragmatic negotiations between Susanita's sister, Angela, who wants to do good works for her community, and her Anglo suitor, "Red" McLane, who will provide her the money to do so in exchange for a marriage that will bring him prestige among the conquered rancheros; to the artistic collaboration between the young ranchero Luis Gonzaga and an older army doctor, Captain Devlin, an artist, who recognizes Luis's talent and wants to help him develop it. All of these peaceful collaborations, and the many others that populate the novel, are juxtaposed against the rigid ideologies of those Anglos and Mexicans whose resistance to the politics of collaboration leads to death and bloodshed on both sides of the border.

Scholars have noticed a protofeminist critique in *Caballero*, especially in two of its most vividly drawn characters, Don Santiago, the patriarch of the rancho, and his widowed sister, Doña Dolores. These characters spend the better part of 350 pages sparring over both gender politics and territorial politics. From their extended debate, readers get not only a critique of the patriarchal standards that governed Mexican life in the nineteenth century, but also a subtle critique of male-centered resistance strategies that characterized emergent Mexican American political institutions during González's own period. Indeed, because of the book's undeniable feminist undertones, some critics contend that *Caballero* represents an early example of what Chicana scholar Sonia Saldívar-Hull has termed "feminism on the border." González and Eimer worked on *Caballero* through the 1940s and 1950s, writing, editing, and revising the manuscript, sharing it with enthusiastic friends, and submitting it to less than enthusiastic publishers. After Jovita and Edmundo Mireles moved to Corpus Christi in 1939, and Eimer left Texas for Joplin, Missouri, the coauthors kept working on the novel, sending revisions to one another via the U.S. mail, but a combination of publisher indifference and the difficulties of trying to work through long-distance revisions of the manuscript eventually brought an end to their collaboration. By the late 1960s, their correspondence seems to have ended. Though *Caballero* remained only a manuscript during González's lifetime, it was finally published in 1996 and has significantly shifted our understanding of this foundational Mexican American scholar.

In her memoirs, Jovita González dedicated a scant three paragraphs on her life after the move to Corpus Christi. Given this cursory treatment, one might get the impression that her life after Del Rio was somewhat uneventful, but nothing could be further from the truth. Though she published less frequently and made fewer public appearances, Jovita González and her husband, Edmundo Mireles, played an enormously important role in establishing Spanish education programs in Texas and the Southwest. And though they met with much resistance at first—as

González notes, "this was a period when the walls of racial prejudice still had to be torn down"—they ultimately succeeded in establishing one of the first elementary-level Spanish programs in the country.[15] In fact, Edmundo Mireles is considered by many to be the father of bilingual education because of the role that he played as an advocate for Spanish education in the public school system of Corpus Christi. González and her husband also collaborated with educator Roy E. Fisher on a series of Spanish textbooks, entitled *Mi Libro Español* (1941) and *El Español Elemental* (1949), designed for teaching Spanish at the grade school level.

González spent a total of twenty-one years as a Spanish teacher at W. B. Ray and Miller High Schools in Corpus Christi, where her students remember her as a vibrant and compelling educator and role model. During this period, González dedicated her summers to training teachers in the "Mireles method" for teaching Spanish and to traveling in Mexico with her husband. For González and Mireles, Spanish instruction meant something more than just developing language proficiency. Their unique instructional method combined González's encyclopedic knowledge of Mexican and Spanish culture, history, and folklore and Mireles's considerable linguistic skills in a potent mix that taught young children the fundamentals of communicating in Spanish, as well as an understanding and appreciation of Mexicano culture. This pedagogical approach was mirrored in the social activity that took up the greater portion of their free time, the establishment and promotion of a quasi-political social club called the Pan American Council, whose principal aims included the study of "Spanish, Latin America, its people, history, geography, population, customs, habits and way of life," the fostering of "good relations between Anglo Americans and Latin Americans," and the encouragement of Latin American professionals to "contribute to the welfare of their community."[16] The Pan American Council also aimed to establish junior Pan American clubs and Pan American parent-teacher organizations in area schools. During this time, González also dedicated herself to the promotion and continuation of Mexicano cultural traditions, directing *pastorelas* (folk pageants) and *posadas* (traditional Mexican Christmas pageants) with Mexican children from the Corpus Christi community, until she retired from teaching in 1967.

Jovita González spent the last years of her life trying unsuccessfully to write her autobiography. Plagued by diabetes and chronic depression, she never finished the project, completing only a scant thirteen-page document before her death in 1983. What we know about this early Latina intellectual must be gleaned from her published folklore studies and the pages of her recently uncovered manuscripts, *Caballero* and *Dew on the Thorn*. This body of work demonstrates that González was one of the first Mexican American scholars to think carefully about the philosophical and political contours of what would come to be recognized as "Borderlands Studies." Like the generation of Latina scholars who emerged in the 1980s, Jovita González moved beyond the rigid binaries that governed traditional thinking in this area to elaborate a concept of the borderlands as a transnational "contact zone" wherein different cultures, languages, histories, and genders collide and recombine into new forms of politics and poetics.

NOTES

1. Jovita González, "Jovita González: Early Life and Education," *Dew on the Thorn,* ed. José Limón (Houston: Arte Público Press, 1997), xi.

2. Mario T. García, *Mexican Americans: Leadership, Ideology, and Identity, 1930–1960* (New Haven: Yale University Press, 1989), 240–41.

3. González, "Jovita González: Early Life and Education," x.

4. David Montejano, *Anglos and Mexicans in the Making of Texas, 1836–1986* (Austin: University of Texas Press, 1987), 107.

5. Jovita González, "Social Life in Cameron, Starr and Zapata Counties" (M.A. thesis, University of Texas, 1930), 108; Montejano, *Anglos and Mexicans,* 114, 161.

6. González, "Jovita González: Early Life and Education," xii.

7. Roger D. Abrahams and Richard Bauman, "Doing Folklore Texas Style," in *"And Other Neighborly Names": Social Process and Cultural Image in Texas Folklore,* ed. Richard Bauman and Roger D. Abrahams (Austin: University of Texas Press, 1981), 4–5; James Charles McNutt, "Beyond Regionalism: Texas Folklorists and the Emergence of a Post-Regional Consciousness" (Ph.D. dissertation, University of Texas, 1982), 226, 235.

8. Jovita González, "Folklore of the Texas-Mexican Vaquero," in *Texas and Southwestern Lore,* ed. J. Frank Dobie (*Publications of the Texas Folklore Society,* no. 6; Austin: Texas Folklore Society, 1927), 241.

9. Quoted in McNutt, "Beyond Regionalism," 350–51.

10. González, "Early Life and Education," xiii.

11. José E. Limón, *Dancing with the Devil: Society and Cultural Poetics in Mexican-American South Texas* (Madison: University of Wisconsin Press, 1994), 61.

12. Jovita González, "Latin Americans," in *Our Racial and National Minorities: Their History, Contributions, and Present Problems*, ed. Francis J. Brown and Joseph S. Roucek (New York: Prentice-Hall, 1937), 509.

13. This story has recently been published, with a commentary. See María Eugenia Cotera, "Engendering a 'Dialectics of Our America': Jovita González's Pluralist Dialogue as Feminist Testimonio," in *Las obreras: Chicana Politics of Work and Family*, ed. Vicki L. Ruiz (Los Angeles: UCLA Chicano Studies Research Center Publications, 2000), 237–56.

14. Leticia Garza-Falcón, *Gente Decente: A Borderlands Response to the Rhetoric of Dominance* (Austin: University of Texas Press, 1998), 78.

15. González, "Jovita González: Early Life and Education," xiii.

16. Garza-Falcón, *Gente Decente*, 97–98.

11

LUISA MORENO AND LATINA LABOR ACTIVISM

Vicki L. Ruiz

> One person can't do anything; it's only with others that things
> are accomplished.
>
> Luisa Moreno

The era of the Great Depression and World War II stands as the golden
era of the American labor movement, the period when auto workers staged
a dramatic sit-in at Flint, Michigan; John L. Lewis organized the powerful
Congress of Industrial Organizations (CIO), a national confederation of
factory workers; and the charismatic A. Philip Randolph mobilized African American railroad porters. Luisa Moreno ranks among these heroes
of labor history, yet her story is still virtually unknown outside of Latino
history. An organizer briefly with Lewis in Pennsylvania and the contemporary of Randolph, Luisa Moreno remains the only transcontinental
Latina union organizer, as her work, indeed her passion, carried her across
the country from the garment shops of New York City, to cigar-rolling
plants in Tampa, to canneries in Los Angeles, with many stops in between.
An immigrant from Guatemala, she was the first Latina vice president of
a major union, the United Cannery, Agricultural, Packing, and Allied
Workers of America, which in its heyday was the seventh-largest CIO affiliate. But her most notable "first" was as the driving force behind *El
Congreso de Pueblos de Hablan Española* (the Spanish-speaking Peoples
Congress), the first national Latino civil rights assembly.

Born Blanca Rosa Rodríguez López on August 30, 1907, Moreno had a most unlikely childhood for a future trade union leader. She grew up surrounded by wealth and privilege in her native Guatemala. Her mother, Alicia López Sarana, who was originally from Colombia, was a prominent socialite married to Ernesto Rodríguez Robles, a powerful coffee grower. With the help of a coterie of servants and tutors, Alicia and Ernesto reared four children, one son and three daughters, on their sprawling estate. Luisa received an education appropriate for her station and gender, spoke Spanish and French, and showed an early aptitude for poetry. She remembered her father as a "real person" but her mother as "a peacock," who never emerged from her boudoir until eleven o'clock in the morning. At the age of eight, Luisa was stricken with a high fever, and the local doctor offered little hope for her recovery. Her father prayed for her life, promising that he would consecrate her to God by sending her to a convent in preparation for religious life. Luisa recovered, and true to his word, in 1916 Ernesto and his nine-year-old daughter boarded a steamship bound for California, where Luisa would attend the Convent of the Holy Names in Oakland.[1]

Moreno had less than fond memories of her four and a half years at the convent. There she experienced her first bout with discrimination. A classmate made a remark about "Spanish pigs so I belted her." Her convent experiences, especially the hypocrisy she witnessed during Lent, when she and the other girls subsisted on bread and water while the nuns dined on sumptuous food, turned her away from Catholicism, in particular, and organized religion, in general. She begged to return home, and finally her parents relented.

Back in Guatemala, Luisa at the age of fifteen desired a university education. When she discovered that Guatemalan women were barred from attending college in their homeland, she began to organize her elite peers into *Sociedad Gabriela Mistral* to push for greater educational opportunities for women. They relied on petition drives and informal lobbying, the traditional political tools for elite women. At approximately the same moment that U.S. suffragists had secured passage of the Nineteenth Amendment, which granted women the right to vote, in 1920, a teenaged Moreno mobilized a cadre of well-heeled young women to claim the right to higher education. One Guatemalan history book, *La Patria del Criollo*, paid them tribute as a generation that made history. With success in sight, Moreno prepared to take her place among the inaugural class of university women. Before entering the halls of academe, however, she experienced a change of heart. Despite her youthful activism, she was fully aware of her family's place in Guatemalan society; the cultural and class expectations weighed heavily on her own future. When one of her siblings married, her father had the fountain on the family compound filled with expensive Veuve-Clicquot champagne. Perhaps filled with a sense of adventure and certainly with a streak of rebelliousness, Luisa chafed at the constraints on her spirit and creativity that her family's most privileged world would require, and thus, she decided to flee Guatemala.

Rejecting her family's wealth and status and permanently straining her relations with her parents and siblings, she ran away to Mexico City. By the age of nineteen, she had ensconced herself in the world of the bohemian cultural elite. Well known for her beauty and poetry, the young Latina flapper supported herself as a journalist, writing children's columns and covering society stories, which brought her into the circles of Mexican artists Diego Rivera and Frida Kahlo. The few possessions she clung to throughout her many travels included her own slim volume of verse *El Vendedor de Cocuyos* (*Seller of Fireflies*) (1927) and a newspaper review of her work, as well as drafts of unpublished poems usually written on scraps of paper. *El Vendedor de Cocuyos* reveals a youthful poet with a deep appreciation of the natural world and the human condition, a woman unafraid of expressing desire openly and honestly. One treasured clipping referred to her as both a gentle compatriot and vanguard feminist. In Mexico, her feminism was situated in self-expression and creativity rather than political action.

In this heady, avant-garde atmosphere, she married caricature artist Miguel Angel de León, a man sixteen years her senior. A dashing figure with a mysterious past, he pursued the young poet. Like Luisa, Miguel had grown up in an elite family in Guatemala, and he, too, had yearned for adventure. In 1914, at the age of twenty-three, he had enlisted in the French Foreign Legion and fought in World War I. Ten years later, he resided in Mexico City, a fixture within the Rivera-Kahlo social scene. They wed on November 27, 1927; Luisa was barely twenty. Although the courtship had been filled with romance and passion, Luisa remembered her dreams were dashed on their wedding night. In a 1984 interview, she related, "He took me to a horrible hotel. . . . [M]y husband said he had business, womanizing . . . . I cried myself to sleep." Amends must have been made, for within months of their marriage, Luisa was pregnant. The couple then made a decision that would change their lives. They would leave their exciting, though sheltered, bohemian community to seek their fortune in New York City. Luisa remarked that she wanted her child to be "a Latin from Manhattan." On August 28, 1928, they arrived in New York harbor on the SS *Monterey*.[2]

With the Great Depression around the corner, 1928 was not a propitious time for the arrival of a Guatemalan artist and poet. By the time their daughter, Mytyl Lorraine, was born in November, they lived in a crowded tenement in Spanish Harlem. Although Miguel and Luisa were fluent in Spanish, French, and English, they had difficulty securing employment. Within months of her daughter's birth, Moreno found herself laboring over a sewing machine and steam press, as she struggled to support her infant and unemployed husband.

Spanish Harlem would provide the seedbed for Moreno's political awakening. Moreno even pointed to *the* event in Spanish Harlem that radicalized her. Although her story could be construed as an apocryphal tale, it encapsulates the hard choices she and other sweatshop workers had to make in a world with few options. One day while walking home from work with a friend, her Latina companion invited Moreno to her apartment to see her baby. As they ascended the stairwell, they heard a baby cry. Her friend started to panic as she recognized her child's voice. The apartment was unlocked, and no babysitter was in sight. In the fading sunlight, the mother carried the infant to the window. As the light struck the infant's face, both women stared in horror: a rat had eaten off half the baby's face. The child died a short time later. Luisa Moreno called this incident the defining moment of her life. She did not know quite what to do, but she knew she had to do something to change the material conditions of her fellow workers. Trade union and political activism became her life course.[3]

In 1930, Moreno joined the Communist Party (CP). Already active in Spanish Harlem's *Centro Obrero de Habla Española*, a leftist community coalition, Moreno began to mobilize her peers on the shop floor into *La Liga de Costureras*, a small-scale garment workers' union. During her days as a "junior organizer," Moreno would hone her skills at building a grassroots local. Although La Liga was initially affiliated with the Needle Worker Trades Industrial Union (which was closely connected to the CP) and later with the more mainstream International Ladies Garment Workers Union (ILGWU), Moreno was pretty much on her own, receiving little financial help and no staff support or advice from the larger unions. As a result, the local remained very small and had little organizing clout. However, Moreno endeavored to build a supportive community among the workers. La Liga thus became a family affair. At a time when only a few male unions had "ladies' auxiliaries," Moreno organized a "fraternal group," or male auxiliary, charged with the task of fund-raising. Taking on the traditional women's work of ticket sales, publicity, and refreshments, fathers, husbands, and brothers of Liga members organized weekly dances to raise funds for the fledgling local. Moreno's own husband, however, was nowhere in sight.

At this point in his life, Miguel de León had as his constant companions his child, his brushes, and his bottles. A cavalier caregiver, he took Mytyl to his favorite neighborhood bar. If he happened to slip away while she napped and she woke up, she quickly learned what to do. "I remember walking across this huge street and these huge street cars and having to cross by myself. I had to be careful not to get hit by the street car." In addition, Moreno would describe her husband as prone to violence.[4]

Luisa's radicalism was rooted in both conviction and refuge. A newly politicized Marxist and tireless organizer, her whirlwind of activism provided physical and psychological distance from a deteriorating marriage. Rarely home, Moreno had reached a crossroads by 1935. Although now a full-time organizer with the ILGWU, she felt frustrated that union leaders evinced little interest in Latina workers. Moreno had immersed herself in a gamut of leftist politics, and in the process she had struck up a friendship with Gray Bemis, a Nebraska farm boy turned New York cabbie. Moreno and Bemis, an activist with the International Workers Order (IWO), attended many of the same political meetings, and he would often give her rides home. Though deeply attracted to him, she hesitated. "I liked him, but he was married and I was married. Although I was in a miserable marriage, I did not fool around with married men." When Luisa decided to leave New York and take a job as an American Federation of Labor (AFL) organizer in Florida, Gray was the one who drove her and Mytyl to the bus station.

In Florida, Luisa Moreno faced a formidable challenge—to organize Latino, African American, and Italian cigar rollers. Moreover, the Ku Klux Klan had a reputation for terrorizing labor activists and other progressives, which was one reason why the AFL was afraid of Florida. While her bosses no doubt recognized her talent, they also considered her young, green, and expendable. According to Moreno, they believed that the Klan would think twice before harming a woman organizer, especially one who was fair-skinned, slender, and only four feet, ten inches tall.

Her organizing days in Florida signaled the birth of "Luisa Moreno." Deliberately distancing herself from her past, she chose the alias "Moreno" (meaning dark), a name diametrically opposite to her given name, "Blanca Rosa" (white rose). Indeed, she conjugated her identity, inventing or inflecting her sense of self, taking to account such constructions as race, class, culture, language, and gender. Simply put, Moreno made strategic choices regarding her class and ethnic identification in order to facilitate her life's work as a labor and civil rights advocate. With her light skin, education, and unaccented English, she could have "passed"; instead, she chose to forgo any potential privileges predicated on race, class, or color. Furthermore, she made these changes in the Jim Crow South, where segregation and white domination was a way of life. The first name "Luisa" could also be seen as a political statement, perhaps a homage to Luisa Capetillo, who had preceded her in Florida twenty years earlier and whose legacy Moreno undoubtedly knew about and built upon in organizing cigar workers.[5]

Rather than emphasizing the primacy of the individual, Moreno focused on the individual in relation to her or his community. As an elderly woman reflecting on her life as labor and civil rights activist in a 1978 interview with the author (then a naive graduate student), Moreno declared, "One person can't do anything; it's only with others that things are accomplished." By nurturing grassroots locals, she cultivated rank-and-file leadership as she fostered a sense of communal investment among workers as union members. This decentering of self would mark her life as an organizer. As a mother, she made painful choices that would have long-term consequences for her daughter.

Given her fears about the Klan, as well as the challenges and erratic schedules inherent in trade union work, Luisa decided to board her daughter with a pro-labor Latino family. From the age of seven until almost thirteen, Mytyl lived with informal foster families; some treated her well, others abused her. In Florida, one head of household routinely molested young Mytyl, while his wife did nothing but sob quietly behind Mytyl's bedroom door. Sixty years later, Mytyl related these incidents with rawness and candor, conveying a little girl's confusion and pain, which she had never confided in her mother. Moreno visited infrequently, sending greeting cards on occasion. Shuttled from place to place, Mytyl recalled from childhood "the feeling of being alone." Moreno, as someone who devoted herself to trade union and civil rights work, knew far too well the sacrifices people made for their children, and she chose to sacrifice any semblance of family for herself and her daughter.

Although Moreno left the Communist Party in 1935, her commitment to Marxism never wavered. Florida labor organizer Berthe Small recalled the first time she met Moreno. As a student at the University of Miami, Small and her friends piled into a jalopy and headed for Tampa to watch a labor organizer in action. "And we got to the union hall. . . . And I see this beautiful woman delivering a speech in English, impressive and revolutionary." Moreno's rhetoric touched a chord among these cigar workers, many of whom, from the days of Luisa Capetillo, held socialist beliefs. In addition to the terrorism of the Klan, AFL leaders also feared the radicalism of the workers, but Moreno felt right at home in their company. Moreno's first step was to address worker grievances, and then later "try to raise the consciousness of the worker." "*Ask the workers*, what are your problems?" she related. "Work on these minor grievances and address them and go on to more major ones . . . . " Bread and butter issues would always take precedence over political education, and as a result, the Marxist study groups that she initiated were few and far between.[6]

In Florida, Moreno refined her skills as a labor leader. Organizing "all races, creeds and colors," she negotiated a solid contract covering 13,000 cigar workers from Ybor City to Lakeland to Jacksonville. When AFL officials revised the agreement to make it more amenable to management, an angry Moreno urged the workers to reject it. In response, the AFL transferred her to Pennsylvania, where she mobilized cigar rollers across three states. In 1937, like many organizers unhappy with the AFL's indifference to unskilled workers and people of color, she resigned to join its newly established rival, the CIO, taking several locals with her. A year later, she joined a fledgling branch of the CIO—the United Cannery, Agricultural, Packing, and Allied Workers of America (UCAPAWA). The union's commitment to rank-and file-leadership and to inclusion, recruiting members across race, nationality, and gender, resonated with Moreno. She would stay with UCAPAWA for the remainder of her career, rising to the position of vice president in 1941. It was the first time a Latina would be elected to a high-ranking national union post. But in 1938, she was a mere UCAPAWA union representative with her first assignment: move to San Antonio, Texas, to take charge of the pecan shellers' strike. From Pennsylvania, Luisa and Mytyl headed for Texas, but again, they would live apart, as Mytyl was boarded with yet another family.

Between 1933 and 1938, before Moreno arrived, Mexican workers had organized a pecan shellers' union in San Antonio. Men, women, and children were paid pitifully low wages—less than $2 a week in 1934. Some employers explained that if they raised the pay scale, Tejanos would "just spend" the extra money on "'tequila and worthless trinkets in the dime stores.'" A twenty-three-year-old member of the Workers' Alliance and secretary of the Texas Communist Party, Emma Tenayuca, emerged as the fiery local leader. Although not a pecan sheller herself, Tenayuca, a San Antonio native, was elected to head the strike committee. During the six-week labor dispute, between 6,000 and 10,000 strikers faced tear gas and billy clubs "on at least six occasions." Tenayuca courageously organized demonstrations, and she and over 1,000 pecan shellers were jailed. In an interview with historian Zaragosa Vargas, Tenayuca reflected on her activism: "I was pretty defiant. [I fought] against poverty, actually starvation, high infant death rates, disease and hunger and misery. I would do the same thing again."

UCAPAWA president Donald Henderson intervened in the strike by assigning Luisa Moreno, then a thirty-two-year-old veteran labor activist, to help move the UCAPAWA affiliate from street demonstrations to a functioning trade union. As the union's official representative, Moreno organized the strikers into a united, disciplined force that employers could no longer ignore. Five weeks after the strike began, management agreed to arbitration. The settlement included recognition of the UCAPAWA local and piece rate scales, which complied with the new federal minimum wage of twenty-five cents an hour. Henderson's decision to send Moreno to San Antonio "infuriated" Tenayuca, who reluctantly stepped aside, and the two women had a tenuous and tense working relationship.[7]

Moreno next traveled to the Rio Grande Valley of Texas. Organizing Mexicano migrants in dire straits, she, too, had few resources. She lived with farm workers, slept under trees, and shared her groceries with those around her. Moreno encountered what she termed a "lynch spirit" among rural white residents, who were hostile to Mexican workers. She had been in the fields only a short time when UCAPAWA pulled her out. The drain on union coffers from farm labor campaigns in California and Texas prompted the union to focus its energies on the more geographically and financially stable cannery and packinghouse workers. Before her next assignment, Moreno requested a leave of absence in order to organize a national Latino civil rights assembly. After stopping in San Antonio to visit Mytyl and pay her board, Luisa headed west. Following an abortive planning meeting in Albuquerque, Moreno journeyed to Los Angeles, where she found sympathetic activists who shared her vision of a national convention, one that would diminish the distance between citizens and immigrants and between Mexicanos and Latinos.

Held April 28–30, 1939, *El Congreso de Pueblos de Hablan Española* was the first national civil rights assembly for Latinos in the United States. Approximately 1,000 to 1,500 delegates representing over 120 organizations assembled in Los Angeles to address issues of jobs, housing, education, health, and immigrant rights. Luisa Moreno drew upon her contacts with Latino labor unions, mutual aid societies, and other grassroots groups in order to ensure a truly national conference. Although the majority of the delegates hailed from California and the Southwest, women and men traveled from such distances as Montana, Illinois, New York, and Florida to attend the convention. In planning this convention, Moreno worked in tandem with local Los Angeles activists, such as Josefina Fierro, Eduardo Quevedo, and Bert Corona, who also assumed leadership roles in El Congreso. The conference attracted a diverse group of delegates from teen-agers, teachers, labor leaders, and even a few politicians."

Over the course of three days, Congreso delegates drafted a compre-hensive platform. They called for an end to segregation in public facili-ties, housing, education, and employment and to discrimination in the disbursement of public assistance. El Congreso endorsed the rights of immigrants to live and work in the United States without fear of deporta-tion. While encouraging immigrants to become citizens, delegates did not advocate assimilation, but rather emphasized the importance of preserv-ing Latino cultures, and called upon universities to create departments in Latino Studies. Despite the promise of the first convention, a national network of local branches never developed, and red-baiting would later take its toll among fledgling chapters in California.

After World War II, red-baiting became a popular tactic in California and one that spread nationally with President Harry Truman's loyalty oaths, the rise of Senators Richard Nixon and Joseph McCarthy, and the "red scare" of the Cold War. Groups against civil rights, the United Na-tions, or any type of activity that they construed as "liberal" would brand their opponents as Communist or as Communist sympathizers. With growing public fear of the Soviet Union during this time period, being labeled a "red" (Communist) or a "pinko" (sympathizer) was not just derisive name-calling; people lost their jobs, and their families, and some labor and civil rights activists were deported. While red-baiting did exist in the 1930s, the national climate was decidedly more liberal with the popularity of the New Deal, the rise of the CIO, and the growth of civil rights organizations, such as the National Negro Congress and El Congreso.

El Congreso brought together Luisa Moreno and Josefina Fierro, women whose lifelong friendship was forged in the fire of community organiz-ing. A native of Mexicali, on the Mexico-California border, Fierro de-scended from a line of rebellious women. Her grandmother and mother were *Magónistas*, followers of socialist leader Juan Flores Magón. While a student at the University of California at Los Angeles, Fierro met Holly-wood writer John Bright at the local cabaret where her *tia* sang. After their marriage, she became a community organizer in East Los Angeles and drew upon her celebrity connections to raise funds for barrio causes. While Luisa

Moreno took the lead in organizing the 1939 national meeting of El Congreso, Josefina Fierro proved instrumental in buoying the day-to-day operations of the fragile southern California chapters. Both Moreno and Fierro believed in the dignity of the common person and the importance of grassroots networks, reciprocity, and self-help. As Fierro commented in an interview with historian Mario García, "Movie stars such as Anthony Quinn, Dolores Del Rio, and John Wayne contributed money, 'not because they were reds, . . . but because they were helping Mexicans help themselves.'" The two women also shared an awareness of the position of women in U.S. Latino communities. The southern California chapters of El Congreso created a women's committee and a women's platform, which expressly recognized the "double discrimination" facing Mexican women. In the words of Josefina Fierro: "We had women's problems that were very deep . . . discrimination in jobs . . . migratory problems . . . schooling. No, we didn't have a Lib Movement so we didn't think in terms of what women's roles were—we just did it and it worked."[8]

After the Congreso, Moreno returned to UCAPAWA and, with a grant from a liberal philanthropic foundation, organized a labor school for Colorado beet workers in Denver. In addition to classes in Mexican and labor history, Moreno taught the fine arts of negotiating contracts, writing pamphlets, and operating mimeograph machines. Margarito Cárdenas, a student at the school, composed a corrido honoring UCAPAWA and Moreno. Two stanzas follow:

> With great sacrifice
> And perseverance of the CIO
> Sister Luisa Moreno
> Organized this school.
> Let's take heed of the past
> And understand reason.
> Divided there's no progress
> Only through the Union.

After several months in Colorado, Moreno made an unexpected move, accepting a desk job with the national office in Washington, D.C., as the editor of *Noticias de UCAPAWA*, the Spanish-language version of *UCAPAWA News*. Taking this post may have been an effort to reestablish a relationship with her daughter, now almost a teenager. With regular work hours, she made an effort to provide a family life. Mytyl recalled with great fondness Christmas in Maryland in 1940, their first holiday together in five years: "I remember having a gift under the tree. . . . I didn't care whether the other kids had five gifts. . . . I was tickled that I had one gift under the tree."[9]

The next Christmas would find the duo in Los Angeles. Anxious to return to the field, Moreno lobbied for a new assignment—to consolidate union organizing among southern California cannery workers, many of whom were Mexican and Jewish women. Moreno, as the newly elected union vice president, threw herself into this task, earning the nickname "The California Whirlwind." Capitalizing on the gendered networks on the shop floor, Moreno harvested unparalleled success, as food processing operatives under the UCAPAWA banner significantly improved their working conditions, wages, and benefits.

The California canning labor force included young daughters, newlyweds, middle-aged wives, and widows. Occasionally three generations—daughter, mother, and grandmother—worked together at the same cannery. Entering the job market as members of a family wage economy, they pooled their resources to put food on the table. "My father was a busboy," Carmen Bernal Escobar recalled, "and to keep the family going . . . in order to bring in a little more money . . . my mother, my grandmother, my mother's brother, my sister and I all worked together at Cal San." One of the largest canneries in Los Angeles, the California Sanitary Canning Company (Cal San) employed primarily Mexican and Russian Jewish women. They were clustered in specific departments—washing, grading, cutting, canning, and packing—and paid according to the production level. Women jockeyed for position near the chutes or gates where the produce was plentiful. "Those at the end of the line hardly made nothing," Escobar remembered. Standing in the same positions week after week, month after month, women workers often developed friendships that crossed family and ethnic lines. Their day-to-day problems (slippery floors, irritating peach fuzz, production speed-ups, arbitrary supervisors, and even sexual harassment) cemented feelings of solidarity. Cannery workers even employed a special jargon when conversing among themselves, often referring to an event in terms of when specific fruits or vegetables arrived for processing at the plant. For instance, the phrase, "We met in spinach, fell in love in peaches, and married in tomatoes," indicated that the couple met in March, fell in love in August, and married in October.

In 1939, Cal San employees had staged a dramatic strike led by UCAPAWA organizer Dorothy Ray Healey. Wages and conditions improved at the plant as workers nurtured their local and jealously guarded their closed-shop contract (that is, joining the union became a condition for employment, so that union members could maintain their bargaining position). When Luisa Moreno arrived, she enlisted the aid of union members at California Walnut and Cal San in union drives at several Los Angeles area food processing firms. Workers organized other workers across canneries, ethnicities, generations, and gender, informing their colleagues at other plants of the benefits and improved wages that they had won under UCAPAWA representation. News traveled across friend and kin networks and in several languages, but predominately in English and Spanish. The result was Local 3, the second-largest UCAPAWA affiliate in the nation. Moreno encouraged cross-plant alliances and women's leadership. In 1943, for example, women filled twelve of the local's fifteen elected positions, and Mexican women were elected to eight of these posts. The union members proved able negotiators during annual contract renewals. In addition to higher wages and better conditions, the local also provided benefits that few industrial unions could match—free legal advice and a hospitalization plan.

Moreno also extended the union's reach beyond Los Angeles to organizing food processing operatives in Fullerton, Riverside, Redlands, Santa Ana, San Diego, and the San Joaquin Valley. Local 2 represented the largest cannery in California, Val Vita of Fullerton, a facility whose deplorable conditions were unmatched. Company supervisors there were notorious for exploiting line personnel, 75 percent of whom were Mexican. Women frequently fainted from exhaustion during speed-up periods. Day care was also a major concern, since many employees had no alternative but to leave their small children locked inside their automobiles in the plant parking lot. Moreno led a hard-fought campaign that resulted not only in a resounding victory complete with certification by the National Labor Relations Board (NLRB), but also in higher wages, more humane conditions, and management-financed, on-site day care.

By the following year (1943), UCAPAWA members had won thirty-one NLRB elections: seventeen in San Joaquin Valley packinghouses, thirteen more in Riverside-Redlands, and one in a Santa Ana onion dehydration plant. The NLRB, created in 1935 by the National Labor Relations Act, or Wagner Act, fostered the success of organized labor across the nation by compelling management to bargain with a labor union that had secured a majority of its workers as members. Owners and supervisors could not legally ignore a union that had won an election certified as valid by the NLRB. Therefore, these elections for union representation were crucial for the future success for workers who sought to improve their wages and working conditions.

In southern California, UCAPAWA provided women cannery workers with the crucial "social space" necessary to assert their independence and display their talents. They were not rote employees, numbed by repetition, but women with dreams, goals, tenacity, and intellect. In addition to extensive committee service, Mexican women in southern California locals held more than 40 percent of executive board and shop steward positions. They shaped local policies and proved skillful negotiators at contract time. A fierce loyalty to the union developed as the result of rank-and-file participation and leadership. Four decades after the strike, Carmen Bernal Escobar declared, "UCAPAWA was the greatest thing that ever happened to the workers at Cal San. It changed everything and everybody."[10]

In tandem with these union victories, Moreno rose in the ranks of the California CIO, becoming the first Latina to serve on a state CIO council. Her greatest professional challenge began in August 1945 as the union launched a campaign among food processing workers in northern California. A year earlier, UCAPAWA had changed its name to the Food, Tobacco, Agricultural, and Allied Workers of America (FTA), and the union, now the seventh-largest CIO affiliate, girded itself for a jurisdictional battle with the International Brotherhood of Teamsters. In May 1945, the AFL national president turned over its northern California cannery unions to the Teamsters; as a result, disgruntled local leaders approached FTA. Directing an ambitious drive that extended from San José to Sacramento to Modesto, Moreno handpicked her organizing team, including veteran activists like John Tisa from New Jersey and new recruits from the rank and file, among them Lorena Ballard, an "Okie" packinghouse worker. Within three months, the team had collected 14,000 union pledge cards and helped establish twenty-five functioning locals. Winning the NLRB election covering seventy-two plants, FTA, under Moreno's leadership, seemed poised to replicate the successes of FTA members to the south. For example, at Pacific Grape Products in Modesto, "one of the largest independent canneries in California," employees negotiated a path-breaking agreement that included a closed shop, higher wages, overtime, and sick leave.

Moreno's professional success, however, masked personal turmoil. Shortly after her arrival in Los Angeles in 1941, Moreno met and married Jacob Shaffer, a local dry cleaner. But thirteen-year-old Mytyl, so recently reunited with her mother, was in no mood for a stepfather. "I wanted my mother all to myself," she explained; "She was nobody else's. She was mine." Though both Luisa and Mytyl characterized Shaffer as a "nice guy," Mytyl and her stepfather "couldn't get along," and, unable to resolve this friction, Moreno separated from her husband within three months of their marriage.

Mytyl continued to test her boundaries, and her teenaged years were marked by rebellion. Recalling her habit of ditching classes at Manual Arts High School, Mytyl candidly revealed: "We used to get the sailors to go into the liquor stores to buy us some booze. Then we'd go into the alley and drink." Mytyl also enjoyed being a "pen pal" to servicemen. "I had boyfriends in the navy; boyfriends in the army." Indeed, Luisa appeared to have little inkling about the antics of her adolescent daughter. In addition to a hectic schedule as a labor organizer, Luisa Moreno worked behind the scenes raising money from union locals for the legal defense of a group of Mexican American youth who had been unjustly convicted in the Sleepy Lagoon murder case; these young men were characterized by the press as dangerous, zoot suit–wearing *pachucos*. Law enforcement looked upon young Latino men, who wore the drapes and chains and identified themselves as *pachucos*, as juvenile delinquents or gangsters. Imagine Moreno's surprise when she caught Mytyl dressed to the nines as a *pachuca*. According to Mytyl: "One time I came home with a dress that was short like a *pachuca*, [the skirt] came straight down [and tight]. And she [her mother] took the scissors and that was the end of that dress." The two would continue to bicker, and Mytyl, just shy of her seventeenth birthday in 1945, eloped with returning veteran Edward Glomboske, the older brother of a girlfriend. During one of our interviews, Luisa Moreno remarked, "I had a choice. I could organize cannery workers or I could control my teenage daughter. I chose to organize cannery workers and my daughter never forgave me."[11]

In the midst of the northern California organizing drive, Moreno would rediscover romance in her own life. Living in San Francisco and absorbed in the logistics of the cannery campaign, Luisa had not planned on attending the CIO V-J Day dance to celebrate the end of the war, but her union compañera Elizabeth Sasuly had goaded her to have "a little fun." At the dance she noticed a handsome naval officer who looked hauntingly familiar. He was Gray Bemis. They danced, and while on the floor, Luisa summoned up the courage to inquire, "How's your wife?" He stopped to take out an envelope from his pocket—it held his divorce papers. Gray and Luisa married seventeen months later. Many who knew the couple attested to their great love for one another. In Mytyl's words:

"I could just feel the tremendous love he had for my mother . . . taking care of her, surrounding her with love." As her attorney and friend Robert Kenny wrote in a letter to Luisa, "Certainly the story of your marriage and devotion is a love story that most novelists would want to claim as their own creation."[12]

The autumn of 1945 thus held much promise for Moreno personally and professionally. However, the northern California cannery campaign was far from finished, despite winning the NLRB election that included seventy-two plants. In February 1946, the NLRB, under intense political pressure, rescinded the results of the 1945 election and called for a second tabulation. The Teamsters immediately negotiated sweetheart contracts with many northern California firms, contracts that stipulated membership in the Teamsters as a condition for employment. Pro-FTA workers lost their jobs, and Teamster goons physically assaulted FTA organizers as well as rank-and-file members. At the Libby's plant in Sacramento, many Euro-American and Mexican women were locked out after refusing to pay Teamster dues. In protest they set up picket lines outside Libby's, and on May 7, as they held hands and sang the "Star-Spangled Banner," they were assaulted by Seafarer Union and Teamster thugs armed with brass knuckles and other weapons. Scabs, recruited from a local bartenders' union to replace the strikers, were so sickened by the spectacle that they refused to enter the cannery.

The sweetheart contracts, rampant red-baiting, and Teamster terror sealed FTA's defeat. Amazingly, Moreno and her team lost by less than 2,000 votes in the second election. The Teamster victory marked the beginning of the end for FTA in California and nationwide. The union would become a battered target of conservative politicians and rival labor leaders, and by 1950, the union could no longer withstand the barrage of red-baiting that was part and parcel of Cold War politics. Indeed, to combat charges of Communists in their midst, the CIO national leadership ultimately purged ten unions for alleged Communist domination; FTA was one of these unions. FTA represented a grassroots democratic union, where local members exercised real power in running their local, and it represented an alternative to what developed in many mainstream unions during the Cold War, a philosophy of business unionism, where professional staff, rather than the workers, ran the affairs of the local and whose interests often coincided with those of management.

In 1947, Luisa Moreno retired from public life. She and Gray Bemis settled in San Diego, where he was a manager for a plumbing firm and she became a homemaker and amateur photographer. However, a year later, she faced deportation proceedings. According to Moreno, she was offered citizenship in exchange for testifying against legendary Longshoremen union leader Harry Bridges, but she refused to become a "free woman with a mortgaged soul." With Gray Bemis at her side, she left the United States in 1950 under terms listed as "voluntary departure under warrant of deportation" on the grounds that she had once belonged to the Communist Party. She died in her native Guatemala on November 4, 1992.

Like Luisa Capetillo decades earlier, Luisa Moreno believed in the dignity of working people and the rights of immigrants. She lived an extraordinary life from pampered rich girl to bohemian artist in Mexico to an American civil rights and labor leader. She had a national presence in trade union circles, but her role has been largely erased. She represents a rich history of labor history activism among Latinos and Latinas, part of a legacy that extends from Luisa Capetillo to Dolores Huerta. Reconciling with her mother, Mytyl became an activist in her own right. For two decades in Los Angeles until her death in 2002, Mytyl Glomboske became a fixture in a mosaic of social justice causes, including the United Farm Workers, animal rights, environmental advocacy, dignity for AIDS patients, and the Bus Riders' Union (to name just a few). Mytyl always couched her own tireless activism as a tribute to her mother.

Mexican American civil rights activists have held tight to the memory of Luisa Moreno. Renowned California organizer Bert Corona paid her homage, as did her good friend Fred Ross, the civil rights leader who was Cesar Chávez's mentor. Cesar Chávez himself acknowledged her historical significance as a charismatic labor leader. In preparing for her immigration hearings, Luisa Moreno clearly articulated her own legacy. "They can talk about deporting me . . . but they can never deport the people that I've worked with and with whom things were accomplished for the benefit of hundreds of thousands of workers—things that can never be destroyed."[13]

NOTES

1. "Data on Luisa Moreno Bemis," File 53, Robert W. Kenny Collection, Southern California Library for Social Studies Research, Los Angeles, California; Interview with Luisa Moreno, August 4, 1984, conducted by the author; Interview with Luisa Moreno, July 27, 1978, conducted by the author; "Handwritten Notes by Robert Kenny," File 53, Kenny Collection.

2. Interview with Berthe Small, Alba Zatz, and Asa Zatz, September 28, 1996, conducted by the author; Moreno interview, 1984; *Jacksonville (Fla.)*

Journal, September 23, 1943; French Foreign Legion Handbook of Miguel Angel de León (in author's possession); Interview with Luisa Moreno, August 5, 1976, conducted by Albert Camarillo; "Data on Luisa Moreno Bemis," File 53, Kenny Collection.

3. Interview with Luisa Moreno, August 12–13, 1977, conducted by Albert Camarillo; Moreno interview, 1984. Moreno related two separate instances of rats attacking Latino babies: one involving the child of a work friend, and the other the infant of an unemployed Mexican couple.

4. Moreno interview, 1984; Interview with Mytyl Glomboske, August 27, 2001, conducted by the author.

5. Moreno interviews, 1976, 1977, and 1984. This concept of conjugating identities derives from interviews with Luisa Moreno and her daughter, Mytyl Glomboske, as well as my reading of the scholarship of Michael Kearney, Chela Sandoval, Stuart Hall, Paula Moya, and Ramón Gutiérrez. I also owe an enormous intellectual debt to all of my *compañeros* in the University of California Humanities Research Institute "Reshaping the Americas" Residential Research Group (Spring 2002). Moreover, I thank Nancy Hewitt for bringing to my attention the importance of Luisa Capetillo's organizing in Florida to Moreno's efforts twenty years later.

6. Glomboske interview; "Handwritten Notes," Kenny Collection; Small, Zatz, and Zatz interview; Moreno interviews, 1977 and 1978. For more information on the radicalism of the Tampa workers, see Nancy A. Hewitt, *Southern Discomfort: Women's Activism in Tampa, Florida, 1880s–1920s* (Urbana: University of Illinois Press, 2001).

7. Moreno interviews, 1976, 1978. For more information on UCAPAWA, see Vicki L. Ruiz, *Cannery Women, Cannery Lives: Mexican Women, Unionization, and the California Food Processing Industry, 1930–1950* (Albuquerque: University of New Mexico Press, 1987); and for the pecan shellers' strike, see Zaragosa Vargas, "Tejana Radical: Emma Tenayuca and the San Antonio Labor Movement During the Great Depression," *Pacific Historical Review* 66 (November 1997): 553–80; and Vicki L. Ruiz, *From Out of the Shadows: Mexican Women in Twentieth Century America* (New York: Oxford University Press, 1998).

8. Moreno interviews, 1977, 1978; Interview with Josefina Fierro de Bright, August 7, 1977, conducted by Albert Camarillo; Carlos C. Larralde and Richard Griswold del Castillo, "Luisa Moreno: A Hispanic Civil Rights Leader in San Diego," *Journal of San Diego History* 14 (Fall 1995): 284–310. For more information on El Congreso, see David G. Gutiérrez, *Walls and Mirrors: Mexican Americans, Mexican Immigrants, and the Politics of Ethnicity in the Southwest, 1910–1986* (Berkeley: University of California Press, 1995); George Sánchez, *Becoming Mexican American: Ethnicity, Culture, and Identity in Chicano Los Angeles, 1900–1945* (New York: Oxford University Press, 1993); Albert Camarillo, *Chicanos in California* (San Francisco: Boyd and Fraser, 1984);

Mario T. García, *Mexican Americans: Leadership, Ideology, and Identity, 1930–1960* (New Haven: Yale University Press, 1989), 158; and Rodolfo Acuña, *Occupied America*, 4th ed. (New York: Longman, 2000). A brief survey of red-baiting, McCarthyism, the Cold War, and their impact on American life can be found in Jacqueline Jones et al., *Created Equal: A Social and Political History of the United States* (New York: Longman, 2003), 800–63.

9. Moreno interviews, 1976, 1977, 1979; Glomboske interview. The corrido is from "Cifras y Datos," Escuela de Obreros Betabeleros Abril de 1940, Denver, Colorado (UCAPAWA publication, 1940), pp. 14–15. The original stanzas in Spanish are as follows:

> Con muy grande sacrificio
> Y empeño del CIO
> La compañera Moreno
> Esta escuela organizó
> Fijemonos en lo pasado
> Comprendamos la razón
> Divididos no hay progreso
> Solamente con la Unión.

10. This discussion is taken from Ruiz, *From Out of the Shadows*, 80–82; and Ruiz, *Cannery Women*, 69–85.

11. Carey McWilliams, "Luisa Moreno Bemis," August 1949, File 53, Kenny Collection; "Data on Luisa Moreno Bemis," Kenny Collection; "Handwritten Notes," Kenny Collection; Glomboske interview; Moreno interview, 1984.

12. Ruiz, *Cannery Women*, 103–7; Moreno interview, 1984; Small, Zatz, and Zatz interview; Glomboske interview; Letter from Robert W. Kenny to Luisa Bemis, February 11, 1950, File 56, Kenny Collection. Given the fact that Gray Bemis was politically active in southern California before he joined the navy, I surmise that he and Luisa had crossed paths earlier, but in her memories, Luisa remembered the CIO dance as the signifying moment of their courtship.

13. Ruiz, *Cannery Women*, 113–18; "The Case of Luisa Moreno Bemis," Labor Committee for Luisa Moreno Bemis pamphlet (in author's possession); U.S. Department of Justice, Immigration and Naturalization Service, "Closing INS Report (Los Angeles District) on Luisa Moreno," December 6, 1950; Steve Murdoch, *Our Times*, September 9, 1949, File 53, Kenny Collection.

12

CARMEN MIRANDA

The High Price of Fame and Bananas

Brian O'Neil

> Carmen Miranda carried her country in her luggage, and taught people who
> had no idea of our existence to adore our music and our rhythm. Brazil will
> always have an unpayable debt to Carmen Miranda.
>
> Brazilian composer Heitor Villa-Lobos

All too often, people garner in death what they had longed for in life. On
August 12, 1955, the Brazilian government returned the embalmed body
of Carmen Miranda to Rio de Janeiro, the late singer's childhood home.
Since 1939, from the time she began living and working in the United
States, Miranda's relationship with Brazilian critics and officials had been
a troubled one. Pundits regularly charged that Miranda had become too
"Americanized" in the process of attaining Hollywood stardom. Further,
they lambasted Miranda's screen portrayals, which consisted almost exclusively of playing stereotypical Latina roles—often providing comic
relief along the "Souse American Way." In response, Miranda, the self-
proclaimed Ambassadress of Samba, continually maintained that she had
done more than anyone to popularize Brazilian music and culture around
the world. Still, the criticisms of her work, and attendant accusations of
disloyalty, tore upon her soul until her untimely death in 1955. Perhaps
Miranda's spirit felt vindicated by the unprecedented funeral procession
that waded through downtown Rio on August 13. More than a million
mourning Brazilians pressed the cortège route as it moved from the

Cinelândia district to the São João Batista Cemetery. The outpouring of grief dwarfed that displayed during Brazilian president Getúlio Vargas's funeral the year before. In death Miranda received her long-overdue esteem among Brazil's cultural elite. Rio's prominent *Diário de Noticias* posthumously proclaimed that Miranda had been the "the greatest interpreter of Brazilian popular music in the United States."

The life and career of Carmen Miranda embodied many of the social and political developments and contradictions of her times. By becoming a transnational, multimedia star, she faced the impossible mission of trying to please both North American and Latin American audiences, of trying to reconcile the nationalist demands of the Vargas regime in Brazil with the United States government's Pan-American push during World War II. Raised in a strict Catholic culture that valorized feminine domesticity and subservience, she became an independent and enormously successful career woman; indeed, by 1945, her income exceeded that of any woman in the United States. Born to European immigrants, she adopted African-Brazilian styles of song and dance, eventually becoming the international symbol of the samba. While always publicly identifying herself as "Brazilian," throughout her adult life she carried a Portuguese passport and lived as a Latina immigrant in Beverly Hills, California. In the end, these tensions took their toll, both personally and professionally, contributing to her rather early death at age forty-six.

At birth, Carmen Miranda was an unlikely candidate to become the international symbolic essence of "Brazilian-ness" and, later, of "Latin American-ness." She entered the world on February 9, 1909, in the small Portuguese town of Marco de Canavezes, where her parents christened her Maria do Carmo Miranda da Cunha.[1] The second daughter in a family of six children, the young Maria do Carmo spent less than two years in her native Portugal. In 1920, her father, a struggling barber, sold his few possessions and migrated to Rio de Janeiro. Within months, the rest of the family joined him. Maria do Carmo spent her formative years in Rio's racially mixed and working-class Lapa district. Close to the waterfront, this somewhat seedy area was known for its high volume of sailors and prostitutes. In 1919, she and her siblings were accepted to a new convent school established by four French nuns of the Order of St. Vincent. Catering to Lapa's disadvantaged children, the Escola Santa Tereza gave Maria do Carmo her first taste of show business. In order to raise money, the Sisters often directed plays and radio programs that featured their students. In these productions, Maria do Carmo's "little voice" immediately stood out. In 1933, after she had already become in a star in Brazil, she recalled that during those early school performances, "when I was on stage, being in the presence of so many people, I felt in my element!"

Maria do Carmo's initial forays into show business were short-lived. At age fourteen, after a mere six years of formal education at Santa Tereza's, she was forced to drop out of school. Two options generally existed for young women in Lapa during the 1920s—becoming a seamstress or a housewife. In order to help contribute to her family's household income, Maria do Carmo found work as an apprentice milliner at La Femme Chic, an upscale hat store in downtown Rio. In retrospect, the job helped cultivate what would become two of Miranda's most famous trademarks: her singing and her headwear. Maria do Carmo loved to sing the popular Argentine tangos of the day while modeling hats for the customers. After work, she began reworking the European-style hats from the store to make personalized designs for herself and her friends. Her creative flair was later echoed in her own unique interpretations of Brazilian popular music.

In 1925, as Maria do Carmo plied her new trade as a singing milliner, her parents decided that the solution to their chronic financial problems was to open a boardinghouse. The da Cunhas bought a house in Rio's market district that was large enough for the family to live upstairs while boarders rented the downstairs rooms. Maria do Carmo's household duties included bringing meals to the boarders, many of whom, as fate would have it, were budding composers and musicians. Such a milieu fueled Maria do Carmo's dreams of becoming a singing star. Increasingly, she sang at local parties and festivals. At one such event in 1928, she met Josúe de Barros, a guitar player and composer who had migrated to Rio from Bahia, the northeastern Brazilian city famous for its musical tradition. Maria do Carmo's charms—her whimsical spunk, energy, and lively green eyes—immediately struck de Barros. He also noticed something that had always been a source of embarrassment to her: a yellow spot in her left eye. Far from a defect, he proclaimed, the yellow splotch swimming on top of the green iris represented the colors of the Brazilian flag.

Spurred on by Josúe de Barros's encouragement, as well as his connections in the music industry, Maria do Carmo began to actively pursue a career as a professional singer. Knowing her conservative father would never approve of such a course, she adopted the public alias "Carmen Miranda," a combination of her mother's maiden name and the Hispanic version of the latter part of her first name. More than a stage name, "Carmen Miranda" signaled a conscious reinvention of self. Whereas Maria do Carmo was rustic, deferential, and proper, Carmen Miranda would be bold, driven, and audacious. Although she would continue to have private moments as Maria do Carmo with old friends and family, most of the world would only ever know the outrageous performer known as Carmen Miranda. Whether smoking in public, driving her own car, or using the coarse slang of the streets, Carmen Miranda reveled in defying the social constraints placed on women in her era. Her strong-willed independence would serve her well in the male-dominated world of the entertainment industry, both in Brazil and later in the United States.

Carmen Miranda's ascent to national stardom in Brazil took place at a meteoric pace. In 1929, she recorded two Josúe de Barros compositions that became minor hits. The following year, she recorded Joubert de Carvalho's "Taí" and became the most popular singing star in Brazil, a position she would maintain throughout the 1930s. The increasing commercialization of popular music helped make Miranda the first truly national pop icon in Brazil's history. By 1930, the Brazilian music industry had become big business. With radio (introduced in 1922) now a ubiquitous feature of Brazil's urban landscape, Miranda's songs literally vibrated all over the cities of Brazil. In November 1930, Miranda negotiated a recording contract with RCA Victor, the Brazilian subsidiary of the American music conglomerate. Since she was not yet twenty-one, Miranda had to seek the approval (and signature) of her father, who, realizing that her success would be a boon to the entire family, reluctantly consented.

During the 1930s, Miranda recorded nearly three hundred songs, many written exclusively for her by Brazil's most renowned composers, such as de Carvalho, Ary Barroso, Sinval Silva, and Dorvial Caymmi. While recording or performing on radio and stage, she counted on Brazil's top musicians. From 1933 to 1939, Brazil's burgeoning film industry, capitalizing on her widespread appeal, featured her in five films, invariably with parts that allowed her to showcase her vocal talent. Whether on screen, stage, the phonograph, or radio, Miranda reigned as Brazil's biggest entertainment star, all the while maintaining a down-to-earth humbleness that her fans identified with. When the Brazilian daily *O País* asked the star what she needed to be truly happy, Miranda responded tellingly, "A good bowl of soup and the freedom to sing."

Miranda's rise to Brazilian stardom was intricately linked to the growing popularity of a distinctly Brazilian style of music: the samba. The samba, with its roots in the musical traditions of Brazil's substantial African population, developed between 1870 and 1930 in the poverty-stricken hillside *favelas* (slums) of Rio de Janeiro. After the abolition of slavery in 1888 and the lifting of the government's ban on the practice of African religions, the samba slowly evolved as a more relaxed version of the fast-paced *batucada*, an African rhythm imported by slaves brought from Angola to labor on the vast sugar plantations in northeast Brazil. The term "samba" most likely stems from the Angolan word *semba*, which means "prayer" and which is also a synonym for *umbigada*, the touching of one's genitals during ritualistic dances. In both name and spirit, the samba fused the sacred with the profane. The music also proved profitable for record companies and radio stations and quickly spread throughout Brazil.[2]

The expansion of the samba, and of Miranda's popularity, was greatly supported by the refiguring of Brazilian nationalism during the regime of President Getúlio Vargas. Taking power in a military coup in 1930, Vargas ruled Brazil until he himself was ousted by a group of military officers in 1945.[3] During the Vargas era, the Brazilian government attempted to re-define the country's national identity around traits perceived to be non-European and indigenous to Brazil. This led, officially at least, to a new attitude toward African and mixed-race Brazilians. While the desire to celebrate Brazil's multiracial and multicultural reality was not shared by all elites—indeed, many highbrow aficionados of opera continued to view popular culture as cheap, gaudy, and scandalous—the government began to actively promote the samba, with Carmen Miranda as its leading in-terpreter, as the most original and quintessential Brazilian musical form. As a white Brazilian of European heritage, Miranda's appropriation of an essentially black Brazilian musical form served as a racial bridge in the popularizing of samba in Brazil. In much the same way that Elvis Presley made African American rhythm and blues music popular among white Americans in the 1950s, Miranda made the samba acceptable to Brazil's (mostly white) urban elites, while simultaneously extending the renown of the African Brazilian art form throughout the nation. The symbolic embrace of Brazil's multiracial society, however, had real limits. During the 1930s, doors opened for Miranda that were closed to black samba sing-ers and performers, who were never invited to work at the swank Rio night-clubs that booked Miranda.

The culmination of the complex racial politics undergirding Miranda's star image in Brazil occurred in 1938 during the filming of her final Bra-zilian movie, *Banana da Terra*. The film called for a scene set in Bahia, the heart of African Brazilian culture. In an attempt to authenticate her role, Miranda wore a colorful turban and ubiquitous jewelry, and she designed her own version of a *bahiana*, the wide, puffed-up skirt commonly worn by the black female food vendors of Bahia. Miranda learned new dance techniques modeled on local traditions and explicitly played the part of a Bahian while performing Dorvial Caymmi's *samba-bahiano*, "O que é que o bahiana tem?" ("What is it that the Bahian woman has?"). The lyrics of the song answer the question by cataloging the distinct clothes, adornments, and dance movements of black Bahian women. After the film, Miranda modified these "Bahian" elements and incorporated them—along with a high, fruit-filled headdress and a shortened blouse that exposed her bare midriff—into her stage show. This image, that of an exaggerated ersatz Bahian with fruit piled on her head, became a trademark for the rest of her career.

In early 1939, Broadway producer Lee Shubert traveled to Rio and got a firsthand look at Brazil's greatest music, stage, and film star. He was in search of new and exciting acts that could compete with the upcoming New York World's Fair. He believed he had found one after seeing Miranda's extravagant stage show at the Cassino da Urca. Shubert immediately offered Miranda a contract to perform in his summer musical, *The Streets of Paris*. Although she was intrigued by the possibility of performing in New York, Miranda refused to accept the deal unless Shubert agreed to also hire her band, the Bando do Lua. The impresario balked at the added expense, saying that there were plenty of great musicians in New York who could back her. But Miranda remained steadfast. She felt that North American musicians would not be able to authentically create the sounds of Brazil. As a compromise, Shubert agreed to hire the six band members, but he would not pay for their transport to New York. At this point, President Vargas, realizing the propaganda value of Miranda's tour, stepped in and announced that the Brazilian government would sponsor the band by providing free tickets on the Moore-McCormack Ship Line between Rio and New York. The wily dictator believed the expedition would do more than just foment bilateral goodwill—he also hoped that the Ambassadress of Samba's trip would help Brazil win a larger share of the American coffee market. Miranda took very seriously the official sanction of her trip and her duty of representing Brazil to the outside world. Before boarding the New York–bound SS *Uruguay* on May 4, 1939, she held a press conference and told her fans: "My dear friends, in New York I'm going to show the rhythm of Brazilian music, the music of our land. I'm afraid and I feel it's a very big responsibility, but always remember me, and I will never forget you."

Arriving in New York on May 17, 1939, Miranda and her band created an instantaneous media splash. The Brazilian consulate sent six officials to meet their nation's greatest star at the pier in order to interview her for a special shortwave radio program broadcast throughout Brazil. Yet, from her first day in the United States, Miranda's image in the American press took on a comic veneer that would later trouble many Brazilians. Knowing little English, the *New York World-Telegram* quoted Miranda as blurting out to the American journalists: "I say money, money, money. I say twenty words in English. I say money, money, money and I say hot dog!"[4] As Brazilian filmmaker Helena Solberg remarks in the narration of her 1995 documentary, *Bananas Is My Business*, Miranda landed on American shores, and "suddenly she sounds like a bimbo. This is not *our* Carmen. This impression would stay forever with the Americans. This is the Carmen that they will love."

And love her the Americans did. Her six-minute performance at the end of the first act of the *Streets of Paris* launched full-fledged Carmen Miranda mania. Her first song, "The South American Way," was a true hybrid. Written as an Anglicized rhumba by Al Dubin and James McHugh, Miranda brought her own flair to the material. Aloysio de Oliveira, leader of the Bando da Lua, provided Portuguese lyrics while Miranda's pronunciation shifted the English chorus from "South" to "Souse." The song, combined with Miranda's bahiana costume and dancing style, became the highlight of *Streets of Paris*. Though only five feet in height (without her signature platform shoes), Miranda stood tall. *Time Magazine* dubbed her the "oomph that stops the show."[5] New York audiences were enchanted by her exotic costume and accessories, her rapid-rhythm, sing-speak delivery, her ability to sing *con movimientos*, her impish and campy gestures, and her haltingly thick accent while singing the four English words contained in the song's title. One critic summed up her surprising appeal: "Her face is too heavy to be beautiful, her figure is nothing to write home about, and she sings in a foreign language. Yet she is the biggest theatrical sensation of the year."[6] Besides performing in *Streets*, Miranda and her Bando also played two sets nightly at the Waldorf Hotel's Sert Room. Her adopted "Bahian look" became an immediate fashion craze. Macy's launched a "South American Turban Tizzy," and Saks Fifth Avenue dressed its window mannequins in modified versions of the bahiana. Miranda's image, which was quickly moving from the "Queen of Samba" to the "Brazilian Bombshell," pervaded New York City. By the end of the summer of 1939, the press lauded Miranda as "the girl who saved Broadway from the World's Fair."[7]

Miranda was quickly courted by Hollywood, which commonly recruited stars of hit Broadway acts during that time. In the fall of 1939, Darryl F.

Zanuck, vice president of Twentieth Century Fox, hired Miranda and her band to perform three numbers for his new Latin-themed musical, *Down South American Way* (later titled *Down Argentine Way*). Miranda's first Hollywood experience was strictly as a so-called specialty act. She had no speaking lines. Nor did she act, or interact, with the stars of the film, Don Ameche and Alice Faye. Rather, the producers filmed her musical performances on a New York soundstage, then shipped the clips to Hollywood and inserted them into the "club" sequences of the film. Opening with Miranda's Technicolor rendition of "Souse American Way," the movie also featured her singing two Brazilian-flavored songs, "Mamãe o Quero" and "Bamboo-Bamboo."

In July 1940, after fourteen successful months in the United States, Miranda returned to Brazil for what would be a traumatic homecoming. Arriving on July 10, she was greeted by thousands of cheering fans, who led her on a triumphal parade through Rio de Janeiro. The following day, however, criticisms of the star surfaced, especially in the conservative press. Many among the Brazilian upper classes had long been concerned that Miranda's act was "too black," which, in their estimation, negatively reflected on Brazil in international circles. The São Paulo paper *A Folha da Noite* sarcastically editorialized: "So that's how Brazil shines in the United States: [Carmen Miranda] singing bad-tasting black sambas." A few nights later, on July 15, Miranda suffered the greatest humiliation of her professional career. Brazil's First Lady, Darcy Vargas, organized a charity concert for Miranda at the Cassino da Urca. All of Rio's high society showed up to see the Queen of Samba's first show since returning to Brazil. She began by addressing the audience with a hearty "Good night, people!" in English, which provoked a deafening silence from the crowd. She then launched into her regular New York club act, beginning with "The Souse American Way." More silence. A smattering of boos greeted Miranda at the end of each number. Crushed, after five songs, she retired to her dressing room and cried. The next day, the press savaged her for having become "too Americanized."[8]

Miranda never fully recovered from the cold reception she received that night. A few weeks later, she responded to the criticisms by recording and performing new songs that explicitly addressed the challenges to her *brasilidade*, or "Brazilian-ness." Two compositions in particular stood out: "Voltei pro morro" ("I Came Back to the Hills") and "Disseram que voltei americanizada" ("They Say I Came Back Americanized"). In the latter song, the translated lyrics read in part:

How can I be Americanized?
I who was born with samba
And who lives in the open air
Dancing to old *batucada*
All night long![9]

Despite the commercial success of her musical retorts to her Brazilian critics, Miranda carried the sting of the July 15 concert for the rest of her life. In late September, she received a telegram from Shubert indicating that Fox wanted to feature her in more Hollywood films. Feeling rejected by her adopted homeland, she left Brazil on October 3, 1940, and would not return again for fourteen years.

In the United States, Miranda reached the peak of her international stardom over the next five years. She appeared in seven more Fox features: *That Night in Rio* (1941), *Week-End in Havana* (1941), *Springtime in the Rockies* (1942), *The Gang's All Here* (1943), *Four Jills in a Jeep* (1944), *Greenwich Village* (1944), and *Something for the Boys* (1944). Her popularity and salary increased with each successive film. Less than six months after her return from Brazil, Hollywood granted the "Brazilian Bombshell" one of the greatest honors of the day. On March 23, 1941, amid a sea of international press and fans, Miranda stamped her diminutive shoe and hand prints in a block of wet cement on the sidewalk outside Sid Grauman's Chinese Theater on Hollywood Boulevard. "To Sid," she wrote, "Viva In the South American Way!" In early 1942, she fulfilled another Hollywood rite of passage by purchasing a palatial house in Beverly Hills. The Spanish mission–style manor at 616 North Bedford Drive became not just Carmen's home, but also that of her mother and sister Aurora. By 1945, Miranda had become the highest-paid woman in America, with an annual income of well over $200,000.[10] In the process, her image came to be one the most easily recognizable in the world, sparking legions of impersonators.

Miranda's career seemed to always echo larger social and political changes. Much as her rise to stardom in Brazil was conditioned by the new nationalism of the Vargas regime, Miranda's ascent to Hollywood fame was shaped by a unique set of international circumstances. Although Miranda's initial enlistment by Hollywood was due in large part to her own talents, a larger sea change in U.S.–Latin American relations helped keep her services in high demand throughout the World War II years. The same year she signed on at Fox Studios, Nelson Rockefeller, grandson of oil tycoon John D. Rockefeller and heir to one of the world's greatest fortunes, had submitted a proposal to President Franklin Roosevelt urging that the United States align itself much more closely with the countries of the Western Hemisphere. Given the growing threat of war with Germany, Roosevelt concurred. By executive order, he created the Office of the Coordinator of Inter-American Affairs (CIAA) in August 1940 and appointed Rockefeller as coordinator. The office's mission was to manage all official relations with Latin America in order to shore up economic ties and thwart Nazi influence in the region. The CIAA essentially specialized in propaganda on all fronts: the press, radio broadcasts, cultural exchanges, and the film industry. The last was considered so important that Rockefeller created a special Motion Picture Section and selected his old friend John Whitney to direct it.[11]

Whitney was fully convinced of the power that Hollywood films could exert in the two-pronged campaign to win the hearts and minds of Latin Americans and to convince Americans of the benefits of Pan-American friendship. To be truly effective at these goals, Whitney reasoned, Hollywood would have to begin to incorporate more Latin American talent into its movies and be "induced to voluntarily refrain from producing and/or distributing in the other Americas pictures that are objectionable or create a bad impression of America or Latin Americans."[12] Throughout the early 1940s, Whitney's office established personal relationships with Hollywood's studio brass and promoted what became an unprecedented hiring of Latin American actors. For their part, studio producers like Zanuck needed little coaxing. With their primary foreign market of Europe engulfed in war, the five major studios sought to offset losses by more aggressively exploiting the Latin American markets. Thus, in the minds of Hollywood producers, patriotism, anti-Nazi sentiment, and, above all, economic interest nicely complemented each other and resulted in a new celluloid Good Neighbor policy. As a result, Hollywood recruited new talent, primarily singers and dancers, from all over the Americas. In addition to Miranda, notable Latin American imports included Desi Arnaz and César Romero from Cuba, Margo from Mexico, the Dominican actress Maria Móntez, and the Colombian baritone Carlos Ramírez.

Hollywood's Good Neighbor policy proved a double-edged sword for Miranda and the other Latin artists brought to Tinseltown. No doubt, the increased visibility of Latin Americans and Latin themes on the movie screen boosted the American public's awareness of and possibly warm feelings toward their southern neighbors. The new demand for Latin performers often brought exceptional financial rewards, as was the case for

Miranda. Yet Hollywood's Latin-themed films also produced unending frustrations for the Latinos involved in their production. While living in Hollywood, Miranda never tired of telling her fans back in Brazil that she was helping inject "authentic" Brazilian music and culture into American movies. Miranda's Hollywood films, however, could never escape being concocted, hybrid representations of Brazil and other Latin locales. Although the industry, in compliance with the CIAA guidelines, had declared its intention to stop the age-old tradition of depicting the region as a culturally homogenous entity, in the eyes of many Latin American critics, the studios failed miserably. A complaint filed at the American embassy in Buenos Aires concerning Carmen Miranda's first film, *Down Argentine Way* (1940), was typical: "Carmen Miranda, a Brazilian star, sings in Portuguese a Tin Pan Alley rhumba called 'Down Argentine Way,' which speaks of tangos. Don Ameche does a rhumba in Spanish with castanets and talks about orchids, as rare in Argentina as in New York. . . . [In short,] everyone who portrays an Argentine in it from the first to the last is outrageously ridiculous. When will they ever get it right?"[13]

The causes of Hollywood's inability to "get it right" were multiple. First, instead of shooting on location, most producers simply inserted short, montage sequences of on-site panoramic footage at the beginning of the narrative. More important, despite the laudable intentions of some individuals, the majority of the writers, directors, and composers involved in the production of these films did not have the cultural knowledge to judge the accuracy of the representations of different Latin American locales. The comments of Mack Gordon, one of Miranda's official composers at Fox, are telling. Queried about the authenticity of his songs for *Week-End in Havana* (1941), he explained, "I feel confident of turning out a good job—I've been smoking Havana cigars for fifteen years!" He also commented on how he had found similar inspiration for a previous Miranda picture: "When we wrote the songs for *That Night in Rio*, we went to Monterey and took an isolated cottage on the bay there. You see, Rio is also on a bay."[14]

On balance, Miranda's characters, and Hollywood's wartime representations of Latin Americans generally, could hardly be characterized as respectful or nuanced. With few exceptions, old stereotypes of alternately docile, stupid, and/or villainous "greasers" gave way to new stereotypical images of Latinos as perpetual fun-seekers, flirts, and flamboyant dancers.[15] Owing to the popularity of new Latin rhythms like the conga and the rhumba, Latin Americans in Hollywood were identified with their music, and consequently, they became mainstays in the immensely profitable musical comedy genre. Film studies scholar Ana López has noted how Latin Americans incorporated into this genre were simultaneously marginalized and privileged. Invariably denied roles with a principal narrative function, they appeared intermittently as agents of exotic entertainment, the locus of pleasure in the production.[16] Taken as whole, the Latin American musicals painted a mythical land where gringos could play with their Latin neighbors. This romantic world of dancing señoritas and debonair caballeros reached its symbolic and popular peak with the eight "exotic locale" fantasies featuring Carmen Miranda produced by Twentieth Century Fox in state-of-the-art Technicolor.

Of the dozens of wartime musicals produced, Miranda's films traded to an unprecedented extent on the Good Neighbor policy. Nearly every one begins or ends with a bilingual paean to the blessings of Pan-Americanism. The rhumba "Chica, Chica, Boom, Chic," composed by Harry Warren and Mack Gordon for *That Night in Rio* (1941), is typical. Miranda, in full Bahian regalia, opens the film rapidly singing in Portuguese, with her trademark sinuous hand and body movements. At the midpoint of the number, Don Ameche enters the imaginary Brazilian set wearing a white, freshly starched admiral's uniform. On cue, with a wink from Miranda, he continues the song in English:

> My friends, I extend my felicitations,
> To our South American relations.
> May we never leave behind us
> All the common ties that bind us.
> One hundred and thirty million people
> Send regards to you.
> Before I return,
> There's one thing you can do . . . .
> Sing the Boom Chica, Boom Chica, Chica, Chica, Boom, Chic.

Even those films which featured non–Latin American locales or themes managed to include a song and dance routine that celebrated hemispheric unity. Although the plot of the 1942 hit *Springtime in the Rockies* contained nary a reference to Latin America and was in fact set in Lake Louise, Canada, the film ends with stars Betty Grable, John Payne, Cesar Romero, and Carmen Miranda joyfully executing a rhumba-samba-conga number called "The Panamericana Jubilee."

Miranda's most notorious and enduring film characterization occurred in Busby Berkeley's 1943 hit *The Gang's All Here*, whose opening sequence explicitly promoted the Good Neighbor message. On a huge nightclub stage, a model of the SS *Brazil* is docking. Quickly, workers begin unloading the ship's cargo, which consists of a veritable inventory of Latin America's major goods for export: coffee, bananas, sugar, and, finally, Miranda herself. As Miranda enters center stage, the nightclub host proclaims: "Well, there's your Good Neighbor policy! Come on honey, let's Good Neighbor it!" Miranda then proceeds to teach the audience the "Uncle Sam-ba." Halfway through the film comes "The Lady in the Tutti-Frutti Hat," the most excessive and spectacular number in Miranda's film career. From above, Berkeley films Miranda being wheeled out onto a faux desert island inhabited by two opposing chorus lines of female dancers, alternately wielding enormous bananas or strawberries. In dance spectacles that the *New York Times* reviewer called "straight from Freud," the banana lines wave up and down over the strawberries before the camera slowly pulls away to reveal Miranda wearing a twelve-story crown of blossoming bananas. The future logo for Chiquita bananas was born.

From today's vantage point, Miranda's films and screen image are troublesome. The sexual politics of her films, for example, consistently represented, and reinforced, the larger asymmetries of power between the United States and Latin America. While Miranda's musical numbers regularly stressed that cultural differences between North Americans and Latin Americans could be transcended through the international languages of music and dance, rarely was a Latin American "neighbor" (usually Miranda and César Romero) permanently mated with the narrative's Anglo protagonists (such as Betty Grable, John Payne, or Alice Faye). The characters portrayed by Miranda, in particular, always remained either contentedly and coquettishly single or hopelessly attached to a Latino playboy. It might be fine to sing, dance, and flirt together, but not to become seriously involved with each other. Moreover, throughout Fox's wartime cycle, Miranda's on-screen character and function were remarkably consistent. Regardless of the narrative or the locale, she remained the same from film to film. Alternately named Carmen, Rosita, Querida, or Chiquita, she always played an exaggerated, homogenized Latina. Through her Hollywood films, the previously self-styled *Brazilian* Miranda, the "Queen of Samba," who often exclaimed that she had "nothing to do with people of Spanish descent," was transformed into an undifferentiated, spectacular Latin Other. Never playing the principal lead, she functioned as an exotic and outrageous fetish, ever ready to entertain. Irrespective of whether a given scene was dramatic or musical, the sources of her entertainment remained consistent: her garishly colorful and frequently fruit-adorned outfits, her rhythmic body gestures and dancing style, her incessantly expressive eye manipulations, and the inherent "foreignness" of her fluent Portuguese combined with the inflated accent and linguistic malapropisms of her spoken English.

Miranda was clearly aware of being trapped in typecast roles. Although she never protested explicitly, she adopted self-parody and humor to subtly press her case. In her stage show, she regularly included her spoken-word piece "Bananas Is My Business," in which she jokingly brainstorms about other career avenues and then concludes, "But why should I, when I make my money with bananas?" Miranda also reveled in the deluge of impersonators that donned tutti-frutti hats in the 1940s and 1950s. In fact, she personally gave Mickey Rooney backstage tips for his turn as the Brazilian Bombshell in *Babes on Broadway* (1941).[17] Some film scholars have argued that the sheer outrageousness of Miranda's image was so excessive and exaggerated that, to some degree, it worked to delegitimize the often racist and sexist stereotypes underlying her Hollywood roles.[18] It may be impossible to known exactly how Miranda or her fans felt about her screen image, but there is no question of her broad appeal. Both men and women enjoyed her performances. And although some elites in Brazil and other Latin American nations decried her images, she always remained popular with working-class Latinos throughout the Americas. Perhaps just seeing a Latin star become so famous engendered pride. Her shows in the Mexican theaters of downtown Los Angeles, for instance, were always standing-room-only events at which the Mexican and Mexican American crowds often referred to Miranda as "our star."[19]

Miranda's career and personal life spiraled downward from the late 1940s to her death in 1955. With the end of World War II, Hollywood's fascination with all things Latin subsided. Like so many other Hollywood stars, Miranda was never able to break free of her established stereotype. She appeared in just six more films.[20] In 1947, she costarred with Groucho Marx in *Copacabana*, a film that she hoped would be her breakthrough as serious actress. The movie, however, flopped. The following year, she got married for the first time, to David Sebastian, a small-time American producer who became her manager. Her marriage, which by all family accounts was an abusive one, came under even more strain after Miranda suffered a miscarriage in 1948. For the remainder of her life, she poured herself into her work, constantly performing on stages around the world. The grueling pace led to an addiction to a dangerous daily cocktail of amphetamines and sleeping pills. Clinically depressed, the fading star suffered an emotional breakdown in 1954. After recuperating (and receiving electroshock treatments) in Brazil during the first months of 1955, Miranda returned to Hollywood and her nonstop work schedule. On August 4, 1955, while taping a segment for the Jimmy Durante television show, Carmen Miranda suffered a mild heart attack. Sometime the following morning, on August 5, she suffered another, this time fatal, heart attack. She was just forty-six years old. Conceding to the wishes of her family, Sebastian allowed her body to be flown back to Brazil, where she was honored in death with a period of national mourning.

The Latina legacy of Carmen Miranda, like the woman herself, is complex and multifaceted. Her Hollywood film images reinforced and extended prevailing stereotypes that subsequent Latina actresses still must combat. Her example speaks to the pitfalls and challenges involved in Latino artists "crossing over" in the American entertainment industry. On his first English-language album, *Nothing but the Truth* in 1988, Panamanian salsa singer Rubén Blades referred to this dilemma in his song, "The Miranda Syndrome." "The basic element of the song," he noted, "was how the world has been fooled by stereotypes and false promises."[21] On the other hand, Miranda's story has served as inspiration for those of humble origins who seek to achieve fame and fortune. Around the world, her image has inspired countless gay male drag queens and others seeking to reinvent themselves in bold and spectacular ways. In Brazil, her life and music is now celebrated and used to promote tourism. Rio's Carmen Miranda Museum welcomes tens of thousands of visitors each year. Contemporary Brazilian artists who have garnered international acclaim, such as Caetano Veloso, see themselves as following in Miranda's footsteps, her musical progeny as it were. Indeed, perhaps more broadly, we are all metaphorically dancing to Miranda's style of hybrid music in the early twenty-first century—an age of increasing transnational flows of peoples, cultures, and, of course, bananas.

NOTES

1. All biographical information has been gleaned from Martha Gil-Montero's *Brazilian Bombshell: The Biography of Carmen Miranda* (New York: D. I. Fine, 1989); David Nasser's *A vida trepidante de Carmen Miranda* (Rio de Janeiro: Edições O Cruzeiro, 1966); and Helena Solberg's excellent documentary *Carmen Miranda: Bananas Is My Business* (1995).

2. See Alma Guillermoprieto, *Samba* (New York: Random House, 1990).

3. Vargas again served as Brazil's president from 1951 until 1954, when he committed suicide.

4. Quoted in Gil-Montero, *Brazilian Bombshell*, 74.

5. "New Shows in Manhattan," *Time*, July 3, 1939, 42–43.

6. Quoted in Allan Woll, *The Latin Image in American Film* (Los Angeles: UCLA Latin American Center Publications, 1977), 69.

7. Gil-Montero, *Brazilian Bombshell*, 74–85.

8. Darién J. Davis, "To Be or Not to Be Brazilian? Carmen Miranda's Fame and 'Authenticity' in the United States," in *Strange Pilgrimages: Exile, Travel, and National Identity in Latin America, 1800–1990s*, ed. Ingrid E. Fey and Karen Racine (Wilmington, Del.: Scholarly Resources, 2000), 233–48.

9. Ibid., 241.

10. Gil-Montero, *Brazilian Bombshell*, 154.

11. For an overview of Hollywood's Good Neighbor policy, see Brian O'Neil, "The Demands of Authenticity: Addison Durland and Hollywood's Latin Images during World War II," in *Classic Hollywood, Classic Whiteness*, ed. Daniel Bernardi (Minneapolis: University of Minnesota Press, 2001), 359–85.

12. Donald W. Roland, comp., *History of the Office of the Coordinator of Inter-American Affairs* (Washington, D.C.: Government Printing Office, 1947), 71.

13. Motion Picture Notes by Joe D. Walstrom, U.S. Embassy, Buenos Aires, September 26, 1941, Records of the Office of Inter-American Affairs, Record Group 229, Box 214, Folder "Reaction," Entry 1, National Archives and Records Administration, Washington, D.C.

14. Quoted in Woll, *Latin Image in American Film*, 69–70.

15. On the prevailing stereotypes of Latinos in Hollywood cinema prior to World War II, see ibid.; and George Hadley-Garcia, *Hispanic Hollywood: The Latins in Motion Pictures* (New York: Carol Publishing Group, 1990).

16. Ana M. López, "Are All Latins from Manhattan? Hollywood, Ethnography, and Cultural Colonialism," in *Unspeakable Images: Ethnicity and the American Cinema*, ed. Lester D. Friedman (Urbana: University of Illinois Press, 1991), 404–24.

17. Other notable cinematic Miranda impersonators have included Bugs Bunny in *What's Cookin' Doc?* (1944), Bob Hope in *Road to Rio* (1947), and Jerry Lewis in *Scared Stiff* (1953).

18. Shari Roberts, "'The Lady in the Tutti-Frutti Hat': Carmen Miranda, a Spectacle of Ethnicity," *Cinema Journal* 32 (Spring 1993): 3–23.

19. *La Opinión* (Los Angeles), March 18, 1941.

20. *Doll Face* (1945), *If I'm Lucky* (1946), *Copacabana* (1947), *A Date with Judy* (1948), *Nancy Goes to Rio* (1950), and *Scared Stiff* (1953).

21. Liner notes of Rubén Blades, *Nothing but the Truth* (Elektra Records, 1988).

13

ANTONIA PANTOJA AND THE POWER OF COMMUNITY ACTION

Virginia Sánchez Korrol

I started to get ideas as to the rights of people: the rights of people to
organize, the rights of people to fight for the problems that affect them.

Antonia Pantoja

All eyes were riveted on the petite, gray-haired senior citizen at the po-
dium. In September 2001, scholars, politicians, community organizers,
educators, and students filled the auditorium precisely because she had
organized the symposium on New York Puerto Rican history. Many came
because she was a legendary figure, regarded as the most influential community activist since the 1950s; some had never met her but knew her
history; and others wondered why she had returned to the city after an
absence of over two decades. With a vigor and fervor belying her seventy-
nine years, Antonia Pantoja addressed the gathering. Concerned about a
number of issues, she reflected upon the status of her beloved Puerto Rican
community. The group's advancement since the mid-twentieth century,
she felt, had diminished. A growing national "English Only" movement,
budgetary shortfalls, and perceived lack of interest among new Latinos
threatened the hard-won gains in bilingual education. Pantoja then announced that she had returned to take up the mantle of leadership, to
shore up educational gains, and to attract supporters. She would promote
the city's vibrant Puerto Rican legacy by accelerating historical research
and energizing collective activism. And as colleagues in this mission, she

would count on the Puerto Rican and Latino community's leading intellectual, political, and corporate figures.

What motivated this resolute woman so identified with Puerto Rican community institutions to return to the scene of her earliest accomplishments? After a lifetime of exemplary contributions, what did Pantoja feel remained undone? Her call to arms received a standing ovation. Some symposium participants, however, felt that Pantoja was out of touch and wondered about her motivations, though few doubted her talents. A builder of institutions, this renowned grassroots activist had championed Puerto Rican and Latino rights in an era when their political currency was largely invisible. A woman who forged national and international enterprises, she created the framework to found a university and received the highest honor given to an American citizen, the Presidential Medal of Freedom, from President William Jefferson Clinton. Although Pantoja maintained a very private personal life, interviews, newspaper articles, and her memoirs reveal her values, goals, and commitment to community empowerment and may shed light on her determination to engage in social change in New York City at an age when other seasoned community organizers tend to ponder their retirement.

Born in 1921 in Puerta de Tierra, Puerto Rico, Pantoja grew up in *Barrio Obrero*, a poor workers' slum in Old San Juan. Daughter of an unwed mother, Alejandrina Pantoja, and an unknown father, Toñita, as she was known in the family, lived with her grandparents. A sickly child, she suffered from asthma, which would cause problems all her life, and she survived tuberculosis during her first year of high school. Her grandfather, Conrado Pantoja Santos, was a self-educated man and union organizer known for his concerns about the plight of the workers in Puerto Rico. A foreman for the American Tobacco Company, he lost his job when the factory moved to avoid making a settlement with striking workers. Years of hardship ensued, but Antonia remembered him as "more an invented figure in my memory . . . a generous and loving man." From him, she learned about inequality, injustice, and the struggles for workers' rights. A voracious and precocious reader, Antonia grasped the importance of collective action, most likely from reading her grandfather's booklets on union organizing, including Lenin's "Letters to the Workers," at an early age. In her own words, she "started to get ideas as to the rights of people: the rights of people to organize, the rights of the people to fight for the problems that affect them."

Her relationship with her grandmother, Luisa Acosta Pantoja, appeared less sanguine, as Toñita perceived her to be undemonstrative and aloof, an opinion that softened as she matured. Antonia's images of woman-hood stemmed from her observations of the women in her life. Her mother, Alejandrina, grandmother Luisa, and aunt Magui provided ex-emplary lessons for Antonia about hard-working individuals who, despite poverty, managed to hold together the family unit. It was in her grand-parents' home that Antonia developed her sense of self-sufficiency, dig-nity, and pride. "As a child," she recalled, "I needed to make decisions and find solutions to issues and events that were never addressed by the adults in my world. I knew that I must be the maker of who I would be-come. . . . In spite of the paucity in their own lives, they transmitted a sense of value for my self and a determination to be self-sufficient and independent."[1]

The Puerto Rico of Pantoja's formative years and young adulthood was steeped in poverty. In 1928, when Antonia was seven years old, the is-land suffered a devastating blow as hurricane San Felipe virtually destroyed the predominantly agricultural economy. The cultivation of coffee, sugar, and other land-based products practically disappeared. A migration of rural workers to urban areas followed, and even the governor of Puerto Rico, Theodore Roosevelt Jr., declared that poverty was so widespread that hunger, to the verge of starvation, was commonplace.[2] Three quarters of the population was rural and survived on an average yearly income of $150. Town workers like Antonia's family fared slightly better. In the rural sectors, four out of five workers were landless due to a system of *Latifundio* (land usage), which put 26 percent of all rural land in the hands of mostly American corporations, partnerships, or private holdings.

By 1932, when Antonia was eleven years old, the Depression had deci-mated the economy of the island, still reeling from the effects of San Felipe. Since Puerto Rico was a United States colony, food, clothing, construc-tion materials, furniture, medicine, and other staples were imported from the U.S. mainland and sold at higher prices. Slums, like the infamous *El Fanguito*, named for its pestilence-laden swamps, where people lived in makeshift wooden shacks without electricity or indoor plumbing, were notorious for widespread disease. Education was a luxury that few could afford, and most children quit going to school after the third or fourth grade out of financial necessity. Some managed to graduate from high school. Others entered seasonal sugarcane work as cheap labor, or took in garment piecework in the home. Yet others remained unemployed, living off whatever the land yielded. Without educated, talented individu-als to take the lead, it was difficult to create programs that addressed pov-erty and progress in Puerto Rico.

A curious and intelligent child, Antonia loved learning and was one of the lucky few who received an education. When she was a student in the public schools, the commissioner of education was the progressive visionary Dr. José Padín. Padín believed that social welfare and economic programs based on sound education were the keys for solving the problems of the island. He supported teaching in the vernacular (in Spanish), a radical departure from the English-only instruction insisted on by his predecessors. He believed that the use of Spanish would lead to cultural growth and development. Furthermore, he viewed rural schools as hubs for community rehabilitation. While his ideas were seen by some as anti-American, and not universally supported, Antonia's early schooling came out of this tradition and may have influenced her perceptions about the role of schools in communities, the importance of the Spanish language and Puerto Rican culture, and individual responsibility for social reform.

When Antonia graduated from the eighth grade, she insisted on continuing her education, but her family, in desperate financial straits, expected her to work. Her uncle Conradito, however, intervened and encouraged her to attend high school, not because he believed in the value of education, but because he feared no one would hire someone with her skinny, sickly appearance. Lacking bus fare and proper clothing, it was difficult for Antonia to leave the working-class confines of *Barrio Obrero*, a diverse, racially mixed community of employed or underemployed workers, musicians, carpenters, and cigar makers, an ambience where she felt most comfortable. High school enabled Antonia to negotiate coming-of-age conflicts and a rigid class structure. Pantoja remembered, "At Central High School, there was no chance but to associate with people whose names and incomes defined their importance and status. Now, thrown together with a different social group and social class, I no longer felt self-assured and confident. Here, social class was the major determinant of who you were and how you were treated and respected."[3] She walked long distances to school, covering the holes in her shoes with cardboard, and worked in the afternoons. Such adversity prepared Antonia to deal with different social situations.

By the time that Pantoja graduated from high school, she was living with her mother, who had married Francisco López. Pantoja and her mother had always maintained a relationship, even though they did not always live together. Enjoying close bonds with her younger half siblings, Pantoja wanted to keep the family together under one roof. As Francisco López often failed to contribute to the household income, survival depended on Pantoja's after-school earnings and her mother's catering business run from the home.

Although money was scarce, Pantoja decided to pursue a college degree because, as she put it, "I was always striving for better opportunities and chances for myself and those around me." With a scholarship and the meager savings she and her mother had managed to scrape together, Pantoja entered the University of Puerto Rico during the late-1930s. The university teemed with writers and poets who pontificated about the essence and substance of Puerto Rican cultural struggles. Although she enrolled in the normal school of the university, which concentrated on preparing teachers, Antonia had access to some of the greatest thinkers of the day. She would have read John Dewey's philosophy of education and perhaps Antonio Pedreira's *Insularismo*, kept abreast of U.S. social science research, and possibly attended a lecture or two by the noted visiting professor José Vasconcelos, architect of the post-Revolutionary Mexican educational system. Pantoja's favorite subjects included English literature, economics, and art and design. In a very nationalistic observation she made years later, she commented, "as I began to develop a clear political consciousness, I would question my childhood love of the English classes and my dates with Americans during the war years."[4]

Graduating in 1942 with elementary school teaching credentials, Pantoja became the breadwinner for her mother and siblings, who could not rely on the erratic earnings of Francisco López. The family faced hardships because World War II caused interruptions in the flow of goods to and from the island. On her teacher's salary, she moved her family to a new housing project, but Pantoja found herself in constant debt. She taught in a one-room, rural school in a mountain town called Cuchilla. To teach in Puerto Rico's rural mountain schools required great sacrifices on the part of instructors, who were often not much older than their students. For Pantoja it meant riding what she described as a "horse with bad habits" up the mountain range to begin her work week and then home again on Friday. Genuinely appreciated by both students and parents in that small, isolated community, she treasured this period of her life. "Every Friday when I left the mountains to return to my home for the weekend, my horse would move very slowly because the children would hold on to his tail. I always left with my arms full of gardenias, pineapples, and oranges. I would hear their voices saying, '¿Maestra, regresará el domingo?' [Teacher, will you return on Sunday?] I would answer, 'Sí, volveré.' [Yes, I'll return.] This period of teaching in the mountains was a most unforgettable experience that helped me to become who I am."

Although teaching offered Antonia a way to make a living, she yearned for greater challenges. Financial binds, coupled with the family's expectations that she should be married or at least dating, conflicted with Pantoja's career interests. She described her life on the weekends as "full of tension and arguments with my mother. I worried about the bills that were always paid late. Sometimes, because of the economic conditions on the island, I did not receive my teaching salary for three months. . . . I had no one to talk to about these conditions and my feelings."[5] Moving to New York City would provide distance from the familial hearth and provide opportunities not available to her in Puerto Rico. In 1944 she left for New York City, one of thousands of migrants forming a massive chain from the island to the United States in search of a better future. Pantoja's scant knowledge about the city was derived from anecdotes told by her aunt and mother, who had both spent time there, from other visitors, and from Hollywood movies and popular books, but the reality of life in New York proved much crueler than anything she had imagined.

The number of Puerto Ricans in the United States escalated from 69,967 in the 1940s to 887,662 in the 1960s. It is estimated that more than 42,000 Puertorriqueños migrated every year between 1946 and 1956, the majority of whom remained in New York City. Some twenty years later, the city's Puerto Rican population would exceed one million individuals.[6] The numbers of women equaled those of men in the migrant flow; wives trailed military husbands recently discharged from service; and children accompanied their parents or came with relatives to join parents who already resided in the city. However, for many of the migrants, New York was not the utopia they imagined. Life in New York rendered them virtually powerless, concentrated into poor neighborhoods without political clout and decent jobs. Racism and discrimination, coupled with lack of knowledge and experience to negotiate good jobs, housing, and safer workplaces, loomed large in the lives of these working-class migrants. The industrial base that had in the past attracted migrants and provided entry-level jobs for newcomers had ceased to expand. Manufacturing rapidly gave way to finance and professional services. Industries, especially garment work—an important sector for hiring Puerto Rican women—relocated to other countries, or to the Deep South, where labor was cheap and plentiful. Advancements in production and automation required fewer unskilled workers and more employees who could read and speak English. Puerto Rican labor, positioned in marginal industries, factories, laundries, restaurants, and janitorial services, rested on tenuous foundations.

Pantoja found lodging with an old high school friend who lived in the South Bronx. She took a series of factory jobs, including being a welder and a garment worker. While she easily doubled her salary from what she earned as a country teacher, she found working conditions for Puerto Rican migrants very disturbing. She remembered, "those jobs in the factories . . . gave me direct experience with the problems that immigrants from Puerto Rico suffered." Pantoja's first attempts to organize workers occurred when she worked as a designer in a lampshade factory. Aware that newly hired Puerto Rican women workers were exploited, she contacted a union organizer from the electrical workers' union to help her form a negotiating committee. Other violations in the workplace prompted Pantoja to organize a union, and after discussions with management, an amicable settlement was reached.

Prejudice and discrimination against Puerto Ricans was often ethno-racial in nature.[7] "In those days, people coming from Puerto Rico usually came in a ship called the *Marine Tiger*. Even though I had come by the SS *Florida*, young people made fun of me when I walked on the streets, shouting 'Marine Tiger,' meaning to hurt and ridicule me," wrote Pantoja of an early Bronx experience. Describing herself as *grifa*—a light-skinned person with kinky hair and Caucasian features—she found that skin color mattered a great deal in the United States. She had experienced racism firsthand when the ship that brought her from Puerto Rico disembarked in New Orleans. Segregated in a coffee shop and on the train she rode to New York, Pantoja understood the negative connotations of the word "Nigger." In Puerto Rico, she had never been denied entrance anywhere because of her features or skin color.

For newly arrived migrants of the postwar era, changes in the New York City's economy and in the Puerto Rican neighborhoods would have as profound an effect as racial discrimination. As city government moved forward, building new bridges, superhighways, and impressive landmark institutions, like Lincoln Center and the New York Coliseum at Columbus Circle, old neighborhoods, many of which were predominantly black and Puerto Rican, were destroyed. As some neighborhoods succumbed to the wrecking ball, their inhabitants spread throughout the city. Dismantling the established infrastructure meant dispersal of old area leaders, small businesses, and closures of *bodegas, farmacias, botánicas,* and other familiar sights. Many early Puerto Rican or Latino organizations, mutual aid societies, trade unions, and professional and sociocultural associations closed their doors. Religious organizations, however, continued to advocate for the welfare of the Puerto Rican communities. The teacher organizations formed in the late 1940s and early 1950s survived, and some groups, like the Home Town clubs, the backbone of the Puerto Rican Day Parade, remained strong. But fraternal associations like the Porto Rican Brotherhood or leftist political groups like the Socialist Party, which had focused on protecting and advancing immigrant or migrant rights, had definitely faded.

Living in the city provided Antonia with the opportunity to discover New York's intellectual and artistic offerings outside of the Puerto Rican community. In the period she calls her "Years of a Bohemian Life," Pantoja surrounded herself with a diverse group of friends interested in music, art, and politics. Her apartment near Greenwich Village became a weekend destination for struggling artists, pacifists, intellectuals, and others interested in discussing modern art and architecture, Marxism, the Spanish Civil War, and the struggle for a Jewish homeland.

Sometime around 1950, Pantoja was hired to work at the 110th Street Community Center, which allowed her to work with Puerto Rican children again. "The job at the Center," wrote Pantoja, "would reconnect me to my Puerto Rican roots, as it required that I interview Puerto Rican families to secure parental consent for their children's participation in the Center's program." To better understand their problems, she took courses on Puerto Rican history at a local school and was amazed to discover heroes like Luisa Capetillo, whose accomplishments were not taught in Puerto Rican schools. A newly formed awareness of the politics of colonialism and emigration led to more study. "This information was a great discovery for me," Pantoja recounted, "but . . . I was afraid of such ideas. I had grown up in Puerto Rico when it was illegal to fly the flag of Puerto Rico. . . . We had been raised in fear of any expressions or actions that could be used to accuse one of treason to the United States."[8] The subsequent closing of the community center coincided with Pantoja's growing desire to return to school to better prepare to serve her community. Learning about free tuition at the City University, she enrolled in Hunter College to complete her baccalaureate degree.

Pantoja's sociopolitical activism began when she joined a group of students and other young Puerto Ricans who shared many of her progressive ideas. Eager to understand why Puerto Ricans in New York suffered discrimination and why they experienced lower standards of living, health care, and education despite being American citizens and wanting to find solutions for these problems, these youthful rebels coalesced into the Hispanic Young Adults Association (HYAA). This group initially focused on the interests of students, young professionals, and college-educated social workers to develop an analytical framework for understanding the Puerto Rican presence in the United States. At first, its members sought to advance the adoption of mainstream American mores and class values. However, Pantoja, who promptly became a spokesperson, pushed for the creation of a responsible leadership corps equipped with the background and knowledge to respond to the needs of the community through action and advocacy. Among the group's members were Puerto Ricans from the island and *Nuyoricans*—those born in New York City. They included politically committed individuals such as Luis and Cecilia Núñez, José and Josie Morales, Josephine Nieves, Eddie González, Alice Cardona, and Yolanda Sánchez, all of whom would work with Antonia over the years in countless ventures and rise to positions of prominence in their own right.

By 1956, the issue of identity provoked the group to rethink its name and mission. Although HYAA's mission remained intact, the term "Hispanic" became hotly debated. Why use Hispanic rather than Puerto Rican? And, as Puerto Ricans, how would assimilation help the community advance when as American citizens they purportedly held the same rights as other citizens? Indeed, Puerto Ricans formed the largest Spanish-speaking group in the city but lived among non-Hispanics who could not differentiate one Spanish-speaking ethnic group from another. Most city organizations that served the Spanish-speaking population were called Hispanic, even though their clientele was predominantly Puerto Rican. Following a contentious HYAA meeting, the organization renamed itself to better reflect its mission and identity. Aggressively promoting a new name, Pantoja pointedly asked the group, "Are we ashamed of calling ourselves Puerto Ricans?" The Hispanic Young Adult Association thereafter became the Puerto Rican Association for Community Affairs (PRACA), one of the most important agencies to serve New York Puerto Ricans.

With staggering numbers of migrants, there was a great need in the early 1950s for an organization like PRACA that could advocate specifically on behalf of the Puerto Rican or Nuyorican community. This great migration had already generated quasi-government agencies, such as the Migration Division, established in 1948 as a New York branch of Puerto Rico's Department of Labor. The agency sought to ameliorate the adjustment obstacles of newly arrived migrants and to mediate between the island and the New York community. The New York office served as a clearinghouse for jobs, housing, welfare, education, and health services, as well as a monitor for seasonal contract labor. By 1955, offshoots of the

Migration Division appeared in Illinois, Pennsylvania, Massachusetts, New Jersey, and Ohio. But, because of its island roots and continued political ties to Puerto Rico, the Migration Division often served to undermine Nuyorican leadership and sought recognition as the sole arbitrator for Puerto Rican affairs.

In Antonia's opinion, the Migration Division, later known as the Office of Puerto Rico, or the Office of the Commonwealth, followed a program that inhibited the growth of self-sufficient communities. What HYAA, PRACA, and Pantoja personally believed was needed to further advance the community was a new model of social action that would take into consideration the diversity of Puerto Rican/Nuyorican society, which encompassed people from different generations and cultural locations, from recent arrivals to settled residents, from those who identified as "Americanized Hispanics" to their neighbors who clung to a traditional island culture, and finally to those who had forged a stateside blend of Puertorriqueño, a synthesis of Puerto Rican and American culture. The impact of race, class, and gender on the development of New York Puerto Ricans needed to be addressed, and a capable leadership had to be hewn from within the community itself, not imposed from outside. As Pantoja reflected years later, "organizations should be developed to handle particular types of problems . . . . [T]hey should concentrate on developmental approaches that would educate to prevent future problems."[9]

By the time Antonia was in her thirties, she was already considered an institution builder by academics, grassroots activists, politicians, and other leaders involved with Puerto Rican and minority affairs. Between 1950 and 1957, Pantoja was instrumental in founding three self-funded community service organizations: HYAA, PRACA, and the Puerto Rican Forum.[10] Though she had natural leadership abilities, she decided to pursue graduate studies that would help her become a more effective and responsible organizer for political and community action. She earned a master's degree in social work from the School of Social Work at Columbia University in 1954, and she would ultimately earn a doctorate in sociology from the Union Graduate School in 1973.

The best known of Pantoja's organizations was ASPIRA, founded in 1961. ASPIRA focused on the educational experience of Puerto Rican youth in an effort to counter soaring dropout rates among high school students, while guiding young people toward professional, business, academic, and artistic goals. ASPIRA's creation was, however, a long and arduous process. Pantoja conceived ASPIRA while she was still involved in her graduate studies, over a period of seven years, as a project called "New Leaders in New York." Pantoja drew upon conversations with students at several PRACA youth conferences. At these student-directed gatherings, speakers often recounted horror stories about their experiences in the public schools. Made to feel ashamed of speaking their native language, students became disaffected and alienated from education. Frightened by gangs and other groups, they also expressed fear of the police. Pantoja searched for ways to change this reality. Years of research and experience finally coalesced into a proposal for a leadership program that would inspire dispirited students to overcome an ineffective educational system and become dedicated community leaders.

Rejected by numerous social service and community agencies, including the Migration Division, Antonia presented the plan to Dr. Frank Horne, then head of the Commission on Intergroup Relations. His immediate faith in the project and in Antonia, along with his connections to city agencies and philanthropic foundations, enabled Pantoja to take the next steps. She recalled, "We wanted an upbeat name, one word to express belief in one's self. The word *aspira* was finally selected . . . . because to aspire is upbeat. . . . The Spanish command form ASPIRA, of the verb *aspirar,* was perfect."[11]

Other community organizations and youth-centered groups, however, did not eagerly embrace ASPIRA because they questioned the need to segregate Puerto Ricans into a separate student program. Furthermore, opponents argued that the group's activities could be folded under the auspices of other, more experienced, community organizations. ASPIRA supporters offered compelling rationale. Given that the Latino community in the New York City was composed predominantly of first- and second-generation Puerto Ricans who continued to appear at the bottom of all social indicators, especially school dropout statistics, aggressive action was needed. Some schools, however, would not even allow ASPIRA chapters to operate on their grounds. The battle for acceptance and recognition was not won until ASPIRA chapters had grown at an impressive rate, and their numbers could no longer be ignored.

With other educators and social workers who shared her vision, Pantoja created ASPIRA chapters in schools, churches, storefronts, and wherever Spanish-speaking young people congregated. These chapters provided nurturing and empowering enclaves where students received tutoring in order to master their core academic courses at school. Classes in Puerto Rican history and culture became cornerstones for developing knowledge, pride, and confidence. Sessions designed especially for parents and students explored college opportunities, admissions, and financial aid. From its humble origins as a small, self-funded agency, ASPIRA grew into a national organization represented in five states, Washington, D.C., and Puerto Rico.

Between 1963 and 1999, ASPIRA served approximately 36,000 Puerto Rican and Latino youth. Graduates of the first ASPIRA clubs enrolled in college and formed the core of student movements that demanded the establishment of Puerto Rican Studies departments at their universities. Thousands of *aspirantes* today occupy influential positions in community service, government, universities, hospitals, schools, the performing arts, and other sectors of American society; among them are the former Bronx Borough president Fernando Ferrer and actor Jimmy Smits. Without doubt, ASPIRA is regarded as Pantoja's most significant legacy to Puerto Ricans and Latinos in general.

In the throes of the civil rights movement of the late 1960s and 1970s, ASPIRA joined with the Puerto Rican Legal Defense and Education Fund in a class-action suit against the largest school system in the nation, the New York City Board of Education, claiming that 182,000 Puerto Rican children with limited or no English-speaking ability were denied the right to an equal education. The courts ruled in the favor of the Spanish-speaking children in the city's public schools. The result was the ASPIRA Consent Decree (1974), which guaranteed equal educational opportunities for language-minority children who were not English speakers, and virtually ensured bilingual education as a method of instruction. This represented a triumph for Pantoja, who had always supported bilingual education and had argued that "total immersion" of Spanish-speaking students in an English-only environment was a "stupid, stupid thing." Puerto Ricans were already bilingual, and their children should not lose their language and speak only English. But, she noted on another occasion, "I am for the fact that our children must learn English for their livelihood and because they should know that other language of the place where they live."[12]

In 1966, Pantoja stepped down from the directorship of ASPIRA, entrusting it to Luis Nuñez, Yolanda Sánchez, and other leaders, and accepted a professorship in the School of Social Work at Columbia University. She taught community organization theory and developed the first courses in the subject. Although she missed ASPIRA, and on the ground, grassroots community organizing, her connections with Columbia University brought other opportunities beyond the classroom. In 1967, Robert Kennedy appointed Pantoja as a delegate-at-large to the New York State Constitutional Convention, where she attracted attention for her advocacy of Puerto

Rican and minority issues. Encouraged by liberal Democrats to run for public office, Pantoja declined because "I did not want my private life examined and exposed to public scrutiny. I did not know who my father was, and I feared that there might be public information that would hurt my mother. Also, I had never married. I had led a bohemian life in my early years, and since then, I had had a number of female companions. I felt that all these things could have been the subject of personal attacks because I knew that political campaigns use low tactics."[13]

Following the convention, Pantoja was appointed to serve on Mayor Lindsay's Bundy panel to decentralize the public schools. Juggling her teaching position at the New School for Social Research, public service, and fighting constant internal community squabbles, she found herself at the brink of exhaustion. Ravaged by chronic asthma attacks throughout her adult years, Pantoja put her community activism on hold and returned to Puerto Rico for two years of recuperation. Family, friends, and the warmth of the island gave her the strength to participate in island youth projects. During her recuperation, she prepared a proposal to establish a research center to study the most pressing problems facing Puerto Ricans.

Funded by the Ford Foundation, the Puerto Rican Research and Resources Center, based in Washington, D.C., came to life in 1971, with Pantoja as its director. Her proposal also called for the establishment of a bilingual college for Spanish-speaking students, laying the foundation for what would become New York City's Boricua College/Universidad Boricua. The idea of a bilingual university was consonant with the pedagogical philosophies that flourished across the nation in the 1970s. Emerging universities and cultural centers, such as New York's El Museo del Barrio and the Oglala Sioux Community College, emphasized multicultural perspectives, nontraditional students and curricula, and community accountability. Pantoja provided an overarching methodology, teaching curricula, and a plan for accreditation, but a resurgence of her asthma prompted her to step aside from making the college a reality. However, she participated in the national search for a president who could carry Universidad Boricua through the accreditation and implementation stages, interviewing leading scholars such as Stanford University's Dr. Frank Bonilla. Ultimately, Dr. Victor Alicea, a professor in architecture and urban planning at Columbia University, was chosen. Led by Alicea and a committee of scholars, Boricua College opened its doors in 1974 in New York City. Named after *Borinquen*, the Taino name for Puerto Rico, Boricua College became a fully accredited, bilingual institution, granting baccalaureate and associate degrees and offering programs in the liberal arts and sciences, business administration, and community organization. Courses in Puerto Rican, Latin American, and Latino culture and history were also included.[14]

Concerned about her health, Pantoja moved to southern California where she was fortunate to meet an ex-New Yorker familiar with Puerto Rican culture, Dr. Wilhelmina (Mina) Perry. A professor of social work at San Diego State University, where Pantoja also taught, Mina would become her life companion. Imbued with the political and intellectual fervor of the 1970s, the two activists surrounded themselves with others eager to bring about social reforms in educating youth of color. "One of the immediate results of the close friendship between Mina Perry and me," recalls Pantoja, "was the change we brought to the curriculum and the faculty of the undergraduate program. First, we changed the philosophy, teaching approach, and readings of the social policy courses. We taught students to analyze the society in which they lived and to identify policies and how these policies affected their lives and the lives of their family, friends, and community."[15]

Dedicated to community-based alternative education, Perry and Pantoja founded the Graduate School for Urban Resources and Social Policy, later known as the Graduate School for Community Development, in San Diego. Located in a downtown redevelopment zone, the school admitted a nationally representative student body of Native Americans, African Americans, Chinese, Filipinos, Mexican Americans, Vietnamese, Puerto Ricans, and European Americans. Pantoja, now in her sixties, showed few signs of slowing down. Receiving acclaim both in the United States and Latin America, she was at the forefront of an important area of study that built on the concept of bringing about positive transformation within grassroots groups. In 1982, Pantoja received a grant to write a book on community development from the U.S. Department of Education's Mina Shaughnessy Scholars Program. This grant provided the financial resources she needed to retire after twelve years of service to the graduate school.

From 1984 to 1998, Pantoja and Perry lived active, productive lives, in what they considered their semiretirement years, in Puerto Rico. They became involved with the Cubuy and Lomas Civic-Social Association where they lived, and created PRODUCIR, a community-based economic development project. With starts and stops, the project managed to produce adequate incomes for some families through the creation of a bakery, a post office, and a credit cooperative, among other ventures. In addition, the community began a Head Start program for younger children and programs for high school students to encourage college enrollment. Disillusioned with an island bureaucracy predicated on a restrictive political relationship with the United States, Pantoja came to realize that dependency had become a way of life in Puerto Rico. Difficult under even the best conditions, economic development could not thrive in a country where "local people are kept dependent upon welfare payment and food stamps that are given to be used to purchase goods shipped from the mainland." However, Pantoja's most significant personal discovery while living in Puerto Rico was that she had become, in every sense of the word, a Nuyorican. "The most important achievement in the process of integration," she writes, "has been finding the answer that I have carried within me for many years and over many spans of geography: 'Where is my home?' I now know that home is New York City."[16]

Determined that there was still much to be done in New York, including fending off increasing threats to bilingual education, Pantoja and Perry returned to the city in 1999. Pantoja put wheels in motion to create an ASPIRA Alumni Association, one that would fund fellowships for a new generation of *aspirantes*. They envisioned the creation of a Latino Educational Media Center that could mount an extensive historical recovery project focusing on the impact of Puerto Ricans in the city.

And so it was that on September 22, 2001, Pantoja organized a symposium on the history and experience of New York Puerto Ricans, the first step in laying the groundwork for her new initiatives. But less than three years after her return to Manhattan, Antonia Pantoja died of cancer on May 24, 2002, at the age of eighty. This visionary activist was survived by Wilhelmina Perry, countless leaders, organizers, and the institutions she helped to create.

NOTES

1. Antonia Pantoja, *Memoir of a Visionary* (Houston: Arte Público Press, 2002), 4; "Puerto Rico Profile: Dr. Antonia Pantoja," *Puerto Rico Herald*, November 17, 2000.

2. Arturo Morales Carrion, *Puerto Rico: A Political and Cultural History* (New York: W. W. Norton, 1983), 213.

3. Pantoja, *Memoir of a Visionary*, 22–23.

4. Ibid., 42. Antonio Pedreira chaired the Department of Hispanic Studies at the university. His classic work, *Insularismo*, was an intellectual catalyst for serious studies on Puerto Rican culture in the 1930s.

5. Pantoja, *Memoir of a Visionary*, 45. Pantoja alludes to the limitations of women's roles, the tensions over dating and marriage, and the family's

traditional expectations of her in a video interview, Bread and Roses Cultural Project, Women of Hope: *Latinas Abriendo Camino: Twelve Groundbreaking Latina Women* (Princeton, N.J.: Films for the Humanities, 1996).

6. Figures are based on "Population Trends of Puerto Ricans on the U.S. Mainland by Region, State, and City, 1950, 1960, and 1970," in U.S. Commission on Civil Rights, *Puerto Ricans in the Continental United States: An Uncertain Future* (Washington, D.C.: Government Printing Office, 1976).

7. There is abundant literature on ethnoracial prejudice and Puerto Ricans. Examples are culled from Gerald Meyer, "Marcantonio and El Barrio," *Centro Bulletin* 1996, no. 192, 76–77. Also see Christopher Rand, *The Puerto Ricans* (New York: Oxford University Press, 1958), 5.

8. Pantoja, *Memoir of a Visionary*, 68, 70.

9. Ibid., 74.

10. HYAA promoted voter registration drives, fund-raisers for charity, and homeless shelters; PRACA was similar to HYAA but extended service to school-age population and families; the Puerto Rican Forum specialized in community development projects and secured funding for small businesses.

11. Pantoja, *Memoir of a Visionary*, 95–99. In addition to ASPIRA, there existed several teachers' organizations dedicated to promoting bilingual education and other means to combat the poor education of Spanish-speaking children in the schools. These included the Society of Puerto Rican Auxiliary Teachers, the Puerto Rican Educators Association, and the Hispanic chapter of the United Federation of Teachers.

12. "Puerto Rico Profile: Dr. Antonia Pantoja."

13. Pantoja, *Memoir of a Visionary*, 131. Before her involvement with the constitutional convention, Pantoja worked with community leaders like Maria J. Canino, Dr. Francisco Trilla, and others to found the Puerto Rican Community Development project. She also helped produce the groundbreaking study by the Puerto Rican Forum: *A Study of Poverty Conditions in the New York Puerto Rican Community* (3rd ed.; New York: n.p., 1970).

14. Boricua College remains one of two bilingual institutions of higher education in New York City. The other is the City University's Hostos Community College.

15. Pantoja, *Memoir of a Visionary*, 161.

16. Ibid., 189–90. Pantoja's ideas were influenced by Richard Weiskoff, *Factories and Food Stamps: The Puerto Rican Model of Development* (Baltimore: Johns Hopkins University Press, 1985).

14

ANA MENDIETA'S ART

A Journey through Her Life

Carlos A. Cruz

The struggle for culture today is the struggle for life.

Ana Mendieta

With these words, Ana Mendieta, the prolific performance artist, defined culture and her own professional and personal quest. To Ana, art as life represented a continual search for lost heritage, identities, and cultural traditions. She sought to enhance knowledge about her diverse cultural background, and in so doing she came to terms with her own sense of personal survival. This obsessive struggle to bring back the essential elements of Latin American and Third World multicultural traditions and incorporate them into a contemporary artistic language is Ana's most important legacy.

Ana is considered a pioneer in integrating her cultural identity into contemporary American art; she is one of the few Latin women artists who became extensively recognized for her contribution and known throughout the international art world. Nevertheless, her largest influence is geared toward the Latin American community of artists inside and outside of the United States. To them, Ana's life and art became a model to follow, particularly among the Cuban artists known as the "eighties generation," who, at the same time, influenced a large number of Latin American artists during the last two decades.

Born in Havana, Cuba, in 1948, Ana was part of an established family with instant name recognition due in great measure to the political connections of her grandfather, Pablo, and great uncle Carlos Mendieta. Pablo Mendieta held the rank of colonel in the Cuban Independence Army in the late nineteenth century and served as commander of the Cuban army after the independent republic was established in 1902. He later served as the Cuban consul to Spain. In 1934, Carlos Mendieta served as the provisional president of Cuba and ruled for five days following a coup led by Fulgencio Batista, who himself would be overthrown two decades later by Fidel Castro. Ana's father Ignacio, like his father before him, had prominent political connections. A lawyer, Ignacio Mendieta had ties to the Batista government, but like many men and women of the Cuban elite, he initially gave his support to the Castro-led revolution against Batista during the late 1950s.

As a child, Ana lived a stable life in Havana, but everything began to change when the rebels took control in 1959. Two years later in 1961, the leader of the revolutionary army, Fidel Castro, declared Cuba a Marxist-socialist country. Along with other former collaborators of the revolution, Ignacio Mendieta reversed his position and openly opposed the Castro regime. During the early 1960s, Cuban intelligence learned that Ignacio Mendieta had received training from the U.S. Federal Bureau of Investigation (FBI). Also suspected of connections to the U.S. Central Intelligence Agency (CIA), Ignacio was sentenced to twenty years in jail in 1965 for his participation in planning the Bay of Pigs invasion. Thirteen years later, Ana's father would be released and reunited with his family in the United States.[1]

Given the social and political upheaval following the revolution, Ana's parents decided to send their daughters to the United States. In 1961, at the age of twelve, Ana and her sister Raquel immigrated to the United States under *Operación Pedro Pan* (Operation Peter Pan). Fearing Communist indoctrination, religious persecution, political retribution, and the rumor of *patria potestad* (the government's assuming legal guardianship of children and the attendant loss of parental rights), Cuban parents sent more than 14,000 children to the United States under this clandestine program sponsored by the Catholic Church.[2] The two sisters were shuffled among a series of Catholic orphanages and foster homes in Iowa and were not reunited with their mother until 1966.

Ana remained in Iowa for many years, and in her early twenties she earned a bachelor of arts degree, and then a master of arts degree, in painting from the University of Iowa. Mendieta's education took place during a time when the university's multimedia and video art program spearheaded experimental, transformative changes in the traditional standards of gallery exhibitions and artistic expression. Art became more diverse by including performance, installation, photographs, and videos, where representation began as an investigation of the artist's own body and how the surroundings affected it. As part of this innovative learning environment, Ana's work would be "clearly indebted to early body-art videos that use makeup and facial expressions to play with identity."[3] At this point, she developed an interest in performance and body art and eventually gave up painting. As she revealed in an interview years later, "I realized that my paintings were not real enough, for what I want the image to convey, and by real I mean I wanted my images to have power, to be magic."[4]

As part of her graduation requirements, Ana performed at the Center for New Performing Arts at the University of Iowa. Her three performances were *Facial Cosmetic Variation*, *Glass on Body*, and *Facial Hair Transplant*, wherein she transformed her body, experimenting with physical representations of gender and beauty. In *Facial Hair Transplant*, Ana expressed sexual issues by pasting a false beard and mustache, which she had shaved off a male colleague, on her own face. Perhaps without realizing it, she was interrogating Cuban manifestations of machismo, male domination as represented by the authoritarian figure of Fidel Castro himself, who was responsible for her family's separation.

Like many women artists who began their careers during the 1970s, Ana identified herself with other feminist artists who were dedicated to exploring gendered identity in relation to the female body. Eventually, her life and art became socially compromised in favor of human values and against man's alienation. The social and political impact of her work soon took a different direction. As she later stated in her own sense of historical connectivity: "The function of an artist is not a gift but an obligation."[5] Moreover, she believed, "Art is a material part of culture but its greatest value is its spiritual role, and that influences society, because it's the greatest contribution to the intellectual and moral development of humanity that can be made."[6]

From 1973 to 1978, Mendieta coordinated the University of Iowa's Summer School of Multimedia programs in Oaxaca, Mexico. Oaxaca represented an important and sacred space in Mesoamerican civilization. There she would find the mythic tradition that she had searched for in support of her artistic experiences. Mendieta believed that "plugging into Mexico was like going back to the source, being able to get some magic just by being there."[7] During her first trip to Oaxaca, she performed *Mutilated Body in Landscape* and *Flowers on Body*. The latter made connections with the beliefs of Mexicanos who thought that death is a tribute to the earth, the place that provides us with everything and where life begins.[8] Ana performed *Flowers on Body* in a Zapotec burial ground, where she lay covered with white flowers. Here, her contoured figure in the landscape (silhouette) became the most remarkable element in the photograph. Noting her Oaxaca experiences, art critic Donald Kuspit observed that Ana had "brought away her first silhouette in the landscape."[9] From this performance, Ana adopted the silhouette, which became a constant theme and the most recognized trademark of her work.

During the height of feminist activism in the United States in the early 1970s, women and art historians protested the fact that female artists were not recognized as important or included in major exhibitions in the male-dominated art world. Feminist artists, curators, historians, and critics mounted their own exhibitions to address the achievements of women artists, such as *Women Artists, from 1550 to 1950*, held at the Los Angeles County Museum of Art. During these years, women artists began their own cooperative galleries, including the highly regarded Artists in Residence, Inc. (A.I.R.) Gallery, the first cooperative gallery in the United States, located in the Manhattan neighborhood of Soho.

Relocating to New York in the 1970s, Ana joined the city's community of feminist and Third World artists. She also discovered an extensive network of Afro-Cuban practitioners of *Santería*, which provided familiar connections to memories of her childhood. *Santería* is the religion of the Yoruba-speaking people of Nigeria who were brought in chains to Cuba. Over time, slaves blended their traditional religion with elements of Spanish Catholicism and European spiritualism. Women are powerful participants and leaders in *Santería* as over half of the *Santería* priests are women. Afro-Cuban beliefs like *Santería* were introduced into New York City during the 1940s and surged in popularity following the exodus from the Cuba after the revolution in 1959. In the mid-1960s, despite the fact that many Cuban immigrants denied any association between the followers of *Santería* and the black nationalist movement, African Americans also became involved in the religion. Attracting people of many different backgrounds, including other Latinos, the number of practitioners in New York City was estimated to be around 6,000 by the 1970s.[10] As anthropologist Gregory Steven has noted, "many artists, dancers and musicians . . . have traditionally been attracted to *Santería* and are largely responsible for its high visibility in New York City."[11]

Like many Latina feminists of her generation, Mendieta combined a quest for a reconnection or reconciliation with her cultural heritage with a dedication to gender equity and feminist consciousness. For Ana, this consciousness was expressed through the spoken word and visual aesthetics of performance art.

In 1976, Ana gave her first one-person exhibition at 112 Greene Street Gallery: *Ñañigo Burial and Filmworks*. In these works, she introduced elements of the Afro-Cuban beliefs collectively known as *Ñañiguismo*. With distinct African roots, *Ñañiguismo* (or *Abakuá*) is an all-male religious practice from which women are excluded; however, they remain central in the mythical representations of the initiation ritual.[12] According to an African legend, a woman called Sikan disclosed her tribe's secret to another tribe. As a consequence, women were deemed untrustworthy and were ostracized from practicing *Ñañiguismo*. To Charles Merewether, a critic who specializes in Latin American art, the principal work in Ana's exhibition "was a *silueta* of herself made from forty-seven lit black candles and presented in a darkened room."[13] Once consumed, the candles left behind an empty black silhouette shape on the gallery floor. In this particular work, Mendieta creatively represented herself as Sikan, the symbol of the exclusion of women who dared to break tradition.

That same year, Ana performed *Anima* (soul) in San Felipe outside of Oaxaca, in which she assumed the passionate role of the *Anima Sola* (lonely soul), yet another symbol of the exclusion of women. In popular Catholic tradition, the *Anima Sola* is a figure of a woman condemned to hell for her sins. The religious handbill of *Anima Sola* is also used in Afro-Cuban religion and is placed behind the main entrance to protect the home. This handbill's prayer is said to spiritually console lovers following quarrels.

In the *Anima* performance, Ana built her silhouette and surrounded it with fire. In traditional rituals, fire is used in the purification of sins. In burning the silhouette, the figure is transformed into smoke and ashes, which can be carried away more easily by nature. The artist representing herself as an *Anima* silhouette thus symbolically threatens to disperse the sin's ashes contained in the spirit of *Anima Sola* all over the world. Ana once described her process of creation in the following manner: "Art must have begun as nature itself, in a dialectical relationship between humans and the natural world from which we cannot be separated."[14] The subtext meaning in her philosophical interpretation of the *Anima Sola*, linked her thoughts with dialectic materialism theory, according to which the material is neither created nor destroyed, but becomes transformed.

In the summer of 1976, Ana's mother was misdiagnosed with cancer, and in response Ana created an emotional series of silhouettes in the sand known as *Fetish*. As Ana explained in an interview, "I am compelled to imagine what it must have been like to walk in the area and stumble on this body molded of wet brown sand. I didn't consciously set out to help her. I just did the pieces, but I think it was connected to death imagery."[15] Like an African sculptor and shaman combined, Ana in one of the *Fetish* pieces molded a human silhouette in the sand and embedded wooden stakes throughout the body. Her performance resulted in an art piece that resembled the Congo nail fetish (*nkisi nkondi*), a wooden figure said to release magical powers when hammered with nails. Believers use this fetish to invoke a spiritual force that can have some degree of control over humans.

El Árbol de la Vida (Tree of Life) series was another performance based on Afro-Cuban tradition. In one piece of this particular series, Mendieta fused body and natural environment by covering her full-figure frame in mud and placing herself in front of the trunk of a tree. She performed this piece in Old Man's Creek, Iowa, in 1977. By the time Ana created *El Árbol de la Vida*, she had worked extensively with Afro-Cuban issues for several years and was well versed in Lydia Cabrera's classic book, *El Monte* (*The Forest*).[16] Since its publication in Cuba in 1954, *El Monte* had become a "bible" for people who practice Afro-Cuban religions such as *Santería*. In the performance *El Árbol de la Vida*, as in the Oaxaca spiritual experiences, Ana returned to traditional culture and the way it related to life and nature. In the first page of *El Monte*, one reads about the relationship between the forest and the people: "we are the children of the forest because life began there. . . . All is found in the forest—the fundamentals of the universe, and we must ask the forest for everything, because everything is given to us there." A follower of Ana's work, Destiny Schevling picked up on this theme in her interpretation of *El Árbol de la Vida*: "She is alive as the tree, she is part of the tree, and the tree is part of her." She is "as much a part of nature as the tree that grows directly from the soil."[17]

Ana's work during those years not only stemmed from the inspiration of Afro-Cuban imagery and myths, but it also incorporated some basic elements of their cosmology. As a performance artist, her works were ephemeral, and yet somehow connected with African ideas, in that the concept of time in her work is viewed as a "two dimensional phenomenon, with a long past, a present and virtually no future."[18]

From series like *El Árbol de la Vida* and *Fetish*, Ana imprinted her own style of body art, sometimes interpreted as the intersection between performance and earth art or earth/body sculptures. As she once described herself: "My art is the way I re-establish the bonds that unite me to the universe. It is a return to the maternal source. Through my earth/body sculptures I become one with the earth. . . . I become an extension of the nature and nature becomes an extension of my body."[19]

After many years of experimentation and performances using her figure and her silhouette in the landscape, Ana exhibited a group of photographs in a solo exhibition titled the *Silueta* series. Presented at the Gallery of New Concepts in Iowa in 1977, this exhibition displayed photographs from her performances from 1973 to 1977. It was the first time the public had the opportunity to view a large portion of her work in one setting. The connection between the photographic images of Mendieta's most extensive and well known artistic expression is the reiteration of the silhouette, which she worked on until 1980. Her art reflected extensive scholarly research and creative imagination. Ana studied literature on cultural issues that she wanted to represent. Her working method (notes, ideas, and sketches) can be found in many catalogues and books written about her. In fact, Ana would become best known for her photographs of her performances rather than the performances themselves. Photography allowed her to work at different creative levels. In her performance art, Ana included the conception, construction, and deconstruction of the silhouettes. As a photographer, she also manipulated her images and added new elements such as titles, sequences, and details to give new meanings to the pieces.

Through the years that followed, Mendieta experimented with a myriad of possibilities through her art. In some of her artwork, she used simple rocks to outline the body and fill the inner cavity with the basic elements of life such as water, fire, and blood. In others, she contoured the body image with flowers or molded the figure into the earth. In her works, weight, volume, and mass were basic and constantly competed for dominance. The relationship was always a constant discourse between absence and presence, figure and background. In addition, Mendieta always maintained the human proportion and used the figure suggested by the natural environment, making ephemeral changes to the landscape. In this way, the earth not only became a material, but it was also the substance and frame where she left the human track. As Ana once stated metaphorically, she used "the earth as my canvas and my soul as my tools."[20] During these years, Ana's work evolved from the nude representation of own body covered with natural components to the representation of her silhouette with nature's elements.

A reconnection to her Cuban cultural background linked Ana with the first avant-garde generation of Cuban artists. During the 1920s, this group of artists took on the role of formally renovating Cuban art, indulging in artistic themes of Cuban nationalism. They were the first generation of artists to incorporate elements of both Afro-Cuban beliefs and urban issues into their art and thus paved the way for a new interpretation of the country's past. Revisiting this theme, Ana incorporated some elements of Afro-Cuban culture in her works, only her representation was more of a compromise with the beliefs and cultural meaning of the group she represented, compared to the earlier generation of Cuban artists. She focused more on the current ideological values of the community that she interacted with in many ways.

In 1978, Ana's sympathy with the movement in favor of human rights and social equality was very visible. As part of her political position, she and many other young Cuban Americans called *Maceitos* joined a group of political exiles involved in dialogue between stateside communities and the island of Cuba. These vital but controversial exchanges between young Cuban exiles and Cuban government officials occurred during President Jimmy Carter's administration. Eventually, these dialogues led to family reunification. As a result of these talks, the Cuban government released a number of political prisoners, including Ana's father. Reunited in the United States in 1978, the two became very close, and he appeared at many of her performances and exhibitions.

As another result of these initial conversations and exchanges, Ana returned to her native country in 1980. During the first flight to Cuba since her childhood exile, Ana saw part of the aerial silhouette of the island and somehow imagined it in a state of repose on the Caribbean Sea. A year later, somewhere outside of Iowa City, she traced the figure of her body with mud directly onto the silt bed of a nearby stream, which she called *Isla*. In a quick process, the stream flowed through the silhouette dissolving the figure. At some point in the process, which Ana recorded, the silhouette resembled the aerial image of Cuba. Ana proceeded to connect her earthwork with the *Isla*, and in the process, she erased the restrictive boundaries between the land and nation. Both concepts are fused in her representations, and Cuba becomes an extension of Ana, herself, as she becomes an extension of Cuba.

By 1980, Ana Mendieta had received her second grant from the National Endowment of the Arts, as well as a prestigious Guggenheim fellowship. As part of her connection with Third World artists and feminist issues, she, along with two other artists, organized *Dialect of Isolation: An Exhibition of Third World Women Artists in the United States* at A.I.R. Gallery. In the introduction to the catalogue, Ana expressed once again her political position against human exploitation, racism, and colonialism.[21]

During this time, her art began to change as she explored more universal cultural themes without a direct correlation to Afro-Latino traditions. She believed that the cosmologies of every culture were related and could have different interpretations, symbols, and images to represent the same meanings, which thus reinforced her deep conviction of women's special bonds with mother earth.

In 1981, as part of the new direction in her artistic expression, Ana incorporated the pre-Columbian cultural legend of the *Venus Negra* (Black Venus) into a project for the feminist art journal *Heresies*. This artwork reflected a mixture of elements taken from many different cultural influences: Spanish, African, Afro-Cuban, Taino, and other indigenous sources. The text of the legend was illustrated with an aerial photograph she had taken some years before at one of her silhouette performances. In this performance, Ana had configured a female image in the earth with a hollow opening that she filled with gunpowder and set on fire, resulting in a figure resembling a prehistoric cave painting. Some of the elements of this performance would foreshadow works that she would later create in Cuba.

During the summer of 1981, Ana visited Cuba at the invitation of the Cuban Ministry of Culture. On this trip, she received a great deal of publicity; official newspapers, magazines, and cultural tabloids published essays about her and her work, and she gave personal interviews on television and radio. Her visit was deliberately used to increase the government's popularity, then in measurable decline due to the Mariel Boatlifts—a massive exodus, which forced as many as 125,000 Cubans to leave the island. For years, the number of Cubans who disagreed with the government's politics increased, and they were sentenced to many years in jail for publicly expressing their own ideas.[22]

All of the attention given to Mendieta's visit was calculated to divert attention away from the forced exodus at Mariel. Although Mendieta realized that the Cuban government had used her, she found little sympathy at home in the United States for her situation. Because of Ana's sponsorship by the Cuban government, the exile community in the United States linked her with pro-Castro circles and excluded her from the list of exiled Cuban artists. She found herself blackballed from their circuit of exhibitions, projects, and other activities. However, some critics hailed Ana's visit, perceiving her inaccurately as a supporter of Fidel Castro.

As part of her stay in Cuba, she created a number of bas-relief representations on the walls of the prehistoric caves of *El Parque Nacional Las Escaleras de Jaruco*, outside of Havana. These petroglyphic sculptures were inspired by pre-Columbian and prehistoric icons of fertility. In her works, she created a free-flowing interpretation of the primordial female goddess, appropriating legends described in scholarly studies about the extinct Taino Indians of Cuba. She gave these sculptures the names of divinities taken from the Taino language: *Guacar* (our menstruation), *Itaba Cahubaba* (Old Mother Blood), *Bacayu* (Light of Day), *Maroya* (Moon). With these bas-reliefs, "Ana created works that self-consciously blurred the lines between art and archeological artifact" and at the same time added contemporary representations to the island's caves.[23] These free-form interpretative ex-pressions of traditional pictographs and concepts in a Cuban context rein-forced the contrasts between her art and the Taino cave paintings.

In November 1981, she exhibited the photographic series of the *Rupestrian* sculptures she had carved in the Jaruco at New York's A.I.R. Gallery.[24] These sculptures represented a break from the ephemeral state of Ana's earthworks and moved toward more permanent installations. With her rock-carving sculptures, Ana Mendieta immortalized herself and forever left her footprints in the Cuban landscape.

During her one-month stay in Cuba, she met several times with young Cuban artists known later as the "eighties generation." Cuban artists from this generation such as José Bedia, Juan Francisco Elso Padilla, Marta María Pérez, Gustavo Pérez Monzón, Ricardo Rodríguez Brey, and Leandro Soto visited her in Jaruco and engaged in long hours of discussion regarding art. Visibly influenced by her work, this group examined their own tradi-tions closely and experimented with new forms and techniques. Lydia Cabrera's books on Afro-Cuban beliefs became mandatory readings for this new generation of Cuban intellectuals. Smuggled secretly into Cuba, the books were passed on from one person to another. Eventually, given the popularity of Ana's influence among the eighties generation, many of them such as Bedia, Brey, Monzón, Elso, and Soto traveled to Oaxaca on a pilgrimage to ceremonial centers that had inspired Ana Mendieta's early work. Today almost all members of the eighties generation maintain their homes outside of Cuba.

Ana's ties with the Cuban cultural scene did not end here. In 1982, her photographs were included in the *Primer Salón Nacional de Fotografía*, in Havana. A year later, the *Museo Nacional de Bellas Artes* in Havana showed her solo exhibition *Geo-Imago*. She was also invited to the *Primera Bienal de La Habana* in 1984. Despite rumors of Ana's disillusionment with the Cuban revolution, and the fact that many of the sculptures she left in Cuba were defaced, her work still represented a link with the Cuban art world, state-sanctioned or not. In 1996, Ana's work was included in the group exhibition *Cuba Siglo XX Modernidad Sincretismo*, supported by the Cuban government. According to the organizers, the Cuban exhibition complemented the exhibition *Outside Cuba*, organized by Cuban exiles in 1987,which had purposefully excluded Ana. In 1998, the *Union Nacional de Escritores y Artistas de Cuba* (UNEAC) (Cuban National Union of Writers and Artists) inaugurated the first *Festival del Performance "Ana Mendieta."*

In 1983, Ana Mendieta, honored with the American Academy Fellowship, moved to Rome, Italy, where she continued to work on her art. A year later, she exhibited her last works in Italy, entitled *Earth Archetypes*. She constructed these major sculptures with only elements found in nature. The *Earth Archetypes* and *Rupestrian* sculptures shared formal similarities. As Ana reflected on her own works, "Now I have been working indoors. I've always had problems with that idea because I don't feel that I can emulate nature. . . . So I've given this problem to myself . . . to work indoors. I found a way and I am involved right now, working with sand, with earth, mixing it with a blender, and making sculptures."[25]

Ana frequently traveled from Rome to New York. Unfortunately, disaster struck on one of these visits. In 1985, while in New York, she fell out of a window of her Manhattan apartment, plunging thirty-four stories to her death. This tragedy occurred after an argument with her husband, Carl Andre, a well-known minimalist sculptor. Mendieta had met Andre at the end of the 1970s, and, in photographs from the 1980s, they appeared to be a happy couple. However, during the time Ana was living in Italy, she wrote several letters to Sue Rosner describing her love-hate relationship with Carl.[26] Carl and Ana had married in January 1985, nine months before her death. The couple was seen arguing frequently in public places, and their relationship quickly become turbulent. Local authorities and Ana's family raised questions about her mysterious death. Based on a police investigation, Carl Andre was arrested and charged with Ana Mendieta's death. At the end of the trial, however, the jury dismissed all of the charges against him. Ana's death has remained a mystery to her family and friends. To many, Andre's acquittal was not only a sign of a failed justice system, but also of a patriarchal disregard of domestic violence.

Following Ana's untimely death, New York feminists staged formal protests of Carl Andre's exhibitions. As part of these demonstrations, the Women's Action Coalition organized a demonstration in front of the new Guggenheim Museum, where Carl Andre exhibited his pieces. During the Guggenheim's inaugural exhibition in 1992 (five years after Ana's death), more than five hundred protesters gathered in front of the museum, several of them carrying a banner that read, "Carl Andre is in the Guggenheim. Where is Ana Mendieta?" Inside the gala event, some protestors managed to cover Carl Andre's sculptures with photos of Ana Mendieta's face.

Since her death, Ana Mendieta's life and art have become a paradigm for the Latin American artistic community in the United States. According to artists and critics like Ana's art professor, John Perreault, "Mendieta was ambitious for her art, and with good reason. She was well on her way to proving that a woman artist, an artist with Third World roots, and a so-called minority artist could establish herself as an innovator."[27] In 1987, the New Museum of Contemporary Art in New York exhibited a retrospective of her artwork. In the introduction of the catalogue to this exhibition, Petra Barreras del Rio wrote: "She was prolific, restless, and intelligent. Her work touched on many relevant issues explored by the visual artists in the seventies and early eighties, but her talent for handling the most elemental materials and grasp of the poetic transcend the moment."[28]

After this critically acclaimed exhibit, Ana Mendieta's works have been displayed in solo exhibitions at the Miami Art Museum of Dade County (1987), Aspen Art Museum, Colorado (1990), Cleveland Center for Contemporary Art (1994), Whitney Museum in New York (1995), Helsinki City Art Museum, Finland (1996), Centro Galego de Arte Contemporánea, Barcelona, Spain (1996), Museo Rufino Tamayo, Mexico (1999), as well as other important venues. Curators at the Hirshhorn Museum in Washington, D.C., are currently planning another retrospective on Ana Mendieta.

Ana Mendieta's work spans from 1972 to 1985. During those thirteen years, she created performances, sculptures, paintings, and drawings and produced many short films and videos. She left behind over two hundred photographs documenting her body works. In addition, from 1979 to 1980, she taught at the College of Old Westbury of the State University of New York. Before her death, Mendieta was working on two book projects: the first would have focused on the photo-etchings of the *Rupestrian* carvings and the second would have included drawings inspired by the myths of the Tainos. Today, Ana Mendieta is a Latina contemporary artist known throughout the international art world, whom critics have compared to the renowned Mexican artist, Frida Kahlo. Both shared common ground in expressing life through their passion for art.

Ana Mendieta's ashes are buried in Iowa, the place where she established her home and where she always returned. With her death, her passion for art echoed throughout the intellectual community. She was literally burned as the forty-seven lit black candles in the *Ñañigo Burial and Filmworks* exhibition. Her legacy serves as the sediment from where new generations of artists may draw their inspiration and grow, similar to the little white flowers representing the new life that emerged from her body in her *Flowers on Body* performance. To paraphrase the old African proverb, from which Ana received inspiration: People who are in touch with their origins are people who will never die.[29]

NOTES

1. Robert Katz, *Naked by the Window: The Fatal Marriage of Carl Andre and Ana Mendieta* (New York: Atlantic Monthly Press, 1990).

2. See Barbara Cruz, "Operation Peter Pan (1960–1962)," *Latinas in the United States: An Historical Encyclopedia*, ed. Vicki L. Ruiz and Virginia Sánchez Korrol (Bloomington: Indiana University Press, forthcoming). For an overview, see Yvonne Conde, *Operation Pedro Pan: The Untold Exodus of 14,048 Cuban Children* (New York: Routledge Press, 1999).

3. Michael Duncan, "Tracing Mendieta," *Art in America* 87 (April 1999): 112; available online at http://articles.findarticles.com/p/articles/ mi_m1248/is_4_87/ai_54432702 (accessed March 2, 2002).

4. Gabriëlle Nederend, "Ana Mendieta," Galerie Akinci, Amsterdam, 1999, available online at http://www.xs4all.nl/~akinci/Ana_Mendieta/ Mendieta.htm (accessed May 13, 2002).

5. Ana Mendieta, "Ana Mendieta escritos personales," in *Ana Mendieta*, ed. Gloria Moure (Barcelona, Spain: Centro Galego de Arte Contemporánea, 1997), 176.

6. Petra Barreras del Rio, "Ana Mendieta: Historical Overview," in *Ana Mendieta: A Retrospective* (New York: New Museum of Contemporary Art, 1987), 6.

7. JudithWilson, "Ana Mendieta Plants," *Village Voice*, August 19, 1980, p. 90.

8. Interview with Guadalupe Rodríguez, conducted by the author in Oaxaca, 1991.

9. Donald Kuspit, "Ana Mendieta, Cuerpo Autónomo," in *Ana Mendieta*, ed. Moure, 22.

10. Beatríz Morales, "Latino Religion, Ritual, and Culture," in *Handbook of Hispanic Cultures in the United States: Anthropology*, ed. Thomas Weaver (Houston: Arte Público Press, 1994), 195.

11. Gregory Steven, "Afro-Caribbean Religions in New York City: The Case of Santería," in *Caribbean Life in New York City: Sociocultural Dimensions*, ed. Constance R. Sutton and Elsa M. Chaney (New York: Center for Migration Studies of New York, 1987), 295.

12. *Ñañigo* exists only in Cuba and remains an important part of the country's cultural components. For an overview on the *Ñañigos* see Enrique Sosa Rodriguez, *Los Ñañigos* (Havana, Cuba: Casa de las Americas Press, 1989).

13. Charles Merewether, "Ana Mendieta," *Grand Street* 17 (Winter 1999): 40–50.

14. Bonnie Clearwater, ed., *Ana Mendieta: A Book of Works* (Miami, Fla.: Grassfield Press, 1993), 11.

15. Jane Blocker, *Where Is Ana Mendieta? Identity, Performativity, and Exile* (Durham, N.C.: Duke University Press, 1999), 72.

16. Lydia Cabrera, *El Monte* (Havana, Cuba: Ediciones Chicherekú, 1954), 1.

17. Destiny Schevling, "Ana Mendieta: About the Artist," http://students.cedarcrest.edu:81/userd/dpschevl/web/final2/MENDIETA.html (accessed October 10, 1999).

18. Sulayman S. Nyang, "Reflections on Traditional African Cosmology," *New Directions: The Howard University Magazine* (October 1980): 31.

19. John Perreault, "Earth and Fire: Mendieta's Body Work," in *Ana Mendieta: A Retrospective*, 38.

20. Duncan, "Tracing Mendieta," 154.

21. Ana Mendieta, *Dialect of Isolation: An Exhibition of Third World Women Artists in the United States* (New York: A.I.R. Gallery, 1980).

22. In 1980, pushed by the rising number of Cuban dissidents on the island, Fidel Castro decided to allow wholesale immigration from Cuba to the United States. Known as the Mariel Boatlifts, an estimated 125,000 came to the United States. Targeting dissidents for removal, Castro called his opponents *escoria* (low life) to justify his actions. Soon the term "low life" was identified with homosexual preferences. People who wanted to leave the island had to walk in public followed by a crowd of people, holding banners proclaiming them to be *tortilleras* (lesbians) or *maricones* (gay men). Personal observations of the author. For an overview on the Mariel Boatlifts, see Alex Larzelere, *The 1980 Cuban Boatlift* (Washington, D.C.: National Defense University Press, 1988).

23. Coco Fusco, "Traces of Ana Mendieta," *Poliéster* 4 (February-April 1993): 56.

24. "Rupestrian" is a term adopted to denominate the rock art done in caves during prehistoric period.

25. Barreras del Rio, "Ana Mendieta: Historical Overview," 39.

26. Mendieta, "Ana Mendieta escritos personales," 217–19.

27. Perreault, "Earth and Fire: Mendieta's Body Work," 10.

28. Barreras del Rio, "Ana Mendieta: Historical Overview," 41.

29. Robert Farris Thompson, *Flash of the Spirit: African and Afro-American Art and Philosophy* (New York: Village Books, 1984), 158.

15

DOLORES HUERTA AND
THE UNITED FARM WORKERS

Alicia Chávez

One thing I've learned . . . is that having tremendous fears and anxieties is
normal. . . . By doing whatever causes your anxiety, you overcome the fear,
and strengthen your emotional, spiritual, activist muscles.

Dolores Huerta

While she appears mild-mannered and even soft-spoken, Dolores Huerta
has been a fearless warrior in her career as an activist. Unflappable as a
union organizer, uncompromising as a contract negotiator, unapologetic
as she lived against the grain of the social and political norms of her era,
she leaves an indelible legacy of labor-organizing in U.S. history. In 1962,
after almost a decade of activism in the Stockton, California, chapter of
the Community Service Organization, a self-help Mexican American civil
rights organization, Huerta joined fellow activist César Chávez in co-
founding the National Farm Workers Association (NFWA) to address the
issues of migrant farm workers in California. In September 1965, the
NFWA joined the Agricultural Workers Organizing Committee, an affiliate of the AFL-CIO, for the famous Delano Grape Strike, and a year later
the two groups merged to form the United Farm Workers Organizing
Committee, also an affiliate of the AFL-CIO. Later, the new union shortened its name to the United Farm Workers of America (UFW).

   With her children in the backseat of her barely operable car, and living on only $5 per week, Huerta embarked on an exhausting and danger-

ous journey of speaking engagements and door-to-door canvassing, activities that established the UFW's membership base. She also did strategic planning for the Grape Strike of 1965, and in 1968 and 1969, she directed the table grape boycott in New York City. In her unyielding style, Huerta became the first woman and the first Mexican American to negotiate a union contract with California growers in 1970. As the UFW extended its reach to the lettuce and strawberry fields, Huerta continued her unflagging organizing while lobbying legislators in both Sacramento and Washington, D.C., for laws that would aid farm workers. Her work as a persuasive lobbyist facilitated the passage of the Agricultural Labor Relations Act of 1975, which for the first time recognized and protected the collective bargaining rights of agricultural laborers in California.

Huerta's work seems all the more extraordinary when combined with her rearing eleven children. In addition, she carried her messages and life lessons to the wider political world around her, speaking out, for example, on women's rights. Her work illuminated how women's activism could be an essential ingredient to a successful Mexican American political movement, and how political engagement could be a path to women's self-determination.

Huerta's activism was sparked by the deleterious impact that transformations in California agriculture had on Mexican communities there. Once marked by individual relationships to the land, agricultural production became a very impersonal agribusiness, with an increasing demand for inexpensive wage labor, on land where there had formerly been tenant farmers. These changes began at the turn of the twentieth century with the technological improvements in farming during the advance of industrialization; by World War II, a lot of agricultural land was owned in large tracts by corporations who sought low-wage workers to perform farm labor. The U.S. government permitted labor contracting in Mexico and other places to meet the increased demand for wartime foodstuffs. The most physically arduous jobs were regarded as menial and reserved for these nonwhite laborers. In this economic milieu, wages and working conditions declined substantially. Life expectancy for California farm workers by the 1960s was only approximately forty-nine years. Exposed to dangerous pesticide chemicals, entire families often had to work and continually migrate with the growing seasons, keeping their children out of school. While Dolores Huerta did not grow up in a migrant family, her evolution as an organizer stemmed from lessons she learned from her parents and her own youthful experiences in a Mexican agricultural community.

Dolores Huerta was born Dolores Fernández on April 10, 1930, to Juan and Alicia Fernández, in the small coal-mining town of Dawson, New Mexico. Huerta's father was a coal miner, but like many of his peers, he supplemented his income with farm labor, traveling to Colorado, Nebraska, and Wyoming for the beet harvests. Fernández also developed a strong interest in labor issues and used his predominantly Latino local union as a base upon which to win election to the New Mexico state legislature in 1938.[1]

When her parents divorced in 1935, five-year-old Dolores and her brothers, John and Marshall, moved with their mother to the central San Joaquin Valley agricultural community of Stockton. Alicia Fernández found it very difficult to support her young family as a single parent in this Depression-era town. Dolores described her mother as "a very genteel woman, very quiet but very hardworking," yet also "a very ambitious woman." Her mother saved the wages she earned at her nighttime cannery shift (a common occupation for Mexican-origin women) and as a waitress during the day in order to buy her own business.[2] First she bought a lunch counter, then a bigger restaurant, and finally, during World War II, a seventy-room hotel. She often offered free lodging to farm worker families and thus modeled for Huerta the value of acquiring resources and knowledge that could meet community needs.[3] Both her parents demonstrated to Dolores the value of leadership and service.

Another crucial lesson Huerta learned from her mother was the value of self-sufficiency for both men and women. With five children in the house, there was plenty of domestic work to be done, but it was divided fairly between the boys and the girls: "My brothers were taught to be self-sufficient. We all had to wash the laundry, clean . . . . From very young, she taught us how to work." Dolores and her brothers labored in their mother's restaurant in the summers, and though it went against her mother's wishes, Dolores also went to work in the fields and the packing sheds in order to experience the work lives of her friends. According to Huerta, her mother's entrepreneurial successes and business acumen enabled her to go to school and enjoy "a more affluent background than the other kids."[4] Dolores Huerta learned from her mother to chart her own course in life, to work with determination, and to take action for those in need.

In recalling her early life, Huerta fondly described the vibrant diversity of her neighborhood in Stockton, with Japanese, Chinese, Jewish, Filipino, and Mexican folks of the working class—all intermingling. She participated in a wide range of youth activities, which, years later, she

indicated had taught her to organize people and to deal with them demo-
cratically. A Girl Scout until the age of eighteen, she also took piano and
violin lessons, studied dance, sang in the church choir, and participated
in Catholic youth organizations. She knew she was more fortunate than
most of her Mexican American peers. Her class status protected her from
the stings of discrimination, particularly in Lafayette grammar school and
Jackson Junior High, where she studied in her early adolescence. "We all
hated the teachers," Huerta declared about the racially mixed groups of
students of which she was a part, "but we didn't hate each other." This
all changed when she got to Stockton High School in 1944. For the first
time, Huerta felt discriminated against in a segregated environment. A
straight "A" student, Huerta experienced memorable disappointment
when a teacher told her that she could not receive an "A" grade because
the teacher did not believe that Dolores had submitted her own original
work.[5] This experience marked the beginning of her political awakening.

As was common for women of her generation, Dolores Huerta married
her high school sweetheart, Ralph Head, after graduation in 1948. He was
an Irish American with whom she had the first two of her eleven children, Celeste and Lori. Though she described him in a later interview as
"a very nice man, very responsible," they divorced after three years. Huerta
then began studying, first at Stockton Junior College and then at the
College of the Pacific in Stockton, where she earned an associate's degree and provisional teaching credentials. Afterward, she taught English
to rural children for one year.[6] Working with the children of farm workers
gave Huerta a very intimate perspective on their lives. She decided thereafter that she could do far more for farm workers by organizing them
around labor issues than by teaching basic lessons to their barefoot,
hungry children.

She found a venue to begin community service work when she met
organizer Fred Ross in 1955. Dolores Huerta has never stopped identifying the day she met Ross as among the most important events of her
life. Ross traveled around California, organizing Mexican Americans into
chapters of the Community Service Organization (CSO), a statewide confederation that mobilized Mexican American communities for voter registration campaigns and improved public services. Upon his arrival in
Stockton, Ross assured Huerta and others that they could "turn everything around" by registering Mexican-origin voters and electing Spanish-
speaking representatives. Huerta, however, was not immediately or easily
convinced. She recalled with some embarrassment: "I thought he was a
communist, so I went to the FBI and had him checked out. I really did

that. . . . See how middle class I was. In fact, I was a registered Republican at the time." Before long, however, Huerta concluded that Ross's organization had potential, as she had "always hated injustice" and "always wanted to do something to change things." "Fred opened a door for me," Huerta declared. "Without him," she insisted, "I'd probably just be in some stupid suburb somewhere." Huerta worked with the CSO to register Mexican-origin voters, to keep the police department from "searching and harassing people arbitrarily," and to get equitable access to the county hospital.[7] Huerta continued her work with the CSO, and through the organization, she met César Chávez in the late 1950s. After a very successful voter registration drive in 1960, Chávez, then executive director of the CSO, decided that Huerta would make a talented lobbyist; in 1961, he sent her to Sacramento where she headed the legislative program of the CSO. Her work laid the foundation of almost everything in that legislative season that benefited California workers. One of Huerta's primary concerns was that many farm workers, as Mexican citizens, were excluded from the social service benefits that had been established in the New Deal era, like social security, disability insurance, and retirement pensions. Huerta pushed for legislation that would ease the burdens that workers experienced trying to navigate their way through life in the United States, regardless of citizenship status or language skills. At the California state capitol, Huerta, with her small children at her side, lobbied successfully with her team for an old-age pension, a welfare bill, the right to register voters door to door, and the right to take the driver's license exam in Spanish.

During her CSO years, Huerta met and married her second husband, Ventura Huerta, also a community organizer. Together they had five children: Fidel, Emilio, Vincent, Alicia, and Angela. Huerta described it as "a terrible marriage," which deteriorated due to incompatible temperaments and disagreements about the manner in which Huerta balanced her public commitments with her private, domestic ones. Huerta later said of the marriage: "I knew I wasn't comfortable in a wife's role, but I wasn't clearly facing the issue. . . . I didn't come out and tell my husband that I cared more about helping other people than cleaning our house and doing my hair." Her second marriage ended in 1961; after it dissolved, she stated, "I put everything into my relationships," but "I have to do what I have to do."[8] Huerta thus alluded to the fact that despite her own personal commitment to her spouse, she refused to let their conflicting visions of her responsibilities prevent her from working as an activist in the Mexican American community, as she felt compelled to do.

Meanwhile, Huerta and César Chávez were becoming more interested in rural labor issues than urban ones, and they tried to give farm workers more visibility within the CSO. When the organization persisted with its primary focus on urban populations, both Huerta and Chávez resigned. In 1962, they co-founded the National Farm Workers Association in Chávez's hometown of Delano, California, and began down the long road of forging an agricultural labor union in California's San Joaquin Valley. Chávez was elected the first president, and Dolores Huerta and their colleague Gilbert Padilla were elected the first vice presidents. From that year forward, Huerta had a key role in shaping the union's fortunes, and she has continued the work for over forty years.

Huerta and Chávez relied on a method they had learned from Fred Ross, called the "house meeting," to earn the trust of individual farm workers and persuade them to join the NFWA. They tried to persuade groups of workers in the neutral, safe space of someone's home, where they could talk to them freely and at length about issues that farm workers faced, knowing that the workers were extremely vulnerable to dismissal and violent reprisals from growers. Labor leader Luisa Moreno (a close friend of Fred Ross) used the same tactic with great success among California cannery workers in the 1940s.

Huerta sent regular correspondence to Chávez about her progress. She often lacked a working automobile, gas money, and a babysitter for her children, and she identified these things to Chávez as the "handicaps" of her organizing. With her children in tow, she canvassed the fields, struggling to garner support for the union and to provide for the needs of her kids at the same time. She told Chávez: "You can only imagine how rough my financial situation is. Any help I get from my two ex-es has to go for grub for my seven little hungry mouths, and I am keeping one jump ahead of PG and E [Pacific Gas and Electric] and the Water Dragons who close off water for non-payment." Living on limited support from her children's fathers and some sparse donations made to the organizing campaign, Huerta revealed a constant need for resources. Working for no regular income, Huerta and Chávez were also anxious in those early years over raising sufficient dues to cover the costs of organizing. She sometimes explained to Chávez, "I have not even tried to have any meetings, because very few of these people up here are working steadily, and it doesn't do me any good to have meetings if I have to wait another month to collect the dues, no?"[9]

Consequently, for Huerta, the possibility of using her educational training to get substitute teacher certification, so that she could work a few days a week to make ends meet, loomed large at that time. However, she ultimately decided to work for the NFWA full-time, giving up gainful employment and everything that goes with it. While Huerta was always briskly conscious of the impact that this sacrifice had on her family, her letters were rife with news of successful advances in the progress of the union. These included frequent reports of new members (with records of their dues payments) and the plans she and Chávez shared for creating a cooperative, a credit union, insurance policies (unemployment, health, life), and a newspaper, *El Malcriado*, all of which eventually came to pass.

Dolores Huerta's advocacy for farm workers took many forms. In 1965, she contacted the Department of Motor Vehicles to get revoked licenses reinstated and persuaded insurance companies to write automobile policies for union members. She also pressured the Welfare Department of Kern County to set clear policies regarding patient access to the county hospital so that Mexicanos seeking medical attention would not be humiliated by hospital social workers.[10]

Dolores Huerta's busy schedule was complicated even further by her continued political lobbying in both Sacramento and Washington, D.C. She began to develop a substantial rapport with legislators who were sympathetic to the union's objectives. One of these was Congressman Phillip Burton of California, who in 1967 introduced a bill to extend the National Labor Relations Act (NLRA) to include agricultural workers—a bill that, despite Huerta's efforts, did not pass. Huerta had forged a working relationship with Burton some years earlier when she had persuaded him to organize donations of stamps to the NFWA. Although César Chávez recognized that support from politicians could clearly help the union, he began to question the amount of time Huerta spent lobbying. She defended her support of the Aid to Dependent Children Bill in the late 1960s by saying, "Let me remind you that at least the workers we are trying to represent will have bread in the winter months." Even as the demands of the NFWA work increased, Huerta continued to see certain legislative victories as paramount to securing true economic justice for farm workers.[11]

One of Huerta's most important goals was the demise of the Bracero program. Begun in 1942 as a wartime emergency measure between the United States and Mexican governments, the program had provided for the legal contracting of large numbers of Mexican nationals to work in the agricultural fields of the Southwest. The program was renewed after the war as growers insisted the *bracero* (worker) migration was still necessary due to continued labor shortages, but these Mexicanos were often ill-paid and ill-treated and had little recourse.[12] Huerta and Chávez knew that as long as these workers were available to growers as "scab" labor (replacement during union strikes), strikers would never be able to force growers to negotiate with the their union.

When Congress abolished the Bracero program in 1964, farm labor activists in California were encouraged by this victory. In the summer of 1965, Filipino workers in the Coachella Valley called a "wildcat" (spontaneous, grassroots) grape strike. Because the hot climate of the area made the crop quickly vulnerable, growers agreed to raise the wages of workers within one week of the strike. Encouraged, these workers moved northward to the San Joaquin Valley, the base of the NFWA, to execute another strike under the banner of the Agricultural Workers Organizing Committee (AWOC), AFL-CIO. They knew that it would be more difficult because of the much larger pool of available scab labor, and they knew that this strike would never be successful without the help of the Mexican workers of the NFWA.

The leaders of the NFWA, including Huerta, were then faced with a momentous decision: to strike or not to strike in solidarity with AWOC. The NFWA plan had been to organize very discreetly for about five years, until they could get the whole San Joaquin Valley organized and acquire some resources, before executing a strike. Despite having no strike fund available, the NFWA members voted to join the AWOC in a grape strike. Perhaps a bit naive, they believed that the strike would last for a few days or a few weeks. Instead it lasted five long years.

In September 1965, Mexican and Filipino workers in Delano, California, walked off the fields, refusing to pick grapes. Three weeks after the initial walkout, the strike had spread, and almost three thousand workers had left the fields. Growers used legal injunctions to stop picketing and resorted to violence to subdue demonstrations and protect their scab replacement workers. In contrast, nonviolent protest to effect social change marked union organizing from the beginning. Both César Chávez and Huerta adhered to the principles of Mahatma Gandhi and Dr. Martin Luther King Jr. Public pilgrimages, growing support from Catholic and Protestant church groups and clerics, and significant financial contributions by the AFL-CIO helped build and sustain the new union—the United Farm Workers Organizing Committee. The 1966 march (known as the *peregrinación*, or Easter pilgrimage) to the state capitol in Sacramento increased the visibility of the union and made the workers' struggle more than a labor issue—it became symbolic of a national civil rights movement among Mexican Americans.[13] Built out of the Filipino AWOC and the Mexican NFWA, the new union, which would soon be known as the UFW, would change the course of American labor history.

Realizing that the battle would not be won in the fields of California, union leaders decided that they would have to carry their message to the marketplace, boycotting table grapes and other produce in supermarkets. Their objective was to force growers to negotiate contracts with the UFW that established increased benefits and improved conditions for union members; while they were successful in securing a few contracts by 1967, dozens of growers, including the powerful John Giumarra Corporation, would not budge. Although the boycott initially targeted only a few labels, Dolores Huerta ultimately moved to New York City, the center of grape distribution, to coordinate the industry-wide boycott in 1968 and 1969. The commercial boycott received tremendous public support and proved very effective, with polls showing that an estimated 17 million consumers supported the boycott by the early 1970s. In the fourth year of the boycott, growers found a powerful ally in the newly elected California Republican governor, Ronald Reagan, who ate grapes at several photo opportunities. In response, the UFW stepped up the boycott aspect of union activities, and by 1970 shipments to the top grape-consuming cities were down by 22 percent.

Finally, on April 1, 1970, after five long years, one grower came through: Lionel Steinberg of the Freedman Ranches signed a contract with the UFW. Shipments of grapes produced on its land were now stamped with the UFW label, signaling the union's approval to consumers. In the economic climate of the boycott, "union" grapes could now be sold for a premium price, and the price of nonunion grapes sunk. As a result, growers began to clamor for the UFW union label on their product, and at that point Dolores Huerta and her colleagues could hardly negotiate the contracts fast enough. Finally, on July 29, 1970, John Giumarra Jr. and the rest of the growers in the Delano area met to sign contracts with the UFW at the union hall in Delano. Dolores Huerta handled the negotiations, and years later, as she reflected on the experience, she insisted, "It never, ever, ever, ever crossed my mind that it couldn't happen. Not once. I always knew that we would be able to do it."[14] Huerta possessed the tenacity and faith that enable one to carry on for years working toward a seemingly impossible goal.

In negotiating these historic contracts, Dolores Huerta earned a nickname among the growers—"dragon lady"—referring to her ability to speak "with fire" as she held fast to the terms and conditions that UFW members demanded. At that time, twenty-six Delano-area growers signed contracts, raising wages to $1.80 per hour plus $.20 per box, as well as establishing provisions for hiring workers directly from the UFW hiring hall, hiring by seniority, and placing strict controls on the use of pesticides.

Growers quickly became familiar with the intensity of Huerta's style, and stories abounded of growers pleading to deal with someone other than Huerta. One representative exclaimed, "Dolores Huerta is crazy. . . . She's a violent woman, where women, especially Mexican American women, are usually peaceful and pleasant." Huerta was called "too quick to attack, too slow to listen," by one politician. Even her successor, David Burciaga, who took over negotiations in 1973, reflected on the new need to "convince, not insult, the growers." However, in Huerta's pathbreaking work with the original contracts, she found the growers very insulting to her and the Mexican-origin members of her union. This explains why she felt her own strong style was justified: "Why do we need to be polite to people who are making racist statements at the table, or making sexist comments?" she questioned. "I think when they do that you have to call them at it because then also you are educating them in the process," Huerta explained. Whatever anyone thought of her style, she did get substantial results.[15] But the events of 1973 convinced her that protecting farm workers would continue to be an uphill battle. The initial contracts were set to expire that year, and growers colluded with the Teamsters Union to sign new contracts directly with the Teamsters without a vote among farm workers. The strike in the fields and the consumer boycott both began again that year. Once again, Huerta was there, serving as a backbone of UFW strategies.

As one might expect in a movement with two determined visionaries, the relationship between Huerta and Chávez could be tense at times. Both believed passionately in their cause and committed their lives to overcoming seemingly insurmountable obstacles to realize its goals. Both raised families while living, working, and organizing in the fields. Both did these things for a sum of money so small, it can hardly be called an "income." It is no surprise that facing such challenges day in and day out would raise tensions. The president of the UFW until his death in 1993, Chávez had become the national symbol of the farm worker movement, and even though he and Huerta did not favor celebrity, they both knew the support it brought to their cause had some positive consequences. Wholly committed to the realization of UFW goals, Huerta often deferred to Chávez's final authority on issues, especially in the beginning. Sometimes she did so calmly, as when she stated, "I bow to your better judgment and experience and will do as you say." Other times, she did so with sarcasm, as when she retorted, "But then again, I am not getting paid to ask questions, right?" On other occasions, and particularly later, she did exactly as she thought best. Whatever the case, she respected Chávez tremendously: "César Chávez is an extremely creative person," she declared; "He is a genius."[16] Huerta knew that they were on the same page about things, and she exercised diplomacy in order to deal with him effectively *and* act upon her own views. For the most part, Chávez and Huerta managed to work together in a manner that enabled the best qualities of each to be put to work toward achieving union objectives.[17]

One of their most important victories came in 1975 with the passage of the Agricultural Labor Relations Act (ALRA) in California. It was modeled after the National Labor Relations Act of 1935 (also known as the Wagner Act), part of Franklin Delano Roosevelt's New Deal. The NLRA protected the right of laborers to organize and bargain collectively, and it established a board to review grievances—but it excluded agricultural laborers from its provisions. The NLRA also established an enforcement arm, the National Labor Relations Board, to provide redress for workers, certify elections, and curb unlawful labor practices by employers. The lack of these basic protections, and especially the lack of governmental redress against grower abuses, had hindered UFW organizing. Dolores Huerta was a major force in lobbying legislators to support the ALRA, which provided the right to boycott, voting rights for migrant seasonal workers, and secret ballot elections and control over the timing of these elections.[18] Also, the ALRA, like the NLRA, established an enforcement board, the Agricultural Labor Relations Board (ALRB), for the redress of grievances and the certification of union elections.

Initially regarded as a victory, ALRB became increasingly conservative during the late 1970s and early 1980s. At that time, a growing conservative political mood in California—particularly after the 1982 election of Republican governor George Deukmejian—led to the appointment of board members who sympathized more with growers than with farm workers. According to Huerta, the ALRB began to rule consistently against the UFW in grievances brought before it. As a result, though the industry-wide grape boycott had been called off in 1978, it was instituted again in 1984.

Huerta continued her lobbying efforts throughout the 1980s. In 1985, she lobbied to outlaw a federal "guest worker program" (a new incarnation of the bracero program), which would once again enable growers to legally bring Mexican nationals into the fields to work for below minimum wages in substandard conditions. When it was introduced, U.S.

congressman from southern California Howard Berman, a longtime ally of Huerta and the UFW, successfully led the opposition to the program.[19] Huerta's primary concern in this period, however, was lobbying to outlaw the use of harmful pesticides. On September 14, 1988, in the course of a peaceful political rally where she spoke on that issue, San Francisco police severely beat Dolores Huerta. She suffered six broken ribs and the removal of her spleen in emergency surgery; she ultimately received an unprecedented monetary settlement from a lawsuit she brought against the offending law enforcement agency.

The longevity of Dolores Huerta's political career is particularly remarkable considering that at its height she embarked on her third marriage and reared another four children. She and Richard Chávez (brother of César) were the parents of Juanita, María Elena, Ricky, and Camilla. Speaking of the demands that her many duties placed on her, Huerta confessed: "I don't feel proud of the suffering that my kids went through . . . but by the same token I know that they learned a lot in the process." Managing this guilt as one of the biggest challenges in her life; she recalls "driving around Stockton with all these little babies in the car, the different diaper changes for each one."[20] Huerta spoke forthrightly about the tremendous pressure she felt to be a conventional mother while she worked as a major American labor leader. Lori De León, her daughter, revealed, "She was always on the road, and we were left to take care of ourselves." Huerta noted that, as in other poor people's movements, farm workers of the UFW were very willing to care for one another's children while other adults performed the work necessary to effect economic justice. Huerta has often insisted that she could only truly improve the conditions of farm workers' lives by living in the same circumstances as the workers. As a result, she could not realistically shelter her children from that reality. "Although criticized for putting *la causa* first, Dolores Huerta has had few regrets. As she informed [historian Margaret] Rose, 'But now that I've seen how good they [my children] turned out, I don't feel so guilty.'"[21] She is filled with parental pride at the course of her children's lives; many of her children now have careers rooted in community service and activism, with some holding advanced professional degrees.

Huerta's own experience as an activist and a mother has given her very particular views about the roles of women in unions and in public life in general. Her first engagement with mainstream U.S. feminism came in the late 1960s, when Huerta's own place in the national spotlight gave her occasion to become acquainted with noted feminist Gloria Steinem. Huerta slowly began to incorporate woman-centered views into her own politics, calling herself a "born-again feminist." As a co-founder of the Coalition of Labor Union Women in 1974, Huerta has lobbied for countless female candidates for political office, addressed the National Organization of Women, and served on the board of the Feminist Majority Foundation. Her work has demonstrated her resolve that the public political agenda should embrace women's issues, and that women should be the ones to bring such issues to the table of political negotiations. She cites her experience in the UFW as an eye-opener on this point: "My mission has crept into my life. I want to see women treated equally in the union. After we fought hard, I found some women were discriminated against. I realized, in about 1978, it was almost like a conspiracy."[22] Huerta is convinced that "the women decided the fate of the union," with the determination that they brought as they struggled to ensure the survival of families during the years of strikes in the fields.[23] Huerta believes her mission is to encourage women to fight on the public side of battles they are often fighting privately—for themselves and for others.[24]

Dolores Huerta's organizing career has been marked by a combination of aggressive efforts to meet her goals and reluctance to take the spotlight. It has been Huerta's personal opinion that the mark of a true organizer was "someone who trains people and then steps back." Huerta did, however, recognize that skill had brought her to the leadership position she occupied in the UFW: "I guess because I'm articulate, I came to the forefront," she confessed. At the same time though, she identified herself humbly as "just a person working at what I'm supposed to be doing."[25] She championed the often unrecognized skills that women brought to the union from their own life experiences, such as management of limited resources, organization, and vision for the long-term well-being of their families. "The energy of women is important," Huerta declared. Though she does not favor the spotlight, she could not help but concede in a 1985 interview: "I know that the history of our union would have been quite different had it not been for my involvement. So I am trying to get more of our women to hang in there."[26] "Hanging in there" precisely describes what Dolores Huerta has done for almost fifty years of struggle as a pioneering civil rights and labor leader.

NOTES

1. Margaret Rose, "Dolores Huerta (1930–): Labor Leader, Social Activist," in *Notable Hispanic American Women*, ed. Diane Telgen and Jim Kamp (Detroit: Gale Research, 1993), 211.

2. For more on Mexican women cannery workers, see Vicki L. Ruiz, *Cannery Women, Cannery Lives: Mexican Women, Unionization, and the California Food Processing Industry, 1930–1950* (Albuquerque: University of New Mexico Press, 1987).

3. Rose, "Dolores Huerta," 210; Dolores Huerta, "Dolores Huerta Talks: About Republicans, César, Children, and Her Home Town," *Regeneración* 2.4 (1975): 20; "Dolores Huerta," p. 1, short biography from archivist's file, Walter P. Reuther Archives of Labor and Urban Affairs, Wayne State University, Detroit, Michigan (hereinafter cited as Reuther Archives).

4. Gloria Bonilla-Santiago, "Dolores Huerta: A Life of Sacrifice for Farm Workers," in *Breaking Ground and Barriers: Hispanic Women Developing Effective Leadership* (San Diego: Marin Publications, 1992), 94; Huerta, "Dolores Huerta Talks," 20. Alicia Fernández married three times and bore a daughter with each of her second and third husbands.

5. Rose, "Dolores Huerta," 211; Huerta, "Dolores Huerta Talks," 20.

6. Bonilla-Santiago, "Dolores Huerta," 95; Nera A. Llamas, "Dolores Huerta (1930–)," in *Significant Contemporary Feminists: A Biographical Sourcebook,* ed. Jennifer Scanlon (Westport, Conn.: Greenwood Press, 1999), 134.

7. Huerta, "Dolores Huerta Talks," 21.

8. Bonilla-Santiago, "Dolores Huerta," Rose, "Dolores Huerta," 212.

9. Dolores Huerta to César Chávez, Folder 14, Box 2, National Farm Workers Association (NFWA) Collection, Reuther Archives.

10. Correspondence of Dolores Huerta, Folder 7, Box 2, NFWA Collection.

11. Dolores Huerta to César Chávez, Folder 12, Box 12, NFWA Collection; Dolores Huerta to César Chávez, Folder 14, Box 2, NFWA Collection.

12. For more information on the Bracero program, see Ernesto Galarza's classic, *Merchants of Labor: The Mexican Bracero Story, 1942–1960* (Charlotte, N.C.: McNally and Loftin, 1964).

13. *Chicano! The History of the Mexican American Civil Rights Movement,* Episode 2: "The Struggle in the Fields" (Los Angeles: National Latino Communications Center and Galán Productions, 1996). See also the companion book to the series: F. Arturo Rosales, *Chicano! A History of the Mexican American Civil Rights Movement* (Houston: Arte Público Press, 1996).

14. *Chicano,* Episode 2.

15. Ibid.; Barbara L. Baer, "Stopping Traffic: One Woman's Cause," *The Progressive* 39 (September 1975): 40.

16. Dolores Huerta to César Chávez, ca. 1963, Folder 14, Box 2, NFWA Collection; Dolores Huerta, "Reflections on the UFW Experience," *The Center Magazine* (July/August 1985): 8.

17. For more on the relationship between Huerta and Chávez, see Margaret Rose, "César Chávez and Dolores Huerta: Partners in 'La Causa,'" in *César Chávez,* ed. Richard Etulain (Boston: Bedford Press, 2002), 95–106.

18. One of the strategies that growers had used to undo the hold that the UFW had on workers was to hold union elections at a point in the growing season when very few workers were available to vote.

19. Olivia Garcia, "UFW Cofounder Still Harvesting Fair Labor Policy," *Bakersfield Californian*, September 5, 1999.

20. Rose, "Dolores Huerta," 213; Barbara L. Baer and Glenna Matthews, "'You Find a Way': Women of the Boycott," *The Nation* 218 (February 23, 1974): 233.

21. Quoted in Vicki L. Ruiz, *From Out of the Shadows: Mexican Women in Twentieth-Century America* (New York: Oxford University Press, 1998), 134.

22. Bonilla-Santiago, "Dolores Huerta," 97. The Coalition for Labor Union Women fostered women's leadership at all levels of policymaking within U.S. trade unions.

23. For an analysis of the variety of contributions women made to UFW efforts, see Margaret Rose, "From the Fields to the Picket Line: Huelga Women and the Boycott, 1965–1975," *Labor History* 31 (Summer 1990): 271–93.

24. Ibid.

25. Huerta, "Reflections on the UFW Experience," 4; Huerta, "Dolores Huerta Talks," 21.

26. Huerta, "Reflections on the UFW Experience," 8.

FOR FURTHER READING

Acosta-Belén, Edna, et al. *"Adiós Borinquen Querida": The Puerto Rican Diaspora, Its History, and Contributions*. Albany, N.Y.: Center for Latino, Latin American, and Caribbean Studies, 2000.

Alvarez, Julia. *Something to Declare*. New York: Plume, 1998.

Aparicio, Frances. *Listening to Salsa: Gender, Latin Popular Music, and Puerto Rican Cultures*. Hanover, N.H.: University Press of New England, 1998.

Aquino, María Pilar, Daisy L. Machado, and Jeanette Rodríguez, eds. *A Reader in Latina Feminist Theology*. Austin: University of Texas Press, 2002.

Belpré, Pura. *Firefly Summer*. Houston: Arte Público Press, 1996.

———. *Once in Puerto Rico*. New York: F. Warne, 1973.

Blocker, Jane. *Where Is Ana Mendieta? Identity, Performativity, and Exile*. Durham, N.C.: Duke University Press, 1999.

Bouvier, Virginia M. *Women and the Conquest of California, 1542–1840: Codes of Silence*. Tucson: University of Arizona Press, 2001.

Brooks, James F. *Captives and Cousins: Slavery, Kinship, and Community in the Southwest Borderlands*. Chapel Hill: University of North Carolina Press, 2002.

Cantú, Norma, and Olga Nájera-Ramírez, eds. *Chicana Traditions: Continuity and Change*. Urbana: University of Illinois Press, 2002.

Casas, María Raquel. *"Married to a Daughter of the Land": Interethnic Marriages in California, 1820–1880*. Reno: University of Nevada Press, 2005.

Castañeda, Antonia I. "The Political Economy of Nineteenth-Century Stereotypes of Californianas." In *Between Borders: Essays on Mexicana/Chicana History*, ed. Adelaida R. Del Castillo, pp. 213–38. Encino, Calif.: Floricanto Press, 1990.

Chávez, Marisela R. "'We Lived and Breathed and Worked the Movement': The Contradictions and Rewards of Chicana/Mexicana Activism in CASA, 1975–1978." In *Las Obreras: Chicana Politics of Work and Family*, ed. Vicki L. Ruiz, pp. 83–105. Los Angeles: UCLA Chicano Studies Research Center Publications, 2000.

Chávez-García, Miroslava. "Guadalupe Trujillo: Race, Culture, and Justice in Mexican Los Angeles." In *The Human Tradition in California*, ed. Clark Davis and David Igler, pp. 31–46. Wilmington, Del.: Scholarly Resources, 2002.

———. *Negotiating Conquest: Gender and Power in California, 1770s to 1880s*. Tucson: University of Arizona Press, 2004.

Cocco-De Filippis, Daisy. *Documents of Dissidence: Selected Writings of Dominican Women*. New York: CUNY Dominican Studies Institute, 2000.

Cotera, María Eugenia. "Engendering a 'Dialectics of Our America': Jovita González's Pluralist Dialogue as Feminist Testimonio." In *Las Obreras: Chicana Politics of Work and Family*, ed. Vicki L. Ruiz, pp. 237–56. Los Angeles: UCLA Chicano Studies Research Center Publications, 2000.

de la Torre, Adela, and Beatríz Pesquera, eds. *Building with Our Hands: New Directions in Chicana Studies*. Berkeley: University of California Press, 1993.

Deutsch, Sarah. *No Separate Refuge: Culture, Class, and Gender on an Anglo-Hispanic Frontier in the American Southwest, 1880–1940*. New York: Oxford University Press, 1987.

Doran, Terry, Janet Satterfield, and Chris Stade. *A Road Well Traveled: Three Generations of Cuban American Women*. Fort Wayne, Ind.: Latin American Educational Center, 1988.

Flores, María Eva. "St. Joseph's Parish, Ft. Stockton, Texas, 1875–1945: The Forging of Identity and Community." *U.S. Catholic Historian* 21 (Winter 2003): 13–31.

Flores, William, and Rina Benmayor, eds. *Latino Cultural Citizenship*. Boston: Beacon, 1997.

García, María Cristina. "Adapting to Exile: Cuban Women in the United States, 1959–1973." *Latino Studies Journal* 2 (May 1991): 17–33.

———. *Havana USA: Cuban Exiles and Cuban Americans in South Florida, 1959–1994*. Berkeley: University of California Press, 1996.

García, Matt. *A World of Its Own: Race, Labor, and Citrus in the Making of Greater Los Angeles, 1900–1970*. Chapel Hill: University of North Carolina Press, 2001.

Gil-Montero, Martha. *Brazilian Bombshell: The Biography of Carmen Miranda*. New York: D. I. Fine, 1989.

Goldman, Anne E. "'I Think Our Romance Is Spoiled' or, Crossing Genres: California History in Helen Hunt Jackson's *Ramona* and María Amparo Ruiz de Burton's *The Squatter and the Don*." In *Over the Edge: Remapping the American West*, ed. Valerie J. Matsumoto and Blake Allmendinger, pp. 65–84. Berkeley: University of California Press, 1999.

González, Deena J. *Refusing the Favor: The Spanish-Mexican Women of Santa Fe, 1820–1880*. New York: Oxford University Press, 1999.

González, Jovita. "Jovita González: Early Life and Education." In *Dew on the Thorn*, ed. José E. Limón. Houston: Arte Público Press, 1997.

González, Jovita, and Eve Raleigh [pseud., Margaret Eimer]. *Caballero: A Historical Novel*, ed. José E. Limón and María Cotera. College Station: Texas A&M University Press, 1996.

Gordon, Linda. *The Great Arizona Orphan Abduction*. Cambridge, Mass.: Harvard University Press, 1999.

Guerin-Gonzales, Camille. *Mexican Workers and American Dreams: Immigration, Repatriation, and California Farm Labor, 1900–1939*. New Brunswick, N.J.: Rutgers University Press, 1994.

Gutiérrez, Ramón A. "Community, Patriarchy, and Individualism: The Politics of Chicano History and the Dream of Equality." *American Quarterly* 45 (March 1993): 44–72.

———. *When Jesus Came, the Corn Mothers Went Away: Marriage, Sexuality, and Power in New Mexico, 1500–1846*. Stanford, Calif.: Stanford University Press, 1991.

Haas, Lisbeth. *Conquests and Historical Identities in California, 1769–1936*. Berkeley: University of California Press, 1995.

Henkes, Robert. *Latin American Women Artists of the United States: The Works of 33 Twentieth-Century Women*. Jefferson, N.C.: MacFarland, 1999.

Hewitt, Nancy A. *Southern Discomfort: Women's Activism in Tampa, Florida, 1880s–1920s*. Urbana: University of Illinois Press, 2001.

Hondagneu-Sotelo, Pierrette. *Doméstica: Immigrant Workers Cleaning and Caring in the Shadows of Affluence*. Berkeley: University of California Press, 2001.

Jensen, Joan M. "'Disfranchisement Is a Disgrace': Women and Politics in New Mexico, 1900–1940." *New Mexico Historical Review* 56 (January 1981): 5–36.

Katz, Robert. *Naked by the Window: The Fatal Marriage of Carl Andre and Ana Mendieta*. New York: Atlantic Monthly Press, 1990.

Latina Feminist Group. *Telling to Live: Latina Feminist Testimonios*. Durham, N.C.: Duke University Press, 2001.

Leonard, Elizabeth D. *All the Daring of the Soldier: Women of the Civil War Armies*. New York: W. W. Norton, 1999.

Leyva, Yolanda Chávez. "Breaking the Silence: Putting Latina Lesbian History at the Center." In *New Lesbian Studies*, ed. Bonnie Zimmerman and Toni McNaron, pp. 145–52. New York: Feminist Press, 1996.

Lucas, María Elena. *Forged under the Sun/Forjado Bajo el Sol: The Life of María Elena Lucas*, ed. Fran Leeper Buss. Ann Arbor: University of Michigan Press, 1993.

Martin, Patricia Preciado. *Songs My Mother Sang to Me: An Oral History of Mexican American Women*. Tucson: University of Arizona Press, 1992.

Matos, Felix V., and Linda C. Delgado, eds. *Puerto Rican Women's History: New Perspectives*. New York: M. E. Sharpe, 1998.

Menjívar, Cecilia. *Fragmented Ties: Salvadoran Immigrant Networks in America*. Berkeley: University of California Press, 2000.

Montoya, María. *Translating Property: The Maxwell Land Grant and the Conflict over Land in the American West, 1840–1900*. Berkeley: University of California Press, 2000.

Mora, Pat. *Nepantla: Essays from the Land in the Middle*. Albuquerque: University of New Mexico Press, 1993.

Moreno, Luisa. "Caravans of Sorrow: Noncitizen Americans of the Southwest." In *Between Two Worlds: Mexican Immigration in the United States*, ed. David G. Gutiérrez, pp. 119–23. Wilmington, Del.: Scholarly Resources, 1996.

Muñiz, Vicki. *Resisting Gentrification and Displacement: Voices of Puerto Rican Women of the Barrio*. New York: Garland, 1998.

Ochoa, María. *Creative Collectives: Chicana Painters Working in Community*. Albuquerque: University of New Mexico Press, 2003.

Orozco, Cynthia E. "Alice Dickerson Montemayor: Feminism and Mexican American Politics in the 1930s." In *Writing the Range: Race, Class, and Culture in the Women's West*, ed. Elizabeth Jameson and Susan Armitage, pp. 435–56. Norman: University of Oklahoma Press, 1993.

Ortiz Cofer, Judith. *Woman in Front of the Sun: On Becoming a Writer*. Athens: University of Georgia Press, 2000.

Pantoja, Antonia. *Memoir of a Visionary*. Houston: Arte Público Press, 2002.

Pedraza, Silvia. "Beyond Black and White: Latinos and Social Science Research on Immigration, Race, and Ethnicity in America." *Social Science History* 24 (Winter 2000): 697–826.

———. *Political and Economic Migrants to America: Cubans and Mexicans*. Austin: University of Texas Press, 1985.

Pérez, Emma. *The Decolonial Imaginary: Writing Chicanas into History*. Bloomington: Indiana University Press, 1999.

Pérez, Gina. *The Near Northwest Side Story: Migration, Displacement, and Puerto Rican Families*. Berkeley: University of California Press, 2004.

Pessar, Patricia. "Sweatshop Workers and Domestic Ideologies: Dominican Women in the New York Apparel Industry." *International Journal of Urban and Regional Research* 18 (March 1994): 127–42.

Pitti, Gina Marie. "The *Sociedades Guadalupanas* in the San Francisco Archdiocese, 1942–1962." *U.S. Catholic Historian* 21 (Winter 2003): 83–98.

Ponce, Mary Helen. *Hoyt Street: An Autobiography*. Albuquerque: University of New Mexico Press, 1993.

Prieto, Yolanda. "Cuban Women in New Jersey: Gender Relations and Change." In *Seeking Common Ground: Multidisciplinary Studies of Immigrant Women in the United States*, ed. Donna R. Gabaccia, pp. 185–210. Westport, Conn.: Greenwood Press, 1992.

Rebolledo, Tey Diana, and Eliana S. Rivero, eds. *Infinite Divisions: An Anthology of Chicana Literature*. Tucson: University of Arizona Press, 1993.

Rodríguez, Clara, ed. *Latin Looks: Images of Latinas and Latinos in the U.S. Media*. Boulder, Colo.: Westview Press, 1997.

Rodríquez-Estrada, Alicia. "Dolores del Rio and Lupe Velez: Images on and off the Screen, 1925–1944." In *Writing the Range: Race, Class, and Culture in the Women's West*, ed. Elizabeth Jameson and Susan Armitage, pp. 475–92. Norman: University of Oklahoma Press, 1993.

Rose, Margaret. "César Chávez and Dolores Huerta: Partners in 'La Causa.'" In *César Chávez*, ed. Richard Etulain. Boston: Bedford Press, 2002.

———. "From the Fields to the Picket Line: Huelga Women and the Boycott, 1965–1975." *Labor History* 31 (Summer 1990): 271–93.

Ruiz, Vicki L. *Cannery Women, Cannery Lives: Mexican Women, Unionization, and the California Food Processing Industry, 1930–1950*. Albuquerque: University of New Mexico Press, 1987.

———. *From Out of the Shadows: Mexican Women in Twentieth-Century America*. New York: Oxford University Press, 1998.

Ruiz, Vicki L., and Virginia Sánchez Korrol, eds. *Latinas in the United States: An Historical Encyclopedia*. Bloomington: Indiana University Press, 2005.

Ruiz de Burton, María Amparo. *The Squatter and the Don: A Novel Descriptive of Contemporary Occurrences in California*, pseud. C. Loyal. San Francisco: Samuel Carson and Co., 1885; rpt., with an introduction and notes by Rosaura Sánchez and Beatrice Pita, Houston: Arte Público Press, 1997.

———. *Who Would Have Thought It?* Philadelphia: J. B. Lippincott, 1872; rpt., with an introduction and notes by Rosaura Sánchez and Beatrice Pita, Houston: Arte Público Press, 1995.

Salas, Elizabeth. "Ethnicity, Gender, and Divorce: Issues in the 1922 Campaign by Adelina Otero Warren for the U.S. House of Representatives." *New Mexico Historical Review* 70 (October 1995): 367–82.

Sánchez, George J. *Becoming Mexican American: Ethnicity, Culture, and Identity in Chicano Los Angeles, 1900–1945*. New York: Oxford University Press, 1993.

Sánchez, Rosaura. *Telling Identities*. Minneapolis: University of Minnesota Press, 1995.

Sánchez González, Lisa. *Boricua Literature: A Literary History of the Puerto Rican Diaspora*. New York: New York University Press, 2001.

Sánchez Korrol, Virginia. *From Colonia to Community: The History of Puerto Ricans in New York City*. 2d ed. Berkeley: University of California Press, 1994.

———. *Teaching U.S. Puerto Rican History*. Washington, D.C.: American Historical Association, 1999.

Sánchez-Walsh, Arlene. *Latino Pentecostal Identity*. New York: Columbia University Press, 2003.

Torres, Lourdes, and Immaculada Pertusa, eds. *Tortilleras: Hispanic and U.S. Latina Lesbian Expression*. Philadelphia: Temple University Press, 2003.

Tywoniak, Frances Esquibel, and Mario T. García. *Migrant Daughter: Coming of Age as a Mexican American Woman*. Berkeley: University of California Press, 2000.

Velázquez, Loreta Janeta. *The Woman in Battle: The Civil War Narrative of Loreta Velázquez, Cuban Woman and Confederate Soldier*, intro. by Jesse Alemán. Madison: University of Wisconsin Press, 2003.

Villarreal, Mary Ann. "The Synapses of Struggle: Martha Cotera and Tejana Activism." In *Las Obreras: Chicana Politics of Work and Family*, ed. Vicki L. Ruiz, pp. 273–95. Los Angeles: UCLA Chicano Studies Research Center Publications, 2000.

Weber, Devra. "Historical Perspectives on Mexican Transnationalism." *Social Justice* 26 (Fall 1999): 39–58.

———. "*Raiz Fuerte*: Oral History and Mexicana Farmworkers." *Oral History Review* 17 (Fall 1989): 47–62.

Whaley, Charlotte. *Nina Otero Warren of Santa Fe*. Albuquerque: University of New Press, 1991.

Whelan, Carmen Teresa. *From Puerto Rico to Philadelphia: Puerto Rican Workers and Postwar Economies*. Philadelphia: Temple University Press, 2001.

Yohn, Susan. *A Contest of Faiths: Missionary Women and Pluralism in the American Southwest*. Ithaca, N.Y.: Cornell University Press, 1995.

Zavella, Patricia. *Women's Work and Chicano Families: Cannery Workers of the Santa Clara Valley*. Ithaca, N.Y.: Cornell University Press, 1987.